THE BRITISH ARMY IN NORTHERN IRELAND

A mobile patrol in Belfast during the third decade of the current troubles. The soldiers are mounted in an armoured Land Rover and are covering their flanks while on the move with a light support weapon in the foreground and an SA80 rifle. Note the caption stencilled on the side of the Land Rover, which encourages the local population to ring a confidential telephone line if they have any 'pertinent information'. **Overleaf:** A mobile patrol stops briefly to report progress back to headquarters. The soldier in the foreground carries an SA80 rifle; his companion covers him while he is on the radio.

THE BRITISH ARMY IN NORTHERN IRELAND

Revised Edition

Colonel Michael Dewar

ARMS AND
ARMOUR

To Lavinia. Alexander, James, Edward and Katharine with love.

Arms and Armour Press
An Imprint of the Cassell Group
Wellington House, 125 Strand
London WC2R OBB

First published 1985
Revised edition published 1996
This paperback edition 1997

© Michael Dewar, 1985, 1996

British Library Cataloguing-in-
Publication Data: a catalogue record for
this book is available from the British
Library

ISBN 1–85409–453–X

Designed and edited by
DAG Publications Ltd.
Printed and bound in Great Britain

Jacket illustrations
Front: A British soldier in Northern Ireland
taking advantage of the cover afforded by
concrete vehicle barriers used to protect
vulnerable targets from IRA vehicle bombs.
Back: A radio operator with the latest radio
equipment designed for Northern Ireland
reports his vehicle's location while on patrol.

ACKNOWLEDGEMENTS

I am most grateful to the staff of the MOD
Library Whitehall, particularly Miss
Thurlow, who gave generously of their
time seeking out original material for me;
also the staff of the Prince Consort's
Library at Aldershot for their invaluable
help. Major-General Gary Johnson and
Lieutenant-Colonel Andrew Pringle were
most generous in allowing me to reproduce material from their articles 'An
Incident in Andersonstown' and 'Operation Vehement'. I should also like to
record my thanks to Major George Hislop
of HQ Northern Ireland, Mr Tom Fitch of
the Airborne Forces Museum, Captain
Derek Oakley of the Royal Marines'
Journal *The Globe and Laurel*, Brigadier
Paddy Ryan of The Royal Artillery Insti-
tution and Major Kelly of the Ulster
Defence Regiment for providing so much
help and advice in their respective areas of
expertise; a thank you also to Lieutenant-
Colonel David Innes of the 2nd Battalion
The Royal Green Jackets and to Corporal
Bert Henshaw of the Light Division Depot
for allowing me to reproduce so many of
their photographs. I owe a particular debt
of gratitude to Lieutenant-Colonel Mike
Kearon for providing me with the material
describing his own part in the Northern
Ireland Campaign. Finally I should like to
thank Jenny Campbell, Margaret
Heywood and Sophie Stones for typing the
entire manuscript, and David Gibbons, at
Arms and Armour Press, for giving so
much excellent advice and, more
important, encouragement.

CONTENTS

NORTHERN IRELAND

Motorways — — Roads — — Border

miles

0   10   20   30

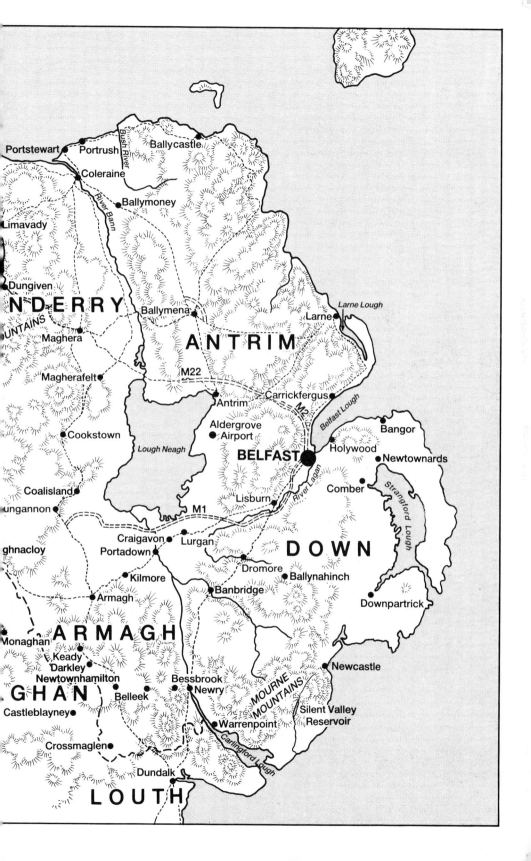

LIST OF ABBREVIATIONS

ADP	Automatic Data Processing
APC	Armoured Personnel Carrier
ASU	Active Service Unit
ATO	Ammunition Technical Officer
BAOR	British Army of the Rhine
CESA	Catholic Ex-Servicemen's Association
CLF	Commander Land Forces
COP	Close Observation Platoon
CSM	Company Sergeant-Major
DOW	Down Orange Welfare
EOD	Explosive Ordnance Disposal
FNE	Fianna N. Eirrean
GOC	General Officer Commanding
GPMG	General-Purpose Machine-Gun
IED	Improvised Explosive Device
IMG	International Marxist Group
INLA	Irish National Liberation Army
IRB	Irish Republican Brotherhood
IRSP	Irish Republican Socialist Party
JNCO	Junior Non-Commissioned Officer
LAW	Loyalist Association of Workers
LCU	Loyal Citizens of Ulster
LDV	Loyalist Defence Volunteers
LES	League of Ex-Servicemen
NICRA	Northern Ireland Civil Rights Association
NORAID	Northern Aid Committee
OIRA	Official Irish Republican Army
OP	Observation Post
OUP	Official Unionist Party
OV	Orange Volunteers
PAF	Protestant Action Force
PD	People's Democracy
PIRA	Provisional Irish Republican Army

PLO	Palestine Liberation Organization
RIC	Royal Irish Constabulary
RSM	Regimental Sergeant-Major
RUC	Royal Ulster Constabulary
SDA	Shankill Defence Association
SDLP	Social Democratic Labour Party
SFWP	Sinn Fein N. – The Workers' Party
SMG	Submachine-Gun
SNCO	Senior Non-Commissioned Officer
SPG	Special Patrol Group
SWP	Socialist Workers' Party
TAOR	Tactical Area of Responsibility
TOM	Troops Out Movement
UCDC	Ulster Constitution Defence Committee
UDA	Ulster Defence Association
UDR	Ulster Defence Regiment
UFF	Ulster Freedom Fighters
UGS	Unattended Ground Sensors
UPA	Ulster Protestant Action
UPV	Ulster Protestant Volunteers
USC	Ulster Special Constabulary
UTOM	United Troops Out Movement
UUAC	United Unionist Action Council
UVF	Ulster Volunteer Force
(U)VSC	(Ulster) Volunteer Service Corps
UWC	Ulster Workers' Council
VCP	Vehicle Check Point
WO1	Warrant Officer Class 1
WO2	Warrant Officer Class 2
WP	The Workers' Pary

INTRODUCTION

'Nobody realizes the waste and sheer stupidity of war more than the British soldier. For it is he who has for centuries had to bear the ordeal of battle, sometimes in opposition to his own feelings.' A. P. N. Clarke, *Contact.*

The events in Northern Ireland since 1969 are among the best documented of our time. Many books have been published on most aspects of the conflict, but there is not one that traces the main course of events of the IRA terrorist offensive between 1969 and 1996 and the counter terrorist campaign fought by the Security Forces, except this second edition of *The British Army in Northern Ireland.* The first edition, which was published in 1985, was completed when there seemed to be little chance of a ceasefire. The IRA had yet to launch its most damaging attacks on the mainland. There was no end in sight to the bloodshed.

Since then, increasing success by the Security Forces and a realization by the IRA that they were losing the propaganda war forced a re-think. This eventually led to the ceasefire of 31 August 1994. For seventeen months it seemed that the 25-year agony might be over. But this time the IRA realized they were losing the peace. Encouraged by international support, an increasing consensus between the people of Ireland – north and south of the border – started to create a real momentum for peace. Sinn Fein-IRA belatedly realized that they were not going to make serious progress towards a united Ireland via the ballot box and so cynically but calculatedly returned to the bomb and the bullet in January 1996.

This book attempts to highlight the important events of military significance during the conflict in Northern Ireland. So that the reader does not lose his or her way, I have included, with the minimum of comment, the essential chronology of the 1969–96 period. In the main, however, I have concentrated on the crucial events of the period. Hence the book is selective. I have concentrated on five regiments of the British Army, and the Royal Marines, as being representative of the whole.

The Parachute Regiment is in some respects in a special category, and its battalions have completed many tours in Northern Ireland. The Royal Green Jackets is representative of the many infantry battalions that have borne the brunt of the campaign; it is my own regiment, and I have served with it in Ulster, so I can speak with some authority. The Royal Artillery is representative of the other arms in the Army who have served with distinction in the infantry role. No account of the campaign in Northern Ireland would be complete without the inclusion of the Royal Irish Regiment (RIR), formerly the Ulster Defence Regiment

(UDR); and finally I have chosen the Royal Marines – not only because of their considerable contribution to the war against terrorism in Ulster – but also because they represent the 'Senior Service' in Northern Ireland.

Most importantly, this book is primarily concerned with the part played by the British Army in Northern Ireland. It does not set out to be an apologia; it does, however, put a case, which I would contend has not been adequately stated in any publication to date. In what I hope is an objective and measured way, *The British Army in Northern Ireland* describes the achievement of British soldiers in Northern Ireland. Though sorely tried, though individual men may have made mistakes, and though inevitably playing the role of 'pig in the middle', the Army has nevertheless in a quite remarkable way managed to do its duty in the professional and humane way we have come to expect of the British soldier throughout history. It has remained impartial and has, with very few exceptions, maintained the tradition of minimum force. It has, where no other modern army has demonstrated similar self-discipline in like conditions, maintained a remarkable degree of restraint, often despite extreme provocation. Whether the legal position of the soldier in Northern Ireland has ever been sufficiently and precisely defined is a matter of some doubt. This question has, in any event, been expertly tackled by my brother Green Jacket, Robin Eveleigh, in his book *Peacekeeping in a Democratic Society*, which is the definitive work on this aspect of the Ulster problem. I have not attempted to cover the legal status of the soldier acting in support of the civil power.

Whether peace has returned to Northern Ireland is still in doubt. If it has, the British Army deserves most of the credit. If it has not, the British Army will continue to do its duty. It has no other choice.

1
HISTORICAL BACKGROUND

Most Irishmen are instant historians. Whereas many Englishmen are blissfully unaware of their country's history and traditions, a good Irishman is more than willing to give an opinion on even the most obscure period of his island's history. The citizens of Eire and the Nationalist population in Ulster are particular experts in the history of what they regard as England's meddling in Irish affairs throughout the centuries. In the case of the Loyalists, their speciality is the details of the Protestant Plantation (settlement) in Ulster and the maintenance of the Protestant ascendancy since that time.

An understanding of the essentials of Ireland's history is, of course, necessary if one is to have any chance of grasping the complexities of the Irish problem as it exists today.

The term Ulster can be used to mean two things. First, it describes the traditional province including Antrim, Down, Armagh, Derry, Tyrone, Fermanagh, Donegal, Monaghan and Cavan. Second, it is the administrative and political unit which, since 1921, has formed the state of Northern Ireland. In this latter sense, Ulster does not include Donegal, Monaghan and Cavan.

The Celts established a pagan civilization of petty kingdoms in Ireland from about 300 BC. The first Christians were refugees from Britain, forced to flee when the Romans withdrew their legions. By AD 432 there was a sufficiently substantial Christian community for the Papacy to dispatch a bishop to Ireland who we now know as St Patrick. But it was still a country of many kingdoms which fell easy prey to the Vikings. In AD 840 the Danes founded the city of Dublin, but in 1014 Brian Boru, having declared himself High King of Ireland, defeated the Danes in battle. This was the first attempt to unite the disparate kingdoms of Ireland. In 1155 Pope Adrian IV (Nicholas Breakspear, the only English Pope) decreed Henry II of England King of all Ireland. Henry encouraged some of his Norman barons to go to Ireland to bring the Irish kings to heel. Many settled and a Norman-Irish aristocracy developed. Henry, jealous of the independent baronage developing in Ireland, visited the country in 1171–72 with an army of 4,000 men. The Normans in Ireland were invited to pay homage to Henry which they duly did. Although the unruly Irish kings were invited to do the same, few complied. In reality, many of the Irish kingdoms still flourished. In 1171 John de Courcy set out from Dublin to subdue the kingdom of Ulster. He defeated King Dunleavy and assumed the title of Earl of Ulster.

Although King John personally crushed a rebellion in Ireland in 1210, successive English kings paid little heed to their Irish possessions. The independent barons continued to resist the power of the Viceroy in Dublin while the Irish kings paid even less attention to the Norman barons and none at all to the Viceroy.

The first English king to take a real interest in Ireland was Henry VIII (1509–47) who determined to break the power of the Irish aristocracy and petty chieftains. However, it was his daughter, Elizabeth I (1558–1603), who was the first monarch to impose effective English rule over all Ireland. Elizabeth's worst fears that Catholic Ireland might be used as a launching pad for the invasion of England by Spain were realized in 1601 when a small Spanish force landed at Kinsale. Since 1595 parts of Ireland had been in revolt under the leadership of Hugh O'Neil, Earl of Tyrone. But when the Viceroy, Lord Mountjoy, immediately defeated this combined Irish-Spanish force, the Tudor conquest of Ireland was complete. English law was enforced and Protestantism declared the state religion.

The Plantation of Ulster started in earnest in 1609. The land was confiscated by the Protestant English gentry and Lowland Scots. It was the huge influx of Scottish immigrants that built the towns, churches and schools. The confiscation of land and displacement of the indigenous Irish not surprisingly bred a deep resentment among the people. In 1641, the native Irish in the North rebelled in an attempt to recover the lands they had lost to the Plantation. The vice-royalty of Thomas Wentworth, Earl of Strafford, during the 1630s had built up a steady revenue for England from Old English as well as Irish landlords. This provoked hostility to the monarchy and, above all, to himself. Such was his mismanagement of affairs in Ireland that he was recalled to London where he faced legal proceedings which ended in his execution. The Dublin administration which succeeded Strafford became more Puritan in outlook and more favourable to the English Parliament. The Ulster rebellion of 1641 against this administration was characterized by considerable brutality and this was magnified in popular belief into a plan to massacre the entire Protestant population.

Thus was created among seventeenth-century English Protestants such fear, distrust and horror of Papists, particularly of Irish Papists, that rational discussion about catholicism became impossible. When the victorious Cromwell landed in Ireland in 1649, having won the English Civil War, he was bent on vengeance against the rebellious

Irish. After he had massacred the garrison at Drogheda he remarked, 'I am persuaded that this is the righteous judgement of God upon these barbarous wretches who have imbrued their hands in innocent blood.' He set about crushing all opposition ruthlessly. The Catholic religion was banned and the confiscation of land intensified. By 1655 nearly four-fifths of Ireland had been granted to English landlords.

The Glorious Revolution of 1688 displaced King James II who was succeeded on the throne by his son-in-law, William of Orange. King James fled to Ireland where he was accepted as King, but when he claimed authority over the whole of the country, the Protestants and Nonconformists in the key towns of Derry and Enniskillen rose in support of King William. In May 1689, when the Protestant Garrison in Derry was besieged by an Irish Army and the city was on the point of surrender, thirteen apprentice boys rushed forward and shut the main gates. Derry was besieged for 105 days until, on 1 August 1689, one of King William's ships broke through the boom in the River Foyle and relieved the garrison and citizens. So was born the legend of the Apprentice Boys and the motto 'No Surrender'.

King William landed with an army the following year. He defeated the Jacobite armies, first at the Battle of the Boyne in County Meath on 1 July 1690, and then more decisively in 1691 at the Battle of Aughrim, County Galway, where his Protestant Army of 18,000 defeated the Catholic Jacobite Army which was more than 25,000 strong.

By 1703 only 14 per cent of the land in Ireland remained in the hands of the Catholic Irish; in Ulster only 5 per cent. During a period of almost exactly one hundred years, the Plantation had seen the systematic introduction of a foreign community into Ireland, but particularly into Ulster. They spoke differently, worshipped apart and represented an alien tradition and way of life.

During the eighteenth century discrimination against Catholics continued and intensified; consequently many emigrated to America. In a notorious affair in 1796, twenty Protestants were killed by Catholics. This incident was the immediate cause of the founding of the Orange Order. Its members pledged loyalty to the memory of King William III of Orange and to the primacy of the Protestant religion. The first Orange marches to commemorate the shutting of the gates of Derry by the Apprentice Boys were held in 1797. Then in 1798 Wolfe Tone led his rebellion against the English. He was supported by a small force of 1,000 French which landed in County Mayo. It was defeated by the British Army at the battle of Vinegar Hill in June. Wolfe Tone committed suicide in prison in November. As a result of the 1798 rebellion the British Government, led by William Pitt the Younger, passed the Union of Ireland with England and Scotland Act in 1801. So long as

Ireland had its own parliament dominated by the Protestant ruling class, Protestant opinion was willing to support Ireland's claim to be regarded as a distinct and self-governing kingdom, joined to Great Britain only by the link of a common sovereign. But by 1800 the Protestants, alarmed by the growing unrest among the Catholic majority, decided it would be politic to accept a parliamentary union with Great Britain.

As the seventeenth century had ended with the consolidation of the Plantation, so the eighteenth century ended with the formal integration of Ireland with England and Scotland. The nineteenth century saw the start of the gradual reversal of this process with the move towards Home Rule.

In 1845–48 the potato crop failed in Ireland, and one million people died in the Great Famine which ensued. Out of a total population of only eight million, two million emigrated to the United States of America, Canada and Australia. Some, who elected not to travel so far from home, fled to the expanding port of Belfast where Catholic ghettos soon formed. Despite Catholic Emancipation in 1829, Catholics remained second-class citizens, particularly in the largely Protestant North. Protestants, realizing that the re-establishment of a separate Irish Parliament would see the end of Protestant ascendancy, resisted every proposal to set up a separate parliament for Ireland, from the Repeal Campaign of Daniel O'Connel to the Home Rule movement of the Gladstonian era. The only area, due to the accident of the Plantation, where widespread popular support for this policy existed was in the province of Ulster. The Protestants of the North were, if necessary, prepared to fight to remain British; the Catholic majority were, if necessary, prepared to fight to gain their independence from Britain. It was out of this impasse that the idea of partition grew.

A résumé of Irish Republican history cannot omit brief mention of the Fenian Rising of 1867. That it was a complete farce is beside the main point. Fenianism was always more of a tradition than a reality. The word derives from 'Fianna', a legendary band of warrior heroes. The movement was the brain-child of James Stephens who had fled Ireland after the abortive 1848 'rising', otherwise known as 'the battle of the Widow McCormack's cabbage garden'. After an enforced sojourn of some years in Paris, he returned in 1856 to set out on a 3,000-mile tour of Ireland, mostly on foot, to gauge the country's revolutionary potential. Clearly convinced that the Irish nation was behind him, he and a handful of fellow conspirators swore in Dublin on St. Patrick's Day, 17 March 1858: '. . . in the presence of God, to renounce all allegiance to the Queen of England, and to take arms and fight at a moment's warning to make Ireland an Independent Democratic

Republic, and to yield implicit obedience to the commanders and superiors of this secret society . . .' The Society was later to become known as the Irish Republican Brotherhood. Soon after forming his own organization in Ireland, Stephens travelled to America where he and a friend from the 1848 'rising', John O'Mahoney, founded a twin American Society named by O'Mahoney (a Gaelic Scholar) the Fenian Brotherhood. Because secrecy was so important, the American title of the organization soon became the title by which the organization was referred to in Ireland.

The Fenian 'Rising' of 1867 was a shambles. The start of the rebellion was to be signalled by a raid on Chester Castle in England on 11 February, with the object of capturing arms. An informer tipped off the police and the whole operation was called off at the last moment. The police had to be content with a large haul of revolvers and ammunition dumped in the vicinity of Chester railway station. An equally abortive 'rising' at Ballyhurst, near Tipperary, in March was put down by soldiers, and its leader, General Bourke, was wounded and captured. Subsequent to the rising, two Fenian prisoners were released from a prison van in Manchester during the course of a raid by fellow Fenians. During this incident Police Sergeant Brett was shot and killed, whether intentionally or accidentally will never be known. Three men were convicted of Sergeant Brett's murder and subsequently executed. Though they had been present at the attack, it is almost certain that none of the three had fired the fatal shot. Allen, Larkin and O'Brien have gone down in Irish history as the 'Manchester Martyrs'. Statues are to be found to them all over Ireland and their deaths are commemorated annually in many places.

Charles Stewart Parnell ('Ireland is not a geographical fragment but a nation') dominated British Parliamentary life in the late 1870s and early 1880s. He was an Irish Protestant landlord who in October 1879 became President of the Land League of Ireland, originally founded by Michael Davitt to protect the rights of smallholders against powerful landowners. Many of the Land League's members, including Davitt, were Fenians who recognized that there was more political capital to be gained from the practical cause of saving fellow Irishmen from starvation than from the achieving of an Irish Republic by force of arms.

During the 1870s cheap American grain began to flood Europe. Inevitably farm prices dropped drastically. Smallholders found themselves unable to pay their rent. The Land League fought for a reduction of rents, initially sensibly but subsequently more and more under the influence of extremist Fenians. The movement became increasingly violent and eventually Prime Minister Gladstone had no option but to order the arrest of Parnell. The Land League movement however now had a momentum all of its own. In February 1882, Gladstone agreed to release Parnell from prison if he agreed to use his influence to cool the situation while the Government undertook to cast a sympathetic eye over the remaining problems on the land. However, the murder of Lord Frederick Cavendish, the new Chief Secretary for Ireland, and his under-secretary, a Catholic Irishman named Thomas Bourke, in Phoenix Park in Dublin later the same year, by a gang of men armed with 12-inch surgical knives was disastrous for Parnell and must have contributed to the defeat of Gladstone's Home Rule Bill in 1886. Parnell died aged 45 in 1891.

The tide of Irish Nationalism was not even halted by the outbreak of the First World War. Only two years later, the Easter Rising of 1916 took the British garrison by surprise. Reinforcements were rushed from England and General Sir John Maxwell was given full powers to crush the rebellion. The Rising had started on 24 April when 700 volunteers seized the Post Office in Dublin. That the British Government had not been alerted by the Royal Navy's interception of a German ship, carrying 20,000 rifles, in the Irish Sea is surprising. Patrick Pearse, the Commander-in-Chief of the Republican volunteers, proclaimed the Republic from the steps of the Post Office. The Rising, which was ruthlessly crushed, has passed into Republican folklore. During the fighting 1,351 people were killed. A total of 97 were sentenced to death of whom sixteen were executed. One of these was Sir Roger Casement, who had been landed in Ireland by a German U-boat and who was captured and executed for treason on 3 August. It was obvious, however, that a solution would have to be found as soon as the war was over. In July 1917, as a gesture of goodwill, the British Government released the remaining prisoners taken after the Rising. From their ranks Michael Collins emerged as leader of the Irish Republican Brotherhood (IRB) which supported a revamped Sinn Fein.

Sinn Fein ('Ourselves Alone') had first appeared in 1907 as a newspaper edited by a young journalist called Arthur Griffiths. Its aim then had been to establish an elected Irish Parliament in Dublin owing allegiance to the British Crown. By 1920 Sinn Fein was dedicated to establishing an independent Irish Republic. Its military arm, the Irish Republican Army (IRA), was waging a guerilla war against the Royal Irish Constabulary (RIC) and the so-called 'Black and Tans', recruited as auxiliaries for the RIC. The need to increase the strength of the RIC to deal with the campaign of terror was obvious. Apart from actual casualties among the RIC, intimidation of policemen and their families had caused many resignations from the force, while at the same time recruitment was almost at a standstill. It was therefore decided that the wastage should be made good from England. Recruitment began on 1 January 1920 and large numbers of ex-soldiers came forward. By the end of May, 1,500 'Black and Tans', as they came to be known by the Irish, had arrived in Ireland. Their nickname came from a famous pack of hounds; the men's uniform was a mixture of khaki and dark green.

The IRA had by this time developed flying columns of 20–30 well-armed men living in the countryside, emerging only to ambush Crown forces. Then on 9 July 1921 Eamon de Valera, also among the prisoners released by the British Government in 1917, met the British C in C in Ireland, General Macready. A truce was signed between the IRA and Crown forces two days later. In London on 6 December, after months of negotiation between an Irish delegation led by Michael Collins and Arthur Griffiths and the British Cabinet, an Anglo-Irish Treaty was signed. Michael Collins, after signing, was reported to have said, 'I have signed my death-warrant.' The effect of the treaty was to give 26 of the 32 counties the constitutional status of the Dominion of Canada. At that time Canada had its own army and navy and control of its own affairs at home and abroad, subject to membership of the British Commonwealth and an oath of loyalty to the Crown. The new state was not the Irish Republic which the IRA had fought for, but an 'Irish Free State'. The six counties were given one month to opt out if they desired. They did. This was the signal for the anti-treaty Republicans to revolt. Michael Collins was shot dead. By July 1922 there was civil war in Dublin. The new Irish Government put 13,000 Republicans in prison and executed 77. This punishment of the Irish by the Irish caused bitterness for a generation.

In 1924 the Boundary Commission finalized the line of the Border, putting the seal on a compromise solution. The new province of Ulster consisted of the counties of Antrim, Down, Armagh, Derry, Tyrone and Fermanagh. Kevin O'Higgins, a member of the Free State Cabinet, said: 'We had the opportunity of building up a worthy State that would attract and, in time, absorb and assimilate those elements . . . we preferred to burn our own houses, blow up our own bridges, rob our own banks, saddle ourselves with millions of debt for the maintenance of an army . . . Generally we preferred to practise upon ourselves worse indignities than the British had practised on us since Cromwell . . . and now we wonder why the Orangemen are not hopping like so many fleas across the border in their anxiety to come within our fold and jurisdiction.'

In Ulster, the siege mentality took root in 1922. Within the Province the polarization of the Catholic minority and Protestant majority worsened inexorably. Partly as a result of Catholic unwillingness to

18

Below: A crowd of people in flight during rioting in 1921 at the corner of York Street and Donegal Street, now the site of the Belfast College of Art.

Above: British soldiers man a check-point and guard post on a street corner in Belfast during the 1922 troubles.

participate in a State whose existence they opposed, and partly as a result of bias by the establishment against a section of the community which it considered traitorous, many institutions in Northern Ireland evolved in such a way as to be heavily biased in favour of the Unionists. The local government franchise, until 1969, reflected property rather than population, excluded non-ratepayers and awarded many people with more than one property extra votes. Housing allocation and gerrymandering of constituency boundaries were used in some instances, notably in Derry, to maintain Unionist majorities. Even by 1961 only 12 per cent of the Royal Ulster Constabulary (RUC) was Catholic and the notorious B Specials were exclusively Protestant.

The RUC were that part of the former RIC that were geographically situated in Ulster. Thus the Irish Free State raised the Garda as their civil police force, the RIC ceased to exist and the RUC was raised as the civil police force in Ulster. They can be compared to the various county police forces on the mainland, though it is true to say that they have always been something of a para-military force as a result of the special circumstances prevailing in Ireland. The police on the mainland have seldom been issued with firearms. In Ireland, both pre- and post-Independence, they often have been. Since the present Emergency started they have carried firearms at all times. The B Specials, on the

other hand, were the only category of the original A, B and C Categories Ulster Special Constabulary (USC) whose role was to augment the full-time police force during periods of tension. Whereas Special Constabulary on the mainland are usually recruited to help the full-time police force in such functions as traffic control, the Specials in Ulster were specifically intended to be for the maintenance of law and order when extra numbers were required. They were permitted to keep firearms at home for this purpose. Over the years they acquired a reputation for brutality and sectarianism.

There was widespread discrimination against Catholics in public employment. This meant, for instance, that State Education was in fact a Protestant education and that the Catholic Church had to subsidize Catholic schools to the tune of 50 per cent. Stormont was only prepared to pay a proportion of the costs of Catholic Schools, arguing that a free State education was available if Catholic parents would only send their children to the appointed local (Protestant) schools.

From 1932 to 1935 there was intermittent violence in the North. Unemployment from 1930 to 1939 never fell below 25 per cent. Despite the IRA bombing campaign in mainland Britain in 1939, and the continuation of that campaign in a very minor form until 1945, 1939 in fact heralded the onset of an industrial and economic boom in

Left: Members of the B Special Constabulary at a road-block near Ballycastle Co. Antrim in 1932.

Northern Ireland. The campaign of 1939 was timed to coincide with the approach of war in Europe and to draw attention to Britain's maintenance of 'partition'. There were a few bomb attacks in London, but the campaign was a complete failure. Nor were efforts to co-operate with German agents during the war any more successful. In the immediate post-war years, and certainly until 1953, there is evidence of real social advance in the Province, with standards of living improving substantially.

Despite the effects of discrimination, the 1960s were a period of relative prosperity in Northern Ireland. The 1956–62 IRA campaign failed because of this increasing prosperity. By and large people were just not prepared to upset a good thing. There was an increase in economic co-operation between North and South. The Nationalist Party agreed to become the Official Opposition at Stormont. Even 'twin towns' were established in North and South. Prospects seemed good, but were about to be destroyed by a combination of Establishment reluctance to improve matters and minority impatience for reform. Why the IRA should have chosen 1956 to launch a campaign in the North is not absolutely clear. It was probably a reaction to the improved relations between Ireland and the United Kingdom which had begun soon after the final rupture between the two countries had been reached in April 1949 with the declaration of the Republic. Although the fortunes of the IRA were at an all-time low, and although its message was becoming increasingly irrelevant, the organization retained just enough vitality to stage one last effort to keep the revolutionary tradition alive.

On 25 July 1953, three men backed a van up to the hut housing the OTC armoury at Felsted Public School in Essex, cut open the rear windows and from the racks took 99 rifles, eight Bren-guns, ten Sten-guns, a Browning 0.3in machine-gun, a 2in mortar and a PIAT (anti-tank projector). Hours later in Bishop's Stortford, an observant constable noticed a van with flat tyres, the driver apparently lost, and rear windows obscured by strips of paper. He stopped the vehicle to point out this serious contravention of the Highway Code and arrested the three occupants of the van with their haul. The leader of this abortive raid was Cathol Goulding, later to become Chief of Staff of the Official IRA. His accomplice, John Stephenson (later Gaelicized to Sean MacStiofáin), emerged as Chief of Staff of the Provisional Irish Republican Army (PIRA). The Felsted raid was one of six, four of which failed. The last was on the Army camp at Aborfield when five tons of arms were removed; they were all recovered in North London. The Aborfield raid was led by Rory O'Brady (later Gaelicized to Ruairi O'Bradaigh) who subsequently became President of Sinn Fein.

Goulding, Stephenson and O'Brady were three leading figures in an ever-decreasing band of IRA activists. Goulding was a Dubliner and had come under the influence of Dublin Communists whose policies were directed at moving the IRA away from their customary rather esoteric attitudes and simple solutions to the problems of Ireland. It was natural that when the IRA split into two wings in 1969, Goulding should lead the Official IRA, who chose not to espouse violence since they reasoned that the time was not yet ripe for revolution. Stephenson, a disaffected Englishman, took the opposite route and was to be a leading figure in the setting up of the Provisional IRA, and later, its Chief of Staff. O'Brady, another Dubliner, though an activist in the 1956–62 campaign, subsequently confined his activities to heading the political wing of the IRA.

The 1956–62 campaign started on 2 December 1956 when 150 men blew up targets in ten areas near the border: a BBC transmitter, a TA building, a courthouse and other similar targets. There was immediate internment in both North and South which bagged most of the key IRA figures. The IRA had not expected internment in the South, and on 26 February 1962 they called off their campaign. They had failed to get the support of the Catholic population and it was not worthwhile carrying on. Six members of the RUC were killed and nineteen wounded; eleven B Specials and two soldiers were wounded. Two members of the IRA were killed by the Security Forces and nine were killed in error by the IRA – 'own goals' in the jargon of the soldier. Internment had been most effective and by 1967 Goulding admitted that the movement was virtually extinct. If only it had been possible to capitalize on this with sensible reform; if only the Catholics had been more patient; if only the IRA had not climbed on the Civil Rights bandwagon; if only . . .

2
THE CIVIL RIGHTS MOVEMENT

It is worth looking in some detail at the history of the Ulster Volunteer Force (UVF) if one is to understand the beginnings of the Civil Rights Movement. The UVF emerged into the limelight again in 1966, partly in reaction to the 1956–62 IRA campaign, but also because extremist Loyalists were taking exception to the increasingly voiced objections of the minority Catholic population to widespread discrimination, sectarianism and gerrymandering.

The UVF may be understood in three distinct ways. First, as the name of Edward Carson's Force, founded in 1912 and reorganized as the Ulster Special Constabulary in 1920. Second, as a broad term describing contemporary paramilitary Protestant organizations, including the Ulster Defence Association (UDA), the Red Hand Commandos, Orange Volunteers, the B Specials Association and Ian Paisley's Ulster Protestant Volunteers. Third, as a specific organization calling itself the UVF, founded in 1966 by Augustus ('Gusty') Spence and later proscribed under the Special Powers Act by Terence O'Neill, Prime Minister of Northern Ireland, 1963–69. Spence completed his National Service as a military policeman in Cyprus in 1959 and took a job at the Harland and Wolff shipyard. He soon became prominent in an organization known as Ulster Protestant Action. From these beginnings he formed an extremist Protestant organization based, as he saw it, on Carson's UVF. Spence's UVF initially had only a handful of members, mostly his drinking friends. After a period of sending threatening letters to moderate Protestants and extremist Catholics, the group's first attack was on 16 April 1966 when they fired at the home of the Unionist MP for Woodvale in a mock IRA attack. Then, on 27 April John Scullion, an innocent drunk singing Republican songs, was shot dead. Charges against Spence for this murder were later dropped. On 25 June, Spence and two accomplices murdered Peter Ward, whom they mistook for a Republican activist, but who was in fact an innocent Catholic youth, and wounded two others. They were all found guilty of his murder.

The UVF was banned by O'Neill the following weekend. Ian Paisley, probably the most vociferous and widely known of all Protestant politicians, decided to dissociate himself from the UVF publicly. In the

light of the fact that the organization was generally consi
product of his own rhetoric, this was received with some sc
most observers of the Ulster scene. The Reverend Ian Kyle l
founder in 1951 of the Free Presbyterian Church, was the ι
long line of fire-breathing, fundamentalist Protestant prea
become involved in Ulster politics. Until the mid 1960s, his n ᴏᵣiety
derived almost exclusively from his opposition to ecumenism. On 19
July, Paisley was sent to gaol for three months after refusing to sign a
pledge of good behaviour, following his arrest in a near riot at the
Presbyterian General Assembly.

The events of 1966 troubled many Catholics and 1967 saw precious
little improvement. Although the UVF's leaders were in jail, the
Catholic minority were still goaded through the pages of *The Protestant Telegraph*. His articles demonstrated Protestant fears, bigotry and
frustration: the Church of England was a 'spiritual brothel, harbouring
theological prostitutes and ecumenical pimps'. The Unionist Party
was a 'political monstrosity, the product of ecumenism and Roman-
ism'. The most rabid invective was reserved for Catholicism: 'Rome
may paint her face and attire her hair like Jezebel of old, but I still
recognize the murderous wrinkles on the brow of the old scarlet-robed
hag. She may clothe herself in the finest attire, but underneath the
gorgeous robes I see the leprous garments of her whoredom.' A series
on 'Love Affairs of the Vatican' proved particularly popular. England
was a country that 'currently wallows – nay revels – in filth, sin and
evil of the most horrible forms. Abortion and sodomy all by law
condoned, even encouraged. Divorce, adultery, fornication, sex perver-
sion, rape, infanticide, murder and illegitimacy flourish.' It was
unbelievably puerile and vicious invective by any standards. No
wonder the minority population felt discriminated against.

Attempts to accentuate the acceptable face of Unionism, most of
them far too late, only drew attention to its shortcomings – the areas of
historic discrimination. The Ulster Unionist Council had been
founded in 1905, bringing together a number of organizations dedicated to preserving the Union with Great Britain. Unionist MPs at
Westminster banded together as early as 1906 in defence of the Union.
Unionism, then as now, was an inextricable mixture of religion and
politics. In 1959, the Unionist Executive Committee stated the policy
and aims of the Unionist Party:

1. To maintain the constitutional position of Northern Ireland as an
   integral part of the United Kingdom and to defend the principles
   of civil and religious liberty.
2. To improve social standards and to expand industry and agricul-
   ture.

Catholic representation on District Councils, 1972

	Catholic population	Unionist Councillors	Non-Unionist Councillors
Co Tyrone:			
Dungannon UDC	50%	14%	7%
Dungannon RDC	52%	16%	6%
Omagh UDC	61%	12%	9%
Omagh RDC	60%	24%	18%
Castlederg RDC	50%	13%	6%
Clogher RDC	51%	14%	5%
Cookstown RDC	55%	12%	7%
Strabane RDC	49%	22%	9%
Other Counties:			
Armagh UDC	58%	12%	8%
Magherafelt RDC	54%	20%	8%
Fermanagh CC	53%	33%	17%
East Down RDC	50%	19%	5%
Lurgan MB	46%	15%	0%

UDC	Urban District Council	CC	County Council
RDC	Rural District Council	MB	Metropolitan Borough

Judicial posts, 1969	Non-Catholic	Catholic
High Court Judges	6	1
County Court Judges	4	1
Resident Magistrates	9	3

After Darby, J., *Conflict in Northern Ireland*, 1976.

3. To welcome to our ranks only those who unconditionally support these ideals.

Until O'Neill's premiership, 'religious liberty' was interpreted as the liberty of the Protestant religion and under no circumstances could Catholics be Unionists. Catholics also suffered in these respects. The basis for the drawing up of the ward boundaries is complicated, but essentially the 1854 Towns Improvement (Ireland) Act stated that wards should be formed having regard to 'the number of persons rated in each ward, as well as the aggregate amount of the sums at which all the said persons shall be so rated'. This act was repealed, but its provisions were included in the Local Government (Northern Ireland) Act 1922. In practice, in many cases a large proportion of poorer property is included in one ward, so that in wealthier wards few votes are needed to return a member. Given the tendency to live in segregated groups, and that the more valuable property is usually Protestant, the division of an area to produce a permanent majority for one side is not difficult. In Londonderry, Armagh and Omagh the percentage of Catholics in the population in 1968 was 69 per cent, 59 per cent and 61 per cent respectively, but the Unionists held twelve out of twenty, twelve out of twenty and twelve out of twenty-one seats on the respective councils. In 1967, in Londonderry, where Catholic voters numbered 14,429 and other voters 8,781, Unionists held twelve seats on the council and non-Unionists eight. The examples are endless and they are equally illuminating in the housing and jobs sectors. The statistics shown on page 26, though selective, are representative of the wider picture.

In the face of this blatant gerrymandering, three strands of society: the growing Catholic middle class, the students of one of Belfast's few integrated academic institutions – Queen's University – and the Catholic working class in their ghettos, were drawn together into the Northern Ireland Civil Rights Association (NICRA). This was founded in February 1967, and was modelled deliberately on the Black Liberation Movement led by Martin Luther King in the United States. Like King's Movement, the Movement chose the popular march as its main means of gaining public attention. The first march took place on 24 August 1968 from Coalisland to Dungannon. The march announced for 5 October 1968 in Londonderry was banned by the Home Affairs Minister, William Craig, himself a hardline Loyalist, well-known for his political extremism and who openly sneered at the Civil Rights Movement. It went ahead, however, and was broken up by two platoons of the Police Reserve Force 'using batons indiscriminately' (Cameron Commission findings). Seventy-five civilians and eighteen policemen were injured. On 4 December there was a riot in Dungannon when a Protestant crowd blocked the path of a Civil Rights march. The two crowds were being kept apart by the police when a shot rang out from the Protestant crowd, the bullet narrowly missing a Pressman. This was the first shot fired in public since the UVF murders of 1966.

Craig, who by this stage was advocating independence for Ulster, was promptly dismissed by O'Neill in an effort to rid Unionism of its more extremist elements. O'Neill realized that Ulster was on the brink of catastrophe. In London, Harold Wilson, the Prime Minister was demanding drastic and radical reform. On 22 November, O'Neill announced a reform programme including a points system of housing allocation, an ombudsman, franchise reform, a review of the Special Powers Act and the dissolution of the Derry Council. In response, NICRA declared a truce on 9 December: there would be a moratorium on marches and demonstrations. On 20 December, however, a less patient organization, calling itself the People's Democracy, its membership mostly disaffected NICRA members, announced a Belfast – Derry march to take place on 1–4 January 1969. It was attacked at

Burntollet on 4 January by a Loyalist mob containing many B Specials in civilian clothes and led by a 'Major' Ronald Bunting who had served in the British Army and was a loyal supporter of Ian Paisley. Burntollet was an unprovoked attack against defenceless marchers many of whom were seriously injured. The incident became part of Catholic folklore and convinced many Catholics that the Establishment was prepared to condone, even encourage, physical attack on the Catholic community.

In the eyes of Protestant extremists the politicians had failed them. They had failed to prevent the erosion of Protestant privilege and they had been blackmailed into compromise by Catholic pressure groups. They decided to try and topple the Prime Minister and at the same time secure the release of Paisley and Bunting who had been imprisoned for organizing an unlawful assembly in Armagh. In their despair they turned to more desperate means. A series of bomb attacks was planned with the purpose of persuading Ulster politicians that they had already gone too far in their appeasement of the Civil Rights Movement and that they were to go no further.

On 30 March four explosions wrecked an electricity substation at Castlereagh. On 20 April an explosion at Silent Valley Reservoir in County Down damaged valves and supply pipes, cutting off two-thirds of Belfast's water-supply. On the same day an electricity pylon at Kilmore, County Armagh was damaged. On 23 and 24 April two more explosions damaged water pipes near Lough Neagh and in County Down. One of those involved in all the explosions, Samuel Stevenson of Newtownards, who was in the pay of the UVF, was convicted and sentenced to twelve years. An accomplice killed himself in a subsequent explosion south of the border. Although these explosions were almost certainly a UVF-inspired operation, none of those involved were brought to trial.

The rapidly worsening situation and the refusal of many Loyalist politicians to go along with O'Neill's reform package left him with only one way out. On 28 April Terence O'Neill resigned and was replaced on 1 May by James Chichester-Clark. The Loyalists had succeeded in forcing the 'collaborator' O'Neill out. The torch of Liberal Unionism was passed to James Chichester-Clark, a cousin of the former Prime Minister and an honest country gentlemen of limited shrewdness and political acumen.

In 1966 Protestant volunteers had reintroduced the gun and the bullet to Ulster politics. In 1969 Protestant bombers forced the resignation of a Prime Minister. Although the present situation in Northern Ireland is immensely complex, and although both communities have contributed towards the present tragic situation, it is perhaps insufficiently highlighted to what extent the Loyalist community were responsible for leading Ulster over the precipice in 1969.

On 2 July, a White Paper on the Reshaping of Local Government, proposed the abolition of the 73 Councils in Ulster and their replacement by seventeen, more accountable councils. This was part of the continuing, albeit belated, effort by the Ulster Government to introduce more representative and accountable local government. But legislation of itself can achieve very little. It needs the willing support and co-operation of the mass of the people. Chichester-Clark did push through the one-man, one-vote reform. Much reform, including placing the housing allocation system on a fairer basis and the replacement of the gerrymandered Derry city administration by a commission, went ahead. But by the time these reforms had begun to take effect, they were irrelevant. Now the very existence of the Unionist Government, which had permitted these abuses to ensure its own survival, was threatened.

On 12 August, the Apprentice Boys' march in Londonderry, an annual event to commemorate the shutting of the gates of Londonderry in May 1689 by thirteen boys to prevent the Catholic James II from entering the town, was attacked by a Catholic crowd and, as a result, the Bogside, a Catholic stronghold in Londonderry, was entered by the RUC.

The subsequent rioting later led to the establishment of a so-called 'Free Derry'. Serious rioting occurred in Dungannon, Dungiven, Lurgan, Newry, Armagh and Belfast. In Belfast, four men and a boy were killed. On 15 August the Queen's Regiment – the first unit of the British Army to be deployed in Belfast in the current emergency – intervened between the Falls and the Shankhill Roads in Belfast, establishing what later became the 'Peace Line'.

The rioting in Belfast in August had been the work of the UVF. In late 1968 they had decided to work through the legal front of the Ulster Protestant Volunteers (UPV). John McKeague, a lean, fair-haired Paisleyite Belfast vigilante, and other UVF old hands joined the Shankill and Willowfield division of the UPV. When they were expelled by the UPV for being too dangerously extremist, even for them, McKeague founded the Shankill Defence Association (SDA). In mid August, when McKeague demanded that the B Specials be deployed in Belfast to protect the Protestant Shankill and neighbouring areas from the possibility of future riots along the Catholic/Protestant Falls/Shankill interface, Chichester-Clark prevaricated. The Protestants put up barricades. In response, the Catholic end of the Crumlin Road also put up barricades. The ensuing violence was the worst that Belfast had ever seen: petrol bombs were hurled in both directions. McKeague and his men followed close behind police baton charges and set houses alight. A machine-gun opened fire from Hooker Street. The police returned the fire. McKeague then rushed to the other end of the Shankill and repulsed an invasion by a howling Catholic mob. More gunfire was exchanged. As the rioting got progressively out of hand, Shorland Armoured Cars were brought in and a 0.3in machine-gun was used against the Divis Flats, killing nine-year-old Patrick Rooney and Trooper McCabe, a British soldier on leave.

The violence of August 1969 was in some respects, no greater in scale than some of the incidents of the preceding year. The difference was the massive coverage by the media which forced the British Government to send in troops to protect the Catholic population against further attacks in Derry and Belfast. The media had not been

Below: An RUC Shorland armoured car on patrol in the Northern Ireland countryside. This version is armed with the 7.62mm GPMG rather than the Browning. These vehicles were designed for rural patrol work, and were seldom, if ever, used again in an urban environment after the Divis flats incident. (Shorts)

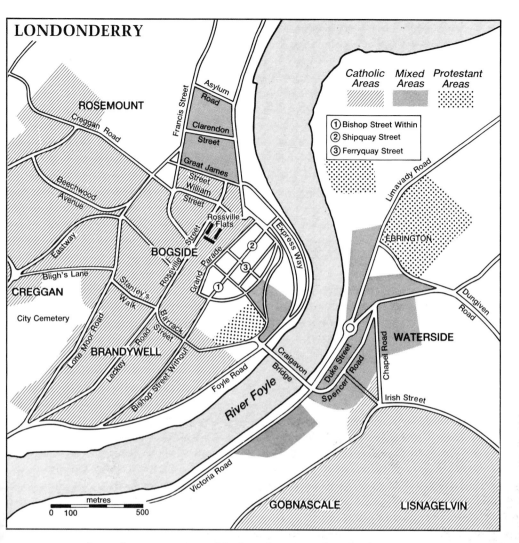

LONDONDERRY

Catholic Areas	Mixed Areas	Protestant Areas

1. Bishop Street Within
2. Shipquay Street
3. Ferryquay Street

ROSEMOUNT

Creggan Road

Francis Street

Asylum Road

Clarendon Street

Great James Street

William Street

Beechwood Avenue

Rossville Flats

Eastway

BOGSIDE

Rossville Street

Grand Parade

Express Way

Limavady Road

EBRINGTON

Bligh's Lane

CREGGAN

Stanley's Walk

City Cemetery

Lone Moor Road

Leckey Road

Barrack Street

BRANDYWELL

Bishop Street Without

Foyle Road

Craigavon Bridge

River Foyle

Victoria Road

WATERSIDE

Dungiven Road

Duke Street

Spencer Road

Chapel Road

Irish Street

GOBNASCALE

LISNAGELVIN

metres
0   100   500

attracted to Ulster in 1968 and before, because the Civil Rights Movement had not yet gathered sufficient momentum to invite much attention. But after Burntollet, the attacks on the Apprentice Boys' march, and the riots in Belfast a few days later, its gatherings became major media events. It was the widespread TV coverage in particular that brought home to the British public, for the first time, the seriousness of the situation and gave the British Government no other option but to send in troops.

The Civil Rights Movement had started something which had gone farther than they had initially intended. After Burntollet, however, the early innocence of the movement became tainted with a new radicalism. At first, the movement had produced reform, but latterly it contributed towards the ever-increasing violence.

3
COMMUNAL VIOLENCE, 1969–1970

Lieutenant-General Sir Ian Freeland arrived as General Officer Commanding (GOC) Northern Ireland on 9 July 1969. Freeland had 2,500 soldiers in the Province, half of them tied up guarding public utilities. On 12 July, only three days after his arrival, rioting broke out in Derry and Dungiven. There were a total of 3,200 RUC available, and it was not long before they had reached the point of exhaustion. On the evening of 12 July, the Ulster Minister for Home Affairs, Robert Porter, consulted with Freeland's Chief of Staff, Brigadier Tony Dyball. Both agreed that troops might be required and a contingent of soldiers was transferred from Lisburn near Belfast across to HMS *Sea Eagle*, a Royal Naval shore station in Derry. In the event, B Specials were mobilized and the troops were not needed.

Wilson and his Government were, at this stage, considering Direct Rule – that is to say, rule direct from Westminster and not via a devolved Parliament of Northern Ireland at Stormont, as constituted in 1922. They were also extremely worried about the legal environment within which British troops would operate. First ideas were based upon the concept of the 'common law constable', that is that all citizens have the power to make a citizen's arrest and, therefore, to be a common law constable. But this begged several questions. Few citizens are put in the position of having to shoot their fellow men. What would happen if a soldier was forced to shoot a United Kingdom citizen? The doctrine of 'equivalent force' was evolved. This meant that a soldier could shoot someone only if that person had been preparing to do something equally drastic to him.

At the end of July, the Cabinet had agreed to provide Chichester-Clark with more troops if he asked for them. Freeland, however, did not appreciate that this decision had already been taken, and watched the situation become daily more serious around him. On 9 August, Whitehall agreed to the use of CS gas by the RUC. CS gas is a form of so-called 'tear-gas', commonly used by many police forces throughout the world, for dispersing unruly crowds, but hitherto never used in the United Kingdom. On 11 August Chichester-Clark and his Cabinet ratified their earlier decision to permit the Apprentice Boys' Parade through Londonderry to go ahead the following day.

Some basic understanding of the geography of Londonderry and Belfast is necessary at this stage. A glance at a map of Londonderry shows that the city is divided by the River Foyle running from South to North through the centre of the city, creating a small enclave of Ulster territory on its West bank. About 80–90 per cent of the population on the west bank, particularly in the Bogside area near the river and in the Creggan housing estate, are Catholic. Whereas in the Victoria, Ebrington and Altnagelvin areas on the east bank, only 20–30 per cent of the population are Catholic.

The same religious divide exists in Belfast, except that there the two communities are not so simply divided. Only study of a map can provide an accurate idea of the situation, but in simple terms a large area of West Belfast including the Lower Falls, Clonard, Beechmount, Whiterock, Turf Lodge, Ballymurphy, New Barnsley and Andersonstown districts, is almost exclusively Catholic. Most of North and East Belfast, on the other hand, is Protestant. This includes the Shankill, Glencairn, Springmartin, Woodvale, Sandy Row, Village, Windsor, Ballysillan and Tiger Bay areas. East of the river, Logan is virtually exclusively Protestant. There are mixed areas and there are 'islands' of Catholicism such as the Markets, Ardoyne and Ligoniel in predominately Protestant Central and North Belfast.

The week from 12 to 16 August 1969 was a watershed: that week the Army became inextricably involved in Ulster. On 12 August the Apprentice Boys' March, as provocative as ever, was attacked as it passed the Bogside. This was the start of a three-day siege of the Bogside and saw the birth of 'Free Derry'. At midnight on 12 August, the RUC used CS gas for the first time in the United Kingdom. Three hundred soldiers were sent to HMS *Sea Eagle* on 13 August. On 14 August the B Specials were deployed in Derry to replace the exhausted RUC. There is some evidence to suggest that some B Specials joined in the rioting and burning of Catholic homes. That same day at 1.30p.m. precisely, RUC Inspector General Peacocke telephoned the Ulster Home Affairs Minister, Robert Porter, at Stormont, to ask for military aid. Chichester-Clark made the request to Downing Street at 3p.m. and at 4.30p.m. Prime Minister Wilson and Home Secretary James Callaghan telephoned their agreement. At 5p.m. the 1st Battalion The Prince of Wales's Own Regiment of Yorkshire (1 PWO) was committed to the Bogside in Londonderry. In Belfast, during the night of 14/15 August, ten civilians were killed and 145 civilians and four policemen were wounded by gunfire.

On the morning of the 15th the devastation was plain to see: one hundred and fifty houses had been destroyed by fire. General Freeland was critically short of soldiers; he had already committed 1 PWO

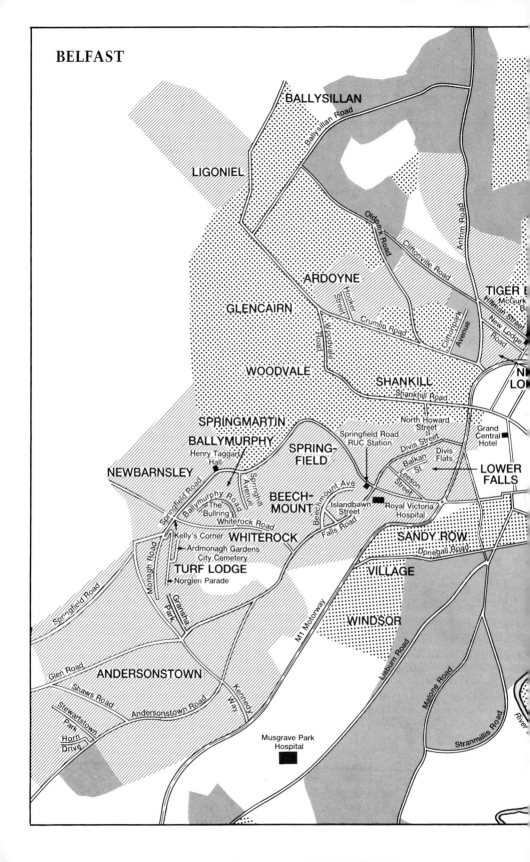

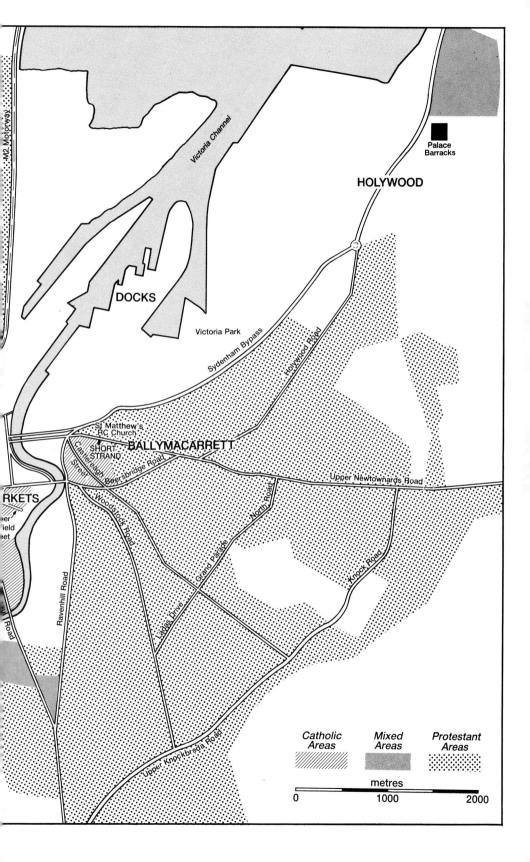

M2 Motorway

Victoria Channel

Palace
Barracks

HOLYWOOD

DOCKS

Victoria Park

Sydenham Bypass

Holywood Road

St Matthew's
RC Church

SHORT
STRAND

BALLYMACARRETT

Castlereagh Street

Beersbridge Road

Upper Newtownards Road

RKETS

er
ield
eet

Woodstock Road

North Road

Ravenhill Road

Grand Parade

Ladas Drive

Knock Road

Road

Upper Knockbreda Road

Catholic Areas	Mixed Areas	Protestant Areas

metres

0   1000   2000

Above: A training facility simulating the urban environment of Belfast and Londonderry in which troops are coached in urban techniques. To the left is a tower from which training staff coach the troops 'on patrol' within the training facility. **Below:** Troops on the streets of Belfast in mid-1969 soon after the first deployment of troops. Note the standard of combat dress – basic camouflage nets on helmets suitable for rural operations, and the lack of any specialist urban counter-insurgency equipment. It took several more years before special-purpose equipment was developed.

Above: The Chief of the Defence Staff, Marshal of the Royal Air Force Sir Charles Elworthy, GCB, CBE, DSO, MVO, DFC, AFC, MA, (foreground left) visits the 'peace line'. He is seen here talking to the Commanding Officer of 1 Para, Lieutenant-Colonel Mike Gray. On the extreme left is Lieutenant-General Sir Ian Freeland, KCB, DSO, Commander-in-Chief Northern Ireland, and fifth from the left is Brigadier Peter Hudson, CBE, Commander of 39 Infantry Brigade, the formation responsible for security in Belfast.

reinforced by a Company of the 1st Battalion The Royal Regiment of Wales (1 RRW) to Derry. For Belfast all he had available was three Companies of the 2nd Battalion The Queen's Regiment (2 QUEEN'S) and two Companies of 1 RRW. On the evening of 14 August, Brigadier Peter Hudson, commanding 39 Infantry Brigade, had toured the trouble spots and quickly appreciated that he needed more troops. Reinforcements were requested by the Stormont Government on the 15th and that night the first elements of the 3rd Battalion The Light Infantry (3 LI) landed at Aldergrove Airport, just outside Belfast. By the beginning of September, Army numbers had increased to 6,000 and on the 4th the barricades in Turf Lodge, a Catholic area of south-west Belfast, were removed, probably as a result of negotiations between residents and the Army.

On 5 September Peter Hudson organized meetings between Tony Dyball, now a Major-General, Father Padraig Murphy, a local priest, and Jim Sullivan, the Republican leader in the Lower Falls. Dyball managed to secure agreement for some of the barriers to come down,

Above: Soldiers of the Parachute Regiment relax between operations in Belfast. The photograph was taken before relations between the Army and the Catholic population deteriorated in early 1970.

this despite a Protestant riot in Belfast on 8 September when the *Sunday Times* reported this military negotiation with the IRA. On 15 September all the Catholic barricades came down after a visit by a Catholic 'team' to 10 Downing Street. General Freeland managed to persuade Wilson's Cabinet that the only realistic approach was to 'talk down' the barricades. The alternative was for infantry battalions to fight their way through the strongly Catholic Falls area which, politically, was clearly quite unacceptable. That a constructive relationship between the Army and the Catholic community survived throughout the autumn of 1969 and into 1970 was a remarkable achievement by the Army given the difficult circumstances which prevailed. But the underlying fact remained; no army, however well it conducts itself, is suitable for police work. Nevertheless, the barricades came down as a result of political persuasion and patient negotiation on the ground by the Army.

On 16 October, the decision to disband the B Specials was taken and it was agreed to form the Ulster Defence Regiment (UDR),* which

*See Chapter 9 for a complete account of the UDR.

would be controlled by Westminster. This so enraged the Protestant community that serious rioting ensued in the Shankill Road area. The Army held its fire for 1½ hours during which time approximately 1,000 rounds were fired at them, injuring 22 soldiers. Authorization was then given for the Army to open fire in self-defence; 66 rounds were fired which killed two Protestant gunmen and wounded others. The riot squads then moved in and made arrests. The Army thus demonstrated its even-handedness by dealing equally firmly with a Protestant mob. The B Specials had come to represent Protestant repression and were regarded as unreformable. They were accountable only to the Ulster Government and they were Protestants to a man. Chichester-Clark wisely decided that they must go and be replaced by the UDR, which would be part of the British Army. The Protestants were profoundly shocked. The B Specials were a part of their mythology – a force recruited exclusively from the Loyalist community to defend them against the IRA. It was being taken from them when they most needed it.

The period over Christmas 1969 and into early 1970 was, by and large, the lull before the storm. It was as if the violence of the summer and autumn of 1969 had caused both communities to stop and think.

The dam broke in the spring. On 1 April 1970 only 70 Royal Scots stood between 400 Catholics on the edge of the Ballymurphy housing estate in Belfast and an excited Protestant crowd in the contiguous Highfield estate; 25 of the soldiers were injured. The next day 600 troops, supported by five Saracen Armoured Personnel Carriers (APCs), moved into the Ballymurphy estate to quell the continuing disorder. A total of 104 canisters of CS gas were fired in response to stoning and riotous behaviour. Inevitably, as the canisters rolled through the estate, the gas affected rioters and innocents alike. Though the use of CS gas was appropriate and, in reaction to stoning, necessary, its use did of course exacerbate the situation. Such is the dilemma of the Security Forces in Northern Ireland. Tension had been increasing for weeks as the Protestant marching season approached, the time when the Loyalist population celebrates old victories over the recalcitrant natives. At the same time, friction between the Army and the minority increased as the Catholic youths began to resent the presence of foreign soldiers in their ghettos. All this came together in April.

It can be argued that the failure to ban the 1970 Orange parades, and the massive arms searches and curfew in the Lower Falls area which followed, was the last chance to avoid the catastrophe that has since engulfed Ulster. The previous August was the watershed, the spring of 1970 the last opportunity for a settlement. Until the spring of 1970, most Catholics regarded the troops as their protectors. The Lower Falls operation changed everything, though the Army was merely doing its job and reacting to events. The first Orange Parade took place on 3 June and ended in rioting by Protestant crowds who objected to the March being diverted.

On 26 June 1970, 45 Commando with the 1st Battalion The King's Own Scottish Borderers (KOSB) and the 1st Battalion The Royal Scots were given the job of keeping protesting Catholics away from marching Orangemen. 45 Commando were responsible for a district which included the Crumlin Road as its focus. To the North lay the Catholic Ardoyne, to the south, the Protestant Shankill. From the row upon row of small red brick homes to the south came a procession of eight Orange Lodges each headed by a band. A crowd of a further 2,000 Protestants followed. That evening, a crowd of some 350 Catholic youths started to hurl stones at the march. 11 Troop of Support Company 45 Commando attempted to block with their 4-ton truck the

side-street from which the youths were advancing, but it afforded little protection against stones, catapulted rivets, iron piping and broken sheets of glass. The glass was skimmed along the street at Marines' shins. Nearly every man was injured and their Troop Commander was hit in the mouth by a brick flung from a mere five yards away. The troop sergeant took over while this wound was dressed, and then the young lieutenant resumed command of his men. By now there were some 1,000 people in two howling mobs, battling to get at one another.

Farther down the road, 400 Commandos prevented another 2,000 Catholics from joining the fray, while the RUC held back 3,000 Protestants. The confrontation lasted throughout the night, but as dawn broke on a summer's day the mobs went home to the south, waving Union Jacks while the Republicans carried the Irish tricolour in the opposite direction. On the following day, Saturday 27th, the marches were again allowed to go ahead. There was rioting through

Left: Commandos hold a Catholic mob at bay in a side-street off the Crumlin Road, Belfast, in June 1970. The 4-ton Bedford truck, adapted to take Macralon armour, is being used as a road-block. Notice that the soldiers are carrying the newly issued riot shields – an early version that was solid metal and only protected a limited part of the body – and batons.

42

Right: A riot scene in west Belfast in 1970. The Army's early riot tactics did not need to take into account the threat from gunmen – it is of interest that only one member of the riot squad (in rear, also holding loud hailer) has his rifle at the ready. The squad is reacting solely to the stone-throwing youths. Such tactics would not be possible today, in view of the danger of a crowd being used to lure soldiers into the open and so set them up for a shooting. Today a greater percentage of soldiers must carry rifles in a riot situation and use armoured vehicles for cover. (*The Times*)

much of Belfast all day and 276 people were injured. In the Marines' area, however, the day passed in an uneasy calm until Protestant marches sparked off an IRA sniper attack in the Ardoyne in which a Protestant civilian was killed. Shortly afterwards one of 45 Commando's medical staff was wounded while giving first aid to a civilian under fire. Petty Officer Freddy Maclaughlin was putting his patient into a clearly marked ambulance when shots ripped through the side of the vehicle and seriously injured him in the cheek. He was awarded the George Medal for his courage.

The Commanding Officer, Lieutenant-Colonel Roger Ephraums, then deployed the remainder of the Commando. By late afternoon they

had succeeded in preventing any further outbreaks of violence, but at
9.0 that night a drunk rammed a stolen bus into a pub and trouble
broke out again. The 23 men of 5 Troop with tear-gas, arc lights and
snatch squads, made seven arrests and then drove the mob back 500
yards. From this mob a gunman fired several shots one of which,
piercing Marine Terence Glover's riot shield, travelled on into the
pouch on his belt and finally landed up in his rifle-cleaning box.
Unable to make any headway against the Marines, the mob resorted to
looting and burning. One group of rioters broke into a wine shop and,
in a wild mood, attacked the police station where a group of some 20
Commandos held off about 300 people. During the riot, RUC Chief

Royal Marine tours in Northern Ireland, 1969–83

This is a record of service in Northern Ireland second to none. Close study of the table will reveal several examples of Commandos being deployed on a short emergency tour as Spearhead battalion, only a few months before a scheduled roulement tour. Where this happens there is no room for substituting another battalion for the second tour, so tight is the equation between troops available and tasks for the available infantry battalions worldwide.

Unit	Dates	Location	Casualties Fatal	Wounded	Role
41 Commando (Spearhead Battalion)	28 Sept– 10 Nov 69	Belfast	—	—	Establishment of Peace Line and Shankill riots
45 Commando	1 June– 31 Aug 70	Belfast	—	1	Butler Street riots
41 Commando	1 Sept– 11 Nov 70	Belfast	—	7	Shankill riots Crumlin riots
45 Commando (Spearhead Battalion)	10 Aug– 1 Sept 71	Province Reserve	—	—	Barricade clearance
45 Commando	17 Oct 71– 18 Feb 72	Belfast, Newry	—	2	IRA Christmas bombing
42 Commando	28 Oct 71– 18 Jan 72	Armagh, Dungannon	—	5	RUC, K Division
40 Commando	14 June– 18 Oct 72	Belfast	2	14	Protestant marches, Op 'Motorman'
45 Commando (Spearhead Battalion)	10–28 July 72	Belfast	—	1	Protestant marches
42 Commando (Spearhead Battalion)	27 July– 1 Sept 72	Belfast	—	4	Shankill/Falls interface, Op 'Motorman'
42 Commando	15 Feb– 16 June 73	Belfast	2	7	Unity Flats, New Lodge areas
40 Commando	16 June– 17 Oct 73	Belfast	1	4	As above
42 Commando	14 Feb– 14 June 74	Belfast	1	1	UWC strike
42 Commando (Spearhead Battalion)	30 Sept– 14 Oct 74	Bessbrook, Newry, Portadown, Armagh, Long Kesh	—	—	Election
45 Commando	2 July– 6 Nov 74	Bessbrook, Newry, Rathfriland, Newtownhamilton, Crossmaglen, Forkhill	2	6	Election

Unit	Dates	Location	Casualties		Role
			Fatal	Wounded	
40 Commando	24 Feb–24 June 75	Belfast	—	—	Turf Lodge, Andersonstown areas
42 Commando (Spearhead Battalion)	6 Oct–5 Nov 75	Portadown, Armagh, Glen Anne, Aughnacloy	—	—	B Infantry Brigade
42 Commando	27 Feb–24 June 76	Belfast	—	2	Turf Lodge, Andersonstown
40 Commando	16 Aug–15 Dec 76	Newry, Bessbrook, Forkill, Crossmaglen	—	6	3 Infantry Brigade
45 Commando	22 June–19 Oct 77	Belfast	1	10	Turf Lodge, Andersonstown
41 Commando	27 Feb–21 June 78	Belfast	—	10	Turf Lodge, Andersonstown
42 Commando	16 July–14 Nov 78	Bessbrook, Crossmaglen, Forkill	2	3	3 Infantry Brigade RUC, H Division
45 Commando (Spearhead Battalion)	6 Aug–14 Aug 78	Belfast	—	—	39 Brigade Reserve for Anniversary of internment
40 Commando	5 Mar 79–12 Mar 80	Ballykelly	—	2	Residential battalion, 8 Infantry Brigade Reserve
41 Commando	16 Aug–31 Oct 80	South Armagh	—	—	3 Infantry Brigade
45 Commando	10 Sept–14 Nov 82	Belfast	1	2	Turf Lodge, Andersonstown
40 Commando	3 Jan–6 June 83	Belfast	—	—	
42 Commando	2 July–12 Nov 84	Armagh	NK		8 Infantry Brigade
45 Commando	July–Nov 86	Belfast	NK		39 Infantry Brigade
42 Commando	May–July 87	Armagh	NK		Op 'Fondant'
40 Commando	23 Feb–18 July 88	Belfast	NK		8 Infantry Brigade
42 Commando	June–Oct 89	Armagh	NK		39 Infantry Brigade
45 Commando	19 Oct 90–12 Mar 91	Fermanagh	NK		8 Infantry Brigade
42 Commando	Nov 91–9 May 92	Armagh	NK		8 Infantry Brigade
42 Commando	1 Oct 94–Mar 95	Casualties	NK		8 Infantry Brigade
		Total	12	87	

The four Royal Marine Commandos, each roughly equivalent in size and capability to an infantry battalion, have undertaken a total of 34 tours in the Province from 1969 to 1994. Only one of these tours was residential, during which 40 Commando took on the role of 8 Infantry Brigade reserve Battalion in Ballykelly from 5 March 1979 to 12 March 1980. 40 Commando has completed seven tours, 41 Commando four tours, 42 Commando thirteen tours and 45 Commando ten tours. By 1983 total casualties were twelve killed and 87 wounded. 41 Commando was disbanded in 1981 as part of the Government defence cuts.

Superintendent Bill Liggett was shot in the neck by a rioter who fired a shotgun at him from only a few yards away, the Superintendent having gone into the Protestant crowd in an attempt to calm the man.

On Sunday morning, 28 June, the Crumlin Road looked like a battleground, bottles, stones, marbles, ball-bearings and bullets littering the area. The air was thick with smoke from burned out cars, petrol stations and private dwellings. 'Y' Company extricated the bus from the pub which it had rammed on the Saturday night, and used it as sleeping accommodation. While some Marines snatched a few hours' sleep, women from the Catholic Ardoyne brought everybody tea and the atmosphere returned to near normal. The Belfast Corporation dustmen came along to sweep up the wreckage and people started going to church.

The Protestant mob had one final go against the police station on the Sunday evening, but this time 45 Commando were ready for them and they were quickly dispersed. So ended 72 hours of almost non-stop rioting, during which, 45 Commando suffered sixteen casualties, though only one of them was serious. Although they themselves had suffered in the rioting, the Marines spent the remainder of their four-month tour trying to bring harmony to the people of their area. The Medical Section treated civilians wounded in the rioting. Regimental Sergeant-Major King was put in charge of community relations. One of his most successful ventures was day outings and camps for local children at a farm near Belfast. The Assault Engineers repaired a community centre, laid a new surface on a basketball pitch and repaired and redecorated an invalid pensioner's home – all before 45 Commando returned to the United Kingdom on 31 August.

The late June disturbances included two shooting incidents in the Crumlin Road/Hooker Street area in which three Protestants were killed. In a second incident in the Short Strand area, the PIRA 'Belfast Brigade' commander, Billy McKee, and his '3rd Battalion' commander, Billy Kelly, supported by local volunteers, defended St Matthew's Church against Protestant gunmen. The shooting went on until 5a.m. by which time two Protestants had been killed; another two died later from their injuries and several more were wounded. One PIRA man was killed and McKee was wounded. The whole incident had taken its course because the Army was so chronically overstretched that night in Belfast. The one spare platoon in the whole of West Belfast was not able to get through rioting Protestants to the Short Strand area. In all, Freeland had barely two battalions in the city. It was too little, too late. Even more disastrously, the IRA had been permitted to play the role of defenders of the minority community. Until this time, IRA activists had been sitting on the fence awaiting a suitable opportunity.

Then, on 2 July, came the Balkan Street arms find in the Catholic Falls area. This consisted of twelve pistols, a Schmeisser submachine-gun (SMG) and assorted explosives and ammunition. Again the problem was insufficient troops available. After the find, one Platoon was effectively besieged in the middle of the Falls. Elsewhere in the same area one Company was stranded. Two more Companies were dispatched to the rescue and they were forced to fire CS. By 5.40 that afternoon the Falls was in chaos. More troops went in to rescue the rescuers. Residents took this for an invasion. By 5.50p.m. nail and petrol bombs were being thrown at the troops and, later, grenades injured five soldiers. Things got seriously out of hand when Brigadier Hudson, who was commanding and controlling operations from a helicopter, was forced to land as it was thought his helicopter had been hit by a bullet. The troops on the ground decided it would be sensible to regroup on the periphery of the Falls. The residents immediately threw up barricades. A simple arms raid had turned into a major confrontation, again not through the Army's fault, but following a seemingly inevitable series of events.

The Official IRA (OIRA) seized the moment to take on the Army. Not surprisingly General Freeland was not prepared to let the IRA get away with it. He decided a show of force was needed and that the Falls had to be brought back under control. At 8.20p.m. on 3 July the Army went in. The IRA opened fire on The Black Watch and Life Guards, the latter unit having just got off the ferry from Liverpool. The Army returned fire and used CS gas and, in order to avoid bloodshed, imposed a curfew at 10p.m. which was not lifted until 9a.m. on 5 July. While the curfew was in force the Army conducted a major arms search which netted 28 rifles, two carbines, 52 pistols or revolvers, 24 shotguns, 100 incendiary devices, 28lb of gelignite and 20,750 rounds of ammunition.

During the period 3 to 5 July, five civilians were killed, four from gunshot wounds and one from a traffic accident involving an APC; two policemen were injured; military casualties totalled eighteen – thirteen from gunshot wounds, five from grenade splinters. A total of 337 people were detained. The events of 3–5 July changed a sullen Catholic Community into a downright hostile one.

The Provisional IRA (PIRA) had been officially formed in January 1970, its founder-members having rejected the socialism of the Official IRA (OIRA). Following the events of early July, PIRA grew from fewer than 100 activists in May–June to roughly 800 in December 1970. By October that year they were sufficiently strong to move to selective terrorism, though they did not yet feel strong enough to take on the Army in a full-scale guerilla war. The split between the two wings of the IRA was now complete. It had started in December 1969, when a group of IRA men repudiated Cathol Goulding's leadership and established the 'Provisional' Army Council. Sean MacStiofáin was appointed its Chief of Staff. He had long opposed the drift away from armed struggle towards the policy of compromise.

The IRA of past history was a rural-based guerilla army, recruited mostly from the poorer farmers, a rather conservative and very Catholic section of the population. However by 1969, in the aftermath of the riots, there were large numbers of poor urban, working-class youths without a future. Many did not come from a Republican tradition, they were merely discontented. Had the Unionist Establishment offered them a fairer deal over the years, they might not have been interested in revolution. The generation that formed the first volunteers for the Provisional IRA came from this background, though its leaders had more traditional Republican roots dating back to the 1940s. The combination of the angry working-class youths and their embittered leaders was to give the Provisional IRA a horrific potential for violence. Goulding's IRA, known after the split as the 'Official IRA', chose, on the other hand, not to act. The time was not ripe, they reasoned, for revolution.

In July the tea stopped flowing in the Falls; by October the Provisional IRA was taking part in selective terrorism, and by December 1970 the honeymoon period between the Catholic community and the British Army had ended. Although the period 1968–70 witnessed the implementation of many reforms, including universal suffrage to local elections, they were swamped in a sea of violence.

Left: The AT-104 was developed from the 1-ton Humber 'Pig' (FV1611) armoured truck. This was the standard British Army armoured transport vehicle deployed in urban areas in Northern Ireland in the 1970s and into the 1980s. This command version is equipped with various radios and a spotlight. In addition, the barbed wire carried on the front of the vehicle provides an instant road-block capability.

4
THE IRA OFFENSIVE AND INTERNMENT, 1971

Although the troop level in the Province had been reduced from a high of more than 11,000 in July 1970 to 7,000 by the end of 1970, the improvement in the situation was more apparent than real.

Lieutenant-Colonel Dick Gerrard-Wright, Commanding Officer of the 2nd Battalion The Royal Anglian Regiment, whose battalion was stationed in Belfast on a 4-month roulement tour, kept in close contact with representatives of the Catholic minority. This has been the practice in late 1969 and early 1970, particularly when the barricades went up in October 1969. The aim was to avoid confrontation by rational discussion. In addition to negotiation the Anglians tried fraternization and opened a disco to which they invited the local girls, but accusations of rape forced the battalion to end this initiative and the girls were invited to film-shows instead. On 10 January, the same girls were stoned after attending a film-show. On 11 January, full-scale riots broke out in the Ballymurphy Estate and continued for a week. On 3 February, 2 R Anglian cordoned and searched the Clonard and Ardoyne areas of Belfast. The riots on 3 and 4 February were probably the worst the Army had faced to date. In one incident in the New Lodge Road, five soldiers were wounded in a burst of machine-gun fire, and another was wounded by a gelignite bomb. On 6 February, Gunner Robert Curtis aged 20, of 94 Locating Regiment, Royal Artillery, was shot dead in the New Lodge Road; four of his companions were wounded, one seriously. That night the Army shot dead one Republican sympathizer, 28-year-old Bernard Wall, and 19-year-old James Saunders, a staff officer in F Company of the PIRA 3rd Battalion. On 10 February, an explosion on a track leading to an isolated BBC transmitter in County Fermanagh killed five BBC technicians. It had been meant for an Army patrol. On 15 February, another British soldier, also a gunner, was shot dead in Belfast.

At this juncture, it is perhaps as well to describe the ground organization of the terrorists which the Army had to face. The IRA 'Army Council' was located in Dublin. Its 'Northern Command' was responsible for Ulster and the border areas; its 'Southern Command' for the Republic. On the ground, its units were organized into self-styled brigades, each brigade being responsible for three battalions. From mid

49

Above: Dereliction and devastation in the Milton Street area of the Lower Falls, west Belfast, in 1971.
Below: A Saracen troop carrier that has fallen victim to a remotely detonated culvert bomb. These devices incorporated large amounts of home-made explosive and were detonated from a distance as military vehicles passed over them.

1970 in Belfast, the city's several hundred volunteers were organized into the First Battalion, raised from the Andersonstown and North Falls areas; the Second Battalion, raised from the heart of the Falls area; and the Third Battalion raised from the outlying Catholic enclaves of north and east Belfast, such as the Ardoyne, the Markets and the Short Strand.

The violence continued throughout February, two policemen being shot dead on the 27th during rioting in the Ardoyne. Then, on 11 March, three young Scottish soldiers were abducted from a pub where they had been drinking and shot in the back of the head in a country road just outside the Belfast suburb of Ligoniel. They were only 17½ years old and had just joined their battalion. It was as a result of this horrific multiple murder that the rule was introduced that no soldier under eighteen should serve in Ulster with a roulement battalion, though service with a resident battalion was permitted provided that the young soldier did not take part in operational duties. This rule remains in force today. The February and March violence resulted in the Unionist Right demanding immediate internment without trial. The Army doubted its efficacy and Westminster took the General's advice. To placate his Party, Chichester-Clark asked for 3,000 more troops. Receiving only 1,300, he resigned. It was 20 March.

He had replaced the dilettante Captain Terence O'Neill in April 1969. Whereas O'Neill had unashamedly upheld the Protestant supremacy while at the same time managing to utter soothing platitudes about equal rights for all Ulstermen, Chichester-Clark had genuinely tried to remove some of the more glaring inequalities. He had, for instance, approved the setting up of the Hunt Commission which, in October 1969, had recommended that the hated B Specials be disbanded. Chichester-Clark was replaced on 23 March by Brian Faulkner, an able middle-class businessman of Presbyterian values, who was prepared to go to almost any lengths to preserve the British connection. A pragmatist, he was the first member of the Ulster middle class to head a government that, for fifty years, had been led by landed gentry. Faulkner came from a family of linen mill owners. He was a canny businessman.

From the end of March 1971 the PIRA bombing campaign started in earnest. There were 37 explosions during April, 47 in May and 50 in June. From January to August, thirteen soldiers, two policemen and sixteen civilians died in the violence. During the same period there were a total of 311 bomb explosions which injured more than 100 people. In July, 194 rounds of ammunition were fired at British troops and in the first nine days of August, 150 rounds. In one hectic 12-hour period in July, no fewer than twenty explosions wrecked pubs, shops and banks, injuring a dozen civilians. The Provisionals had now embarked upon a full-scale guerilla war, striking indiscriminately at civilian and military targets in an endeavour to make the Province ungovernable and so bring about the collapse of the State and the withdrawal of the British who, the terrorists believed, would not be willing to pay the price in soldiers' and civilians' lives, in wrecked infrastructure and, perhaps most important, international odium. The bombs were mostly car bombs, of commercial explosives, at that time easily obtainable in the Republic. The Provisionals' expertise at this stage was not exceptional, as was witnessed by the number of IRA men killed by bombs exploding prematurely, but it was sufficient to cause mayhem throughout the Province.

Sometimes, however, the bombers were frustrated. In early 1971, 25-year-old Sergeant John Green, who was detached from 94 Locating Regiment stationed in Celle in West Germany to 32 Heavy Regiment in Northern Ireland, was called upon to carry out a task not usually performed by a Grade A1 Surveyor. As a result of an anonymous telephone call, he took out a patrol to check a TV mast near the Eire–Ulster border. On arrival at the mast he found an explosive device apparently actuated by an alarm clock. He disconnected the clock thereby breaking the circuit. The Army has naturally always welcomed favourable publicity in Northern Ireland. On this occasion the following report appeared in *The Daily Express* on 8 January 1971:

Three seconds – and a steady hand – made John Green a hero. Sgt Green is from 94 Loc Regt serving with 32 Hy Regt in Northern Ireland. Three seconds more and he risked being blown up with the Ulster television transmitter he was trying to preserve.

Sgt Green – untrained in bomb disposal – was at the Bessbrook Army base in Co Armagh when an anonymous phone caller reported that the transmitter was due to 'go up'. He set out with a four-man patrol to the site, five miles away on Fathom Mountain. Beneath the transmitter they found the biggest bomb uncovered so far by Ulster's troops – 48lb of gelignite linked to an alarm clock and battery. It was timed to go off in three minutes.

'There was no time to call out an explosives expert,' said 25-year-old Green. 'I knew I had to defuse it myself.' He worked lying on his stomach as the seconds ticked by. First he disconnected the four-and-a-half volt battery from the clock. Then the clock from the detonating mechanism. Brrrr – the alarm clock went off as he tossed it over his shoulder. He'd beaten the bomb by three seconds.[*]

On 9 August, a soldier was shot in the head in Belfast and died instantly. Throughout that day mobs roamed the streets burning and looting. There was now no doubt that the Provisionals had launched a full-scale terrorist campaign against the civilian population of Northern Ireland. The police had lost control in many Catholic areas; witnesses, intimidated by the IRA, would not give evidence; even juries were in danger if they convicted. In a situation where terrorist

[*] Reproduced by kind permission of *The Daily Express*.

Above: An unusual photograph showing an explosive device attached to the underside of a car – in this instance, the bomb was discovered before detonation. Security force members are taught to look under their cars as an automatic drill, before unlocking the car. It is a favourite IRA tactic to place bombs underneath or in the engine compartments of cars belonging to members of the security forces during the night, so that when they drive them away next morning a trembler device detonates the explosive. The same method was used to murder Airey Neave, MP, in 1979, when he was driving away from the House of Commons car park.

intimidation plus some degree of sympathy with the terrorists among a sizeable section of the community exists, the successful arrest and conviction of terrorist criminals becomes virtually impossible; in such circumstances some alternative must be found for the normal procedures of criminal justice. In Ireland, both North and South, this has traditionally been detention and internment without trial. During the inter-war and post-war years, it had been accepted that the use of internment was necessary to public order. Neither Whitehall nor the Army were particularly keen on the idea. Reluctantly, in the face of increasing violence in August, and under pressure from Faulkner, Reginald Maudling, who was then Home Secretary in the new Conservative administration led by Prime Minister Edward Heath, gave his consent. The arrest operation began at 0430 hours on 9 August and predictably caused a violent reaction throughout the Province. The net was cast fairly wide and internees ranged from known terrorists to comparatively harmless pamphleteers. On 23 July a dawn raid on PIRA and OIRA homes and establishments in Belfast and nine other towns had netted documents from which lists for internment were derived. Of a total of 450 on the 'wanted' list, 342 had been arrested by the evening of 9 August. Some, suspecting imminent internment, had fled. In Belfast that night, there were riots in Leeson Street where troops used CS gas to disperse crowds. From 8a.m. Ballymacarrett and the Ardoyne were barricaded by local residents using buses to block roads. In the Ballymurphy area youths roamed the streets and an attempt was made to burn down Mackie's factory. 1 RGJ came under attack in the Falls Road, 1 DWR dispersed crowds in North Queen Street and 2 PARA came under sniper fire at Henry Taggart Hall.

Internment was a political disaster, nor was it particularly effective in military terms, yet it was inevitable given Stormont's failure to accept radical reform years before. Although internment without trial

Above: The Army rounds up suspects after an incident in the Markets area of Belfast in 1971.

was a traditional remedy in Ireland, both North and South, for it to happen in a part of the United Kingdom in 1971, in one of the oldest democracies in the world, presented the Westminster Government with a conundrum it would have preferred to have avoided.

Early in the internment operation a small batch of suspected terrorists were chosen for in-depth interrogation by Army experts. The same methods were regularly used by the Army to train their soldiers to themselves resist interrogation. The methods were inevitably frightening and psychologically disorientating, and intentionally so. But they did not involve physical force nor was any physical injury inflicted. The techniques used involved sensory deprivation, disorientation, keeping prisoners standing for long periods facing a wall in the classic search position, a certain amount of sleep deprivation and subjection to the so-called 'white noise' – a monotonous, nagging tone.

In March 1972 the whole question of in-depth interrogation was examined by a Committee under Lord Parker. The Committee found that the duress to which those under interrogation had been subjected did not amount to brutality. Above all it found that the information gleaned from these methods was indispensable in the fight against the IRA. The Government, however, decided to follow the advice of Lord Gardiner who, in a minority report, advised that the practice be discontinued. Bearing in mind international opinion, the Government had no other choice. Much was written subsequently about the use of 'white noise' and other methods of disorientation. Much later, Britain was put in the dock in the European Court of Human Rights which, in the rarified atmosphere of a courtroom, was bound to find against the practice. In reality the Army had used highly sophisticated and clinical, though admittedly, and intentionally, very frightening, methods to get vital information from evil men. Whether their continued use would have changed the course of events since 1972 we shall never know.

On 6 October, Faulkner announced that three more battalions would be deployed in Ulster, bringing the troop level to 13,600. By now the Army had worked out a system for meeting the demand for troops in Ulster. There were three categories: first, some battalions formed part of the permanent garrison of the Province. These lived in permanent barracks and their tour of duty lasted for two years. Second, the majority of battalions were sent to the Province on 4-month (later 4½-month) tours of duty (called roulement tours by the Army) and were billeted in Emergency accommodation such as requisitioned halls or schools or specially constructed 'Portakabin' camps. Permanent garrison battalions were accompanied by families and all the paraphernalia of an infantry battalion in any normal garrison. Roulement battalions, on the other hand, left their families as well as a Rear Party, the latter to administer vehicles and heavy equipment, in their permanent barracks on the mainland or in Germany.

The third category consisted of battalions undertaking Emergency or unplanned tours to meet a particular situation. These often lasted for a matter of weeks and were usually undertaken by the 'Spearhead' or standby battalion. Most of these additional troops were deployed in the border areas where men cratering border crossing-points (in an attempt to prevent illegal crossing of the border by vehicles possibly carrying explosives) regularly came under fire from terrorist groups inside Eire.

The last months of 1971 saw PIRA extending its attacks to members of the newly formed Ulster Defence Regiment (UDR), especially to members off duty at home in front of their families to deter recruitment, and to the assassination of prominent citizens. The year ended with the introduction of the car bomb and the death of fifteen people in an explosion at McGurk's Bar, Belfast. During 1971, 43 British soldiers were killed. The newly formed UDR, composed mainly of part-time soldiers, had five men killed, the RUC another eleven. In addition, 61 civilians died in violent circumstances during the year. The only consolation – if it can be called that – was that 52 Republican terrorists were killed by the Security Forces.

The Army now knew it was committed to a long and hard campaign. The year 1971 had seen the situation change from communal disturbances to a terrorist offensive. Sir Harry Tuzo, who had taken over as GOC Northern Ireland in February, braced himself to meet the storm.

Left: A typical Orange parade staged by Loyalists in the summer 'marching season'. These demonstrations of 'tribalism' are matched by similar Nationalist marches. Throughout the Northern Ireland troubles they have been a constant source of aggravation – from whichever side they might come.

5
THE HEIGHT OF THE BLOODSHED, 1972

The street battle in Londonderry on 30 January 1972, when thirteen people were killed, was dubbed 'Bloody Sunday' by the Press. The scenes on television that night horrified the nation: a crouching priest, carrying a white handkerchief as a flag of truce, begged paratroopers to let him and several other men carrying a grievously wounded civilian reach an ambulance. Helmeted paratroopers took cover on street corners, ready to engage gunmen. These are images that, for those who saw them, will remain forever etched on the memory.

An illegal march, which began in the Creggan and Bogside areas of Londonderry, had swelled to some 3,000 strong by the time it reached a Security Forces barrier at about 3.30p.m. This Sunday afternoon protest march was infiltrated by some 150 hooligans who were determined to provoke a confrontation with the troops policing the march, and who were throwing stones, bricks and even stolen CS gas at the Security Forces with increasing violence as the afternoon wore on. The Brigade Commander decided to mount an operation to attempt to arrest some of the hooligans.

1 PARA had been stationed in Palace Barracks, Holywood in Belfast since September 1970. They were commanded by Lieutenant-Colonel Derek Wilford and became the Province Reserve as part of 39 Brigade. They had had a busy tour and had been involved in a number of gun battles with known IRA terrorists. In a typical incident, one of many, the previous February, one of D Company's 'Pigs' had been hit by three petrol bombs. These vehicles are the standard vehicle in use by the British Army in Northern Ireland. Designated AT–104,* they were produced in 1972 by GKN Sankey to meet the requirements of urban Internal Security operations. Utilizing Bedford civilian truck parts already in production, in order to keep down costs, they were among the first to have been specially designed for IS work. The result is a simple and rugged vehicle, hard to drive, difficult to see out of, uncomfortable to ride in – hence they have been dubbed 'Pigs' by the Army.

As the crew evacuated the vehicle an exploding bomb injured one trooper in the thigh. The soldiers were able to return fire and subsequently it was confirmed that one gunman had been killed. Meanwhile

* The AT-104 is an up-armoured version of the original 'Pig', the FV 1611.

the 'Pig' burned out with the loss of three rifles and a submachine-gun. It was 1 PARA who were being held in reserve in Londonderry on 30 January. They were experienced and seasoned troops and had been in Ulster for fifteen months. They were ideal for the job in hand: they knew what to expect, they would be steady under fire, they would be able to identify any terrorists, they were, in short, the most experienced troops in Ulster at this time. At 5.55p.m. a shot was fired at soldiers of 1 PARA who were occupying a house in William Street. Immediately following this incident two 1 PARA soldiers shot dead a man lighting a nail bomb. Minutes later, 1 PARA went into the area of the Rosseville flats from three directions in an attempt to cut off as many of the hooligans as possible. As they dismounted from their 'Pigs' they came under fire. A burst from what was probably a Thompson submachine-gun struck the ground around them; it seemed to come from the Rossville Flats. Simultaneously one or more gunmen opened fire from the direction of the flats. Then several nail bombs were thrown at the Paratroopers. What looked like three armed men were spotted running across the open ground in front of the flats and were engaged with fire.

It was at this stage and during the minutes that followed that thirteen civilians died of gunshot wounds. Their death attracted great publicity and 1 PARA were accused of 'sheer unadulterated murder' by the Londonderry City Coroner. The IRA propaganda machine immediately produced 'witnesses' for the Press of the 'irresponsible and indiscriminate shooting by the Paras of unarmed civilians'. This gave rise to the sobriquet 'Bloody Sunday'. Simon Winchester in *The Guardian* reported, 'soldiers, firing into a large group of civil rights demonstrators, shot and killed 13 civilians . . . the streets had all the appearance of the aftermath of Sharpville . . . and, while it is impossible to be absolutely sure, one came away with the impression, reinforced by dozens of eye-witnesses that the soldiers, men of the 1st Battalion The Parachute Regiment, flown in specially from Belfast, may have fired needlessly into the large group'. Irish newspapers went berserk. The British Government had no choice but to order an inquiry by Lord Chief Justice Widgery in person.

Perhaps the only constructive way to comment on the affair is to quote verbatim the relevant conclusions of the Widgery Report which was published on 10 April 1972:

There would have been no deaths in Londonderry on 30 January if those who organized the illegal march had not thereby created a highly dangerous situation in which a clash between demonstrators and the security forces was almost inevitable.

The decision to contain the march within the Bogside and Creggan had been opposed by the Chief Superintendent of Police in Londonderry but was fully justified by events and was successfully carried out.

If the Army had persisted in its 'low key' attitude and had not launched a large-scale operation to arrest hooligans, the day might have passed off without serious incident.

The intention of the senior Army officers to use 1 PARA as an arrest force and not for other offensive purposes was sincere.

An arrest operation carried out in Battalion strength in circumstances where the troops were likely to come under fire involved hazard to civilians in the area which Commander 8 Brigade may have under-estimated.

The order to launch the arrest operation was given by Commander 8 Brigade. The tactical details were properly left to CO 1 PARA who did not exceed his orders. In view of the experience of the unit in operations of this kind it was not necessary for CO 1 PARA to give orders in greater detail than he did.

When the vehicles and soldiers of Support Company appeared in Rossville Street they came under fire. Arrests were made; but in a very short time the arrest operation took second place and the soldiers turned to engage their assailants. There is no reason to suppose that the soldiers would have opened fire if they had not been fired upon first.

Soldiers who identified armed gunmen fired upon them in accordance with the standing orders in the Yellow Card. Each soldier was his own judge of whether he had identified a gunman. Their training made them aggressive and quick in decision and some showed more restraint in opening fire than others. At one end of the scale some soldiers showed a high degree of responsibility; at the other, notably in Glenfalda Park, firing bordered on the reckless. These distinctions reflect differences in the character and temperament of the soldiers concerned.

The standing orders contained in the Yellow Card are satisfactory. Any further restrictions on opening fire would inhibit the soldier from taking proper steps for his own safety and that of his comrades and unduly hamper the engagement of gunmen.

None of the deceased or wounded is proved to have been shot whilst handling a firearm or bomb. Some are wholly acquitted of complicity in such action; but there is a strong suspicion that some others had been firing weapons or handling bombs in the course of the afternoon and that yet others had been closely supporting them.

There was no general breakdown in discipline. For the most part the soldiers acted as they did because they thought their orders required it. No order and no training can ensure that a soldier will always act wisely, as well as bravely and with initiative. The individual soldier ought not to have to bear the burden of deciding whether to open fire in confusion such as prevailed on 30 January. In the conditions prevailing in Northern Ireland, however, this is often inescapable.

The Widgery Report exonerated the soldiers from the IRA charges of firing indiscriminately at a crowd running away from them and of opening fire before they themselves were fired upon. These charges might perhaps have been more pertinently refuted by the proven ballistic characteristics of a 7.62mm round and its inability to differentiate among a crowd of several thousand, between male and female, young and old, or children and adults. Seen in this context, the fact that those killed were all male aged between 18 and 26 years speaks for itself. Paragraph 95 of the Report says it all:

In the events which took place on 30 January the soldiers were entitled to regard themselves as acting individually and thus entitled to fire under the terms of Rule 13 without waiting for orders. Although it is true that Support Company operated as a Company with all its officers present, in the prevailing noise and confusion it was not practicable for Officers or NCOs always to control the fire of individual soldiers. The soldiers' training certainly required them to act individually in such circumstances and no breach of discipline was thereby involved. I have already stated that in my view the initial firing by civilians in the courtyard of Rossville Flats was not heavy; but the immediate response of the soldiers produced a brisk and noisy engagement which must have had its effect on troops and civilians in Rosseville Street. Civilian, as well as Army, evidence made it clear that there was a substantial number of civilians in the area who were armed with firearms. I would not be surprised if in the relevant half hour as many rounds were fired at the troops as were fired by them. The soldiers escaped injury by reason of their superior field-craft and training.

At the inquest in Londonderry, an open verdict was recorded on the victims of 'Bloody Sunday'. As a military operation the PARA sortie into the Bogside was highly successful; the political consequences though were catastrophic. The consequences did not wait on the judicial report. The Irish Republic recalled its Ambassador from London while a Dublin mob burned the British Embassy. The Catholics in the North identified the Security Forces with the Protestant cause, and 'No-Go' areas were proclaimed in Belfast and Londonderry. The Government's reluctance to risk heavy casualties to re-establish the rule of law in these areas enraged the Loyalists. The hatred between the two communities escalated during these months and was particularly exacerbated by the erection of Protestant barricades in the Shankill.

Army PR in Northern Ireland is now well under control. The Army has a good image in Northern Ireland, the public is largely sympathetic and the Army now trains its senior commanders to talk to and deal with the Press. It was not always so. In the early days, until about 1972, the Army over-reacted to the success of the crude IRA propaganda of the 1970–71 period. Consequently there was a breakdown of confidence between the British Press and the Army PR system. The Army took a while to learn that Ulster was a very different proposition from the colonial campaigns of the post-war period, which were sufficiently far removed from home for the Press to be relatively disinterested or easily misled. In Ulster, scores of highly competent journalists were able to see everything at first hand. Official statements were often overly defensive. On Bloody Sunday, the initial statement said that all the civilians that had been shot were wanted members of the IRA. In fact, not all were, and the statement was later retracted. On another occasion a young man was shot by a Marine during a demonstration in Strabane. The first statement said that he had been waving a pistol. It became clear later that he was, in fact, a wildly gesticulating deaf-mute and the object in his hand was a spent rubber bullet. The Marine had thought that he was about to be shot at; it was one of those tragic mistakes which happen during a riot. Nor probably did the PR men intend to mislead; they listened to the first version of events and

Right: A military spokesman being interviewed by a BBC team after the bombing of the James Dorrian pub in Belfast. Soldiers of all ranks must be prepared to comment to the media almost instantaneously after an incident.

Above: Devastation at the Parachute Regiment Officers' Mess in Aldershot after the IRA bomb attack of 22 February 1972. **Below:** A paratrooper takes a young girl in his arms to comfort her after she had been injured in the bomb blast in Donegal Street, Belfast, on 20 March 1972. Four people were killed in the incident, two of them policemen. The revenge bombing by the IRA in Aldershot did not in any way diminish the humanitarian reaction of individual paratroopers in their subsequent operations. (Press Association)

released this before checking. The machine is very smoothly oiled now, but it took a few years to sort itself out.

The IRA took their revenge on 22 February only three weeks later, when they bombed a Parachute Officers' Mess in Aldershot. The bomber found it relatively easy to gain access to an open-plan barracks

---

The Paras

The Parachute Regiment is deservedly one of the most famous in the British Army. Since its formation during the early years of the Second World War it has repeatedly distinguished itself in campaigns all over the world: the 6th Airborne Division drop into Normandy in June 1944 secured the eastern flank of the Allied landings; at Arnhem the 1st Airborne Division guaranteed for themselves a place in history. In Palestine in 1946, in Cyprus in the 1950s, in the Suez Operation in 1956, in the Radfan and in Aden 1965–7 and, of course, in the Falklands in 1982, the Parachute Regiment played a leading role. And, not least, the Paras have undertaken more tours in Northern Ireland than most.

The 1st Battalion were the first to be involved in Ulster when they took over responsibility for the Shankill Road district of Belfast from October 1969 until February 1970. Since that time the 1st Battalion has served two residential tours of about two years and six further emergency $4\frac{1}{2}$-month tours. The 2nd Battalion, which relieved the 1st Battalion in February 1970 in Belfast, has since undertaken a further eight emergency tours, a 20-month residential tour and completed a second residential tour in 1995 while the 3rd Battalion has added seven emergency tours and one residential tour to the regiment's total. The Parachute Regiment, therefore, has served in the Province for a period totalling $17\frac{1}{2}$ years during the emergency.

The best measure of the regiment's contribution in Northern Ireland can perhaps be illustrated by the fifteen awards for gallantry: one George Cross, two Military Crosses, one Distinguished Conduct Medal, one Military Medal, one Distinguished Service Cross, six Queen's Gallantry Medals and three Queen's Commendations. Further honours earned by the Regiment include three OBEs, three MBEs and six BEMs, and 24 Mentions in Dispatches. The George Cross was earned posthumously by Sergeant Michael Willets of the 3rd Battalion the Parachute Regiment who saved the lives of two adults and two children by shielding them from the effect of an explosion in the Springfield Road Police Station on 25 May 1971. A terrorist had dumped a suitcase in the hall of the police station and fled; Sergeant Willets, who had heard the alarm, went to the hall where he held the door open to allow four civilians out. Then he used his body as a screen to shield them from the explosion. This tally of medals had been earned by 1985. Statistics for the past ten years are not available.

The Parachute Regiment's contribution to the defeat of terrorism in Northern Ireland has been immense. They have, perhaps more than any other Regiment, been the butt of much IRA vilification and propaganda, most of this arising from 'Bloody Sunday'. The whole nature of IRA propaganda is best summed up by a Belfast housewife whose house was searched by 2 PARA without causing any offence. The *Irish News* printed a story that soldiers had first broken the lavatory pan and then urinated on the woman's son. The next day she came to collect some articles which had been taken for examination during the search. The Company Commander drew her attention to the story and, after agreeing that it was without foundation, the woman commented cheerfully, 'Oh, never mind, that's just our propaganda'.

If it were never more serious than that, it would be a laughing matter. But the seven men and women in the Para Brigade Officers' Mess at Aldershot, and scores more innocent people, have died at the hands of the IRA because so many people have learned to hate and, through hatred, to condone or encourage murder. Propaganda is as dangerous and evil a weapon in the hands of terrorists as a gun or a bomb.

built in the 1960s with the intention of fusing the military with the local people. Either their bomb went off early or their idea of the time at which British Army Officers eat their lunch was inaccurate. In any event the bomb went off too early to kill those at whom it was aimed. Instead, the RC Padre, one male civilian and five women Mess staff were killed.

The Stormont Government refused to accept the package of reform proposed by Prime Minister Heath. Devolved government became unworkable and on Tuesday 28 March 1972 the Stormont Parliament was prorogued and replaced by direct rule from Westminster. Since partition, Ulster had enjoyed devolved Government. It was this government that the Catholic population believed had created and perpetuated over the years the grievances of the minority. There are those who hold that it would have been better to prorogue the Stormont Government at the outset of the troubles in 1969 and that Direct Rule from Westminster might have averted the subsequent crisis. No one will ever know. Part of the package was an immediate adoption by the military of a low profile in Catholic areas. Seen in retrospect, this was a mistake; it allowed the IRA to regroup, extend their influence and establish the 'No-Go' areas. At the time, however, it seemed a sensible option. A low profile meant less patrolling, fewer arrests and fewer house searches.

The bombing campaign, which had started in 1971, reached its height in 1972. There were in fact 1,853 bomb incidents among the most horrific of which were the Aldershot Officers' Mess bomb in February, which killed seven people and which was a direct retaliation by the IRA against a Para installation following the events of 'Bloody Sunday'; the Abercorn Restaurant explosion in March, which killed two girls and injured many more innocent people; the many bombs of 'Bloody Friday' (21 July), a day which Belfast will never forget. Nine were killed, 77 women and girls and 53 men and boys were injured, many seriously. Targets included the Smithfield Bus Station, the Brockvale Hotel, the Oxford Street Bus Station, the Great Northern Railway Station, the York Hotel, the Liverpool Ferry Terminus, the Gas Department offices, the Cavehill Shopping Centre, where three people died, one a mother of seven, another the 14-year-old son of a clergyman; the indiscriminate destruction continued with the virtual wiping out of the village of Claudy on 31 July by three enormous car bombs which killed six people.

Right: An armed member of the IRA on guard at a sandbagged emplacement on the edge of the 'no-go' area in the Bogside, Londonderry, in April 1972. He is armed with a Thompson submachine-gun, a weapon since discarded by the IRA. The remarkable sight of armed IRA gunmen openly 'guarding' the 'no-go' areas persisted until the 'Motorman' operation in July. (Press Association)

The aim of the IRA campaign was to show the world that the British could no longer govern the Province. The bombing in Ireland was an attempt to prove that the IRA could strike anywhere. These were very bad times for the Security Forces and there is no doubt that however abhorrent the vast majority of people found this IRA strategy, it was effective. Whether the Government was close to losing its nerve will never be known, but many can be forgiven for wondering if the Security Forces were capable of containing the situation and if the Government would be prepared to pay the price for refusing to be intimidated.

Enough was enough. At 4.0a.m. on 31 July, Operation 'Motorman' to enter and re-occupy the 'No-Go' areas was launched. A total of 21,000 troops were concentrated in the Province for the operation, and the intention to re-occupy the 'No-Go' areas was broadcast ahead of the event in order to give the IRA the opportunity to leave the areas peacefully and so avoid bloodshed. As a result, Operation 'Motorman' met virtually no resistance.

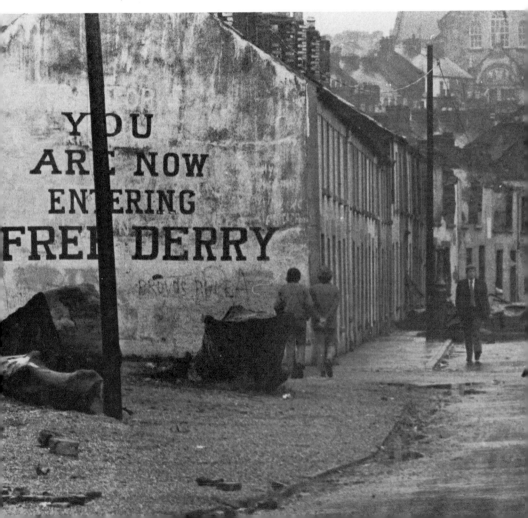

1 RGJ was one of the battalions involved. It had been stationed in the pretty Hanoverian town of Celle in West Germany. Battalion Headquarters, A, C and Support Companies had returned from training at Vogelsang in the Moselle region on 12 July. B Company had returned from training at Hohenfels in Southern Germany on 23 July. At this stage most members of the battalion had plans for leave during August or September and indeed by late July the Commanding Officer, Lieutenant-Colonel Bob Pascoe (complete with family, car and caravan) was heading south for Spain. One major and two captains were sunning themselves in the South of France, to say nothing of nearly 80 members of the battalion on leave or on courses in England. Then it happened. At thirty minutes past midnight on Wednesday 26 July, the Second-in-Command was called to the telephone by Brigade Headquarters and told that the battalion was off to Northern Ireland, the Advance Party within 24 hours and the Main Body on Friday and Saturday. By 0300 hours a list of 85 names and addresses was telephoned through to the Duty Officer at the Depot in Winchester, who

Left: A Ferret armoured car leaving the Bogside area of Londonderry. The message on the wall is a left-over from the 'no-go' era. (Pacemaker Press)

The following infantry battalions (accounting for about 12,000 of the 21,000) were in Ulster on 31 July 1972

Belfast:
1st Battalion The Welsh Guards (1 WG)
2nd Battalion The Queen's Regiment
  (2 QUEEN'S)
2nd Battalion The Royal Regiment of
  Fusiliers (2 RRF)
2nd Battalion the Royal Anglian
  Regiment (3 R ANGLIAN)
1st Battalion The King's Regiment
  (1 KING'S)
1st Battalion The Prince of Wales's Own
  (1 PWO)
1st Battalion The Light Infantry (1 LI)
1st Battalion The Royal Green Jackets
  (1 RGJ)
1st Battalion The Parachute Regiment
  (1 PARA)
2nd Battalion The Parachute Regiment
  (2 PARA)
40 Royal Marine Commando (40 Cdo)
42 Royal Marine Commando (42 Cdo)

Londonderry:
1st Battalion The Coldstream Guards
  (1 COLDM GDS)
2nd Battalion The Scots Guards
  (2 SCOTS GDS)
1st Battalion The Royal Scots (1 RS)
3rd Battalion The Royal Regiment of
  Fusiliers (3 RRF)
2nd Battalion The Light Infantry (2 LI)
3rd Battalion The Queen's Regiment
  (3 QUEEN'S) (6–31 August 1972)

Elsewhere:
1st Battalion The Queens Own
  Highlanders (1 QO HLDRS):
  Dungannon
1st Battalion The Gordon Highlanders
  (1 GORDONS): Armagh

Below: Following the introduction of internment in 1971, the British Government opened the Maze Prison (formerly Long Kesh) to house Republican and Loyalist paramilitary prisoners. This forbidding establishment has entered Ulster folklore.

telephoned local police stations to ask them to contact the 1st Battalion men in their area with the message to return to Germany immediately. Within 24 hours, all but one were back in Celle.

1 RGJ's area of responsibility in Operation 'Motorman' was the Andersonstown area of Belfast, where the IRA had held almost complete control since earlier in the year. All but the main roads were barricaded, IRA check-points controlled who entered the area, few people paid their rent, electricity or gas bills. Stolen cars were used quite freely, and many cars were untaxed or uninsured. Normal services such as refuse collection and road sweeping had not been done properly for up to two years, street lights had been shot out in gun battles and never replaced, and gunmen roamed the streets with almost complete freedom, meting out their own justice. The police had not dared enter for fear of their lives for many months, and intimidation and fear were so rife that a member of the Security Forces could be wounded in the street and nobody would so much as look at him.

By the time such 'No-Go' areas had become firmly established it was too late to do anything about them without risking enormous civilian casualties. In accordance with the British tradition of minimum force to solve any given situation, the government of the day bided its time and acted when it judged the least civilian casualties would be caused. In order to keep civilian casualties to a minimum, an announcement of the pending operation was made and in the event there was virtually no opposition. Once 1 RGJ had entered the area they took over two school buildings, fortified them against attack, made them habitable and set about dominating the area.

The Marines were even able to incorporate a beach landing in Operation 'Motorman'. Four landing craft from HMS *Fearless* made the 25-mile passage up the Foyle estuary to land Royal Engineer Centurion bulldozer tanks to remove the barricades in Londonderry. Escorted by the minesweeper HMS *Gavington*, the craft reached the landing beach just before midnight, coming ashore over trackway which had been quietly laid by hand so as not to attract undue attention. When the bulldozers had cleared the barriers in the Creggan and the Bogside, they returned to the beach and were taken off soon after dawn. In the course of this operation, a gunman and a petrol bomber were shot dead. In the Bogside, arms finds included an anti-tank rifle and a 0.30in Browning machine-gun.

In Belfast, eleven battalions moved into likely trouble spots in a co-ordinated operation: 42 Cdo into Ligoniel, 2 PARA into the Ballymurphy and Whiterock areas, 1 PWO and 2 RRF into Andersonstown, 1 LI into the Ardoyne, 40 Cdo into New Lodge, 1 WG into the City Centre and the Markets, 3 R Anglian into the Beechmount and 1 King's into the remaining parts of the Falls Road area. 19 Field Regiment Royal Artillery and the Life Guards were also involved in the operation. Total arms finds for Operation 'Motorman' were:

Weapons: 32   Ammunition: 1,000 rounds (+)
Explosives: 450lb   Bombs: 27

Operation 'Motorman' was an outstanding success. For months the Provisionals had controlled the Creggan and Bogside areas of Londonderry as well as parts of Belfast. The situation had been allowed to persist only because Intelligence had indicated that an attempt to take the 'No-Go' areas, in which gunmen openly patrolled and manned roadblocks, would result in massive civilian casualties. The political decision was therefore taken not to interfere, thus permitting gun law to rule for a time in parts of two cities in the United Kingdom. Although perhaps hard for a soldier to understand, this policy was in line with the British policy of minimum force to solve any given terrorist situation that was adopted throughout the years of withdrawal from Empire in many parts of the world. In Aden in 1967, the GOC, General Philip Tower, did not re-occupy Crater, the heart of Aden town, which had been taken over by elements of the South Arabian Army (SAA) and Aden Police, because to do so successfully would have required considerable force, including probably the 76mm guns of the Saladin Armoured Cars. Instead he waited and the Argylls chose their moment to re-enter Crater stealthily by night when most of the rebels were sleeping, and so virtually without opposition. The comparison with the re-occupation of the 'No-Go' areas in Londonderry and Belfast is similar in many respects. Such a policy cannot be popular with men who are trained to find quick and efficient solutions to problems; it says a great deal for the British Army that it has always been able to understand the wider implications of a situation and to react accordingly. This cannot be said of all armies, even of some of those of our Western allies.

August 1972 was spent consolidating the success of Operation 'Motorman'. In the Andersonstown area of Belfast, 1 RGJ patrolled, searched and observed. Every garage, every garden, every drain and every shed was searched and re-searched. As patrolling continued the Battalion gained more information as seemingly unrelated snippets gradually built up the Intelligence jigsaw. No scrap of information was rejected. Though it may not have been relevant at the time, it often became so in conjunction with further information days or weeks later. As August went on two rifles were found under a bridge, more houses were searched, suspects were detained, questioned and released; an IRA 'hospital' was discovered in a derelict house and some ammunition was found. On Sunday 13 August a 5lb bomb exploded beside a patrol commanded by Second Lieutenant Alex Van Straubenzee, injuring four members of his patrol. Riflemen Willet, Day and Lawrence were injured by flying metal, but all were out of hospital within a fortnight. Lance-Corporal Harrison was less fortunate and received severe facial injuries requiring 72 stitches in his face. Investigations afterwards showed that a bomb had been placed against a wall on a street corner and wires ran back to a car 100 yards around the corner. Some young boys stood about 50 yards away in the open ground opposite the bomb and when the patrol was opposite the bomb they turned and ran away. This was the signal for two men in the car to detonate the bomb, after which they dropped the wires and drove off. It was not possible to prosecute the boys; running across open ground near one's home is not an offence.

The ensuing four months were extremely busy. Perhaps the best way of putting over the 'feel' of this tour is to quote verbatim from an eloquent account of an incident in which he was involved, by one of 1 RGJ's Company Commanders, Major Gary Johnson, MC, MBE:*'We lay panting under the hedge and around the red-brick walls of the council houses. Our uniforms were soaking from crawling through the damp grass. We craned our necks to see without being seen and Colour-Sergeant Ambrose shouted hoarse orders to his platoon. A hundred yards away across the open gulley, two lookouts lay tense and alert, scanning the row of houses across the bottom of the waste land. I called for my signaller, but there was no answer. Suddenly, from the long grass in the middle of the gulley came a loud shuddering groan. Everything fell silent. Then someone behind me said softly, "It must be Dave Card," and I knew we had to go back . . .

It had been quiet in the Ops Room the previous night. The radios hummed softly in the corner and occasionally the duty signaller passed some routine traffic or checked communications with 7 Platoon who were out in the housing estate, patrolling. It was a dark night and drizzling steadily. This would make it unpleasant for those out on foot, but should dampen any potential aggro-stirrers. The Intelligence Sergeant worked at his table, sifting and collating the mass of documents which had arrived earlier from Tac HQ. On the far side of the class-room the Company Sergeant-Major was sorting out next-of-kin cards. We were settling down to a routine after the first few hurried days following our sudden arrival from Germany to take part in Operation 'Motorman', the plan to take over the Catholic 'No-Go' areas in Ulster.

*Now General Sir Garry Johnson, KCB, OBE, MC. Account first published in Greenjacket *Chronicle*, vol. vii, 1972.

Paul Evans came in with his platoon at midnight. One of the corporals, he told me, thought he had smelt gelignite when passing a garage on a street corner in the middle of the estate. I thought for a few moments; both officer and NCO were new and inexperienced, and people always smelt, heard and saw strange things at the beginning of a tour. Still, it wouldn't hurt to check the report, so Colour-Sergeant Ambrose was briefed to visit the garage during his 2-hour patrol just starting.

Half an hour later the Second-in-Command phoned from the Tac HQ. They had just received an anonymous phone call saying some gunmen were using a garage in a certain road. It was the same one that Ambrose was to visit and he was told by radio to move with caution.

Silence returned to the Ops Room. The Intelligence Sergeant went to bed. I dozed in my chair.

The shooting started shortly after one o'clock, jerking everyone into wakefulness. The Sergeant-Major ran out to check the black-out and Robin Laugher hurried in to take his place as Duty Officer on the radios. Phones and radios chattered to life; our sentries at the front of the school had seen the terrorists' muzzle flashes and had fired back – two men had run across the road in shadows – no hits; C Company base had been fired on at the same time – no casualties to either side – two men seen running towards the long open gulley which bisected the estate and formed the boundary between our two company areas. I was pulling on my bulky flak jacket and buckling on my belt, the Browning heavy by my side, as the information came in. Lance-Corporal Rowledge, his face impassive as always, put his head in the door and said the vehicle crew were stood to. I ran out with him and climbed

---

The Royal Green Jackets

Although a relatively junior regiment in the British Army List, The Royal Green Jackets have a distinguished history. The oldest of the Regiment's antecedents, the 43rd Regiment, was raised in 1741. The most junior, The Rifle Brigade, was raised by Colonel Coote Manningham in 1800 to fight against Napoleon's Army in the Peninsular War.

The Regiment's battle honours include Waterloo, Inkerman, Afghanistan, Ypres, The Somme, Calais and El Alamein. Since the end of the Second World War the battalions of the Regiment have served in Malaya, Kenya, Cyprus, British Guiana, Hong Kong, Gibraltar, Borneo, Brunei, the Falkland Islands and, of course, Northern Ireland. It is perhaps of note that the Regiment has in its relatively short history amassed 56 Victoria Crosses. In 1995 the Regiment boasted two Field Marshals, five serving Generals, seven serving Brigadiers and seven full Colonels. This again is a remarkable achieveent for a small regiment and is representative of The Royal Green Jackets' ethic of the pursuit of excellence.

The Royal Green Jackets have undertaken 30 tours in Northern Ireland between 1969 and early 1995, and 2 RGJ commenced a tour in July 1995.

into the front seat of the armoured Land Rover. Lance-Corporal Card and another signaller in the back had the radios working. I gave some quick orders to Ambrose, arranged where to meet him and turned to the driver: "All right. Move it."

He revved the engine and the escorts swung up on to the tailboard, cocking their rifles with loud metallic clacks. The sentry ran out of the sangar to open the gates and we were away. The roads were deserted and the street lights threw glistening yellow pools on to the damp pavements. We drove fast and without lights, ready to slam to a stop and leap out if ambushed. Then Ambrose's bulk loomed into view, hand raised. He was panting from running his platoon into position to cut off the gunmen moving away from C Company's base. Stealthily we combed the empty streets, stalking shadows through the silent gardens, but there was no sign of life. The doors stayed shut and the curtains drawn. Through the night sights we watched a section of C Company moving through the gulley, acting as beaters towards our stops. After another hour or so we called it off; our quarry had escaped.

On the way back to the Company base we stopped to look at the suspect garage. It was quite ordinary. Three brick walls, a corrugated iron roof and two wooden doors secured by a padlock. We sniffed hard at all the cracks in the doors, but there was none of the tell-tale almond scent of gelignite. It seemed, however, that the telephone call Simon had received was genuine – the gunmen had obviously met there prior to having a go at the bases.

On our return I arranged with Colour-Sergeant Ambrose that he should take his platoon out at dawn to check the gulley to see if they could find any traces of the terrorists chased across it by C Company. We knew the IRA, when hotly pressed, had a trick of leaving their weapons hidden to pick up later.

Very early the next morning, I was shaken awake by the Colour-Sergeant on duty in the Ops Room. Ambrose's people had found two weapons. The Land Rover was ready by the time I was dressed, the soldiers smiling and chatting despite the early hour and their lack of sleep. Ambrose met me at the head of the gulley. He was a strongly built man, but seemed larger than ever in his loose green anorak worn against the continuing drizzle.

"What about it then, sir? Trust 6 Platoon to make the first find."

They were all elated and buoyant with their success. This platoon had achieved quite a reputation as searchers on our previous tour and they were running true to form. Ambrose led me down the gulley, pointing out where he had placed riflemen on the banks to cover our movement. The weapons were tucked under a hedge, wrapped in plastic and an old blanket. A .303 SMLE rifle of the old British Army pattern and an American MI carbine nestled into an assorted mound of ammunition. The weapons were in good condition. Tac HQ gave permission to search the house behind the hedge, and we made our way up the garden and knocked loudly several times on the back door. There was no answer, so Ambrose put his shoulder to the door and the bolt gave easily. The occupants, a young married couple, appeared from upstairs in answer to our calls. Sleepy-eyed and clutching dressing-gowns, they accepted dully and without comment our intention to search their home. The house was cleaner than many we had seen and sparsely but neatly furnished. I doubted whether we would find anything but decided to go through the motions. The search did not take long and revealed nothing of interest except, tucked under clothing in a chest of drawers, a small printed sheet bearing a doggerel poem in honour of an IRA leader who had been shot recently by the Army. I knew him to have been the man responsible for the ambush and killing of Corporal Bankier of our Company the previous year, and pocketed the sheet.

Lance-Corporal Card came into the kitchen, the long aerial from the radio on his back rattling against the top of the door frame. Tac wanted a sitrep. I went outside with Card and gave details of our find to the Duty Officer as Ambrose had the young man sign the clearance chit agreeing we had done no damage to his property. Then we moved out through the garden, picked up the weapons and ammunition and spread out across the gulley back to my Land Rover. We were in the middle of the open area when a rifle bullet cracked very close above our heads. It was followed quickly by more shots as we dropped flat on our faces on the wet ground. The grass was longish with summer growth and we crawled as fast as we could through it to the cover of the row of houses we had just left . . .

I don't remember telling anyone to come with me, but when I reached the wounded man, Ambrose and two of his NCOs were close behind me. Card lay on his left side, bleeding heavily from a hole the size of a florin in the side of his neck. He was conscious and groaning loudly. Goudge held a field dressing over the wound and the rest of us tried feverishly to unstrap the radio from Card's back so we could move him. But it was no good. The unseen gunmen fired intermittently just over our heads and we could not stand, or even kneel upright. The radio handset lay in the grass squeaking angrily. I grabbed the microphone and told Tac briefly what had happened, demanding the doctor urgently. Sergeant Goudge kept the dressing on the wound and Corporal Shepherd jammed his thumb on a pressure-point to reduce the bleeding. Then we waited, pressed flat to the earth. Other platoons were deploying quickly to cordon the area and flush the gunmen, the doctor was on his way and we were stuck in that damnable patch of grass, unable to move without provoking a bullet from the hidden sniper. Ambrose alternatively swore steadily and viciously in a low voice and shouted orders to his scattered platoon, urging them on to find the terrorists' position and shoot back. Shepherd muttered encouragement in Card's ear, but he gave no sign of hearing. I lay with the radio headset by me giving directions for the doctor and wondering when a further sniper would open up from a position where he could see us more clearly. In the bedroom of one of the nearby houses a man was getting dressed in a calm unhurried manner. He buttoned his shirt and put on his tie, watching our small group with the same casual disinterest that he might have shown to a group of sparrows clustered round some crumbs in his garden. Some of our riflemen thought they had pinpointed the sniper now and the odd shot rang out from the gardens around us.

Then, after what seemed an interminable time, but was in fact only a few minutes, there was a crashing and slithering as the doctor and his orderly threw themselves down the bank and arrived with us, dragging a stretcher. He gave Card a shot of morphia and we cut the straps of the radio harness and rolled him onto the stretcher. The shooting seemed to have stopped now but we were taking no chances and, one at each corner of the stretcher, we pushed and pulled our burden up to the gardens and loaded our friend into the armoured ambulance and slammed the doors. The cordon was moving piecemeal into position around the area. The gardens were alive with crouching, watchful riflemen and armoured 'Pigs' ground through the streets in low gear. By this time the Colonel had arrived and joined me in the shelter of an alley-way where he told me his plan and my part in it. I found 'B' Company's other two platoons and put them quickly into position. They were silent and grim, angry at our loss and with the people whose complicity had made it possible. They searched all civilians trying to pass through the cordon and were none too gentle with anyone foolish enough to object. The Press were around too. A television camera team was at work, getting the locals' version of events, as they stood in their doorways. The riflemen watched them with guarded suspicion.

Then it hit me. Of course! If the two rifles we had found were those used to fire at 'C' Company's base, where else should those used for firing at our base be but in that garage we had been suspicious of the previous night! I was there in a couple of minutes. 'A' Company HQ was there, on the corner.

"Come on, Bill," I said, "I'm poaching in your area but we've got to have a look in these garages. I think there's something in them. Let's start with that one."

A platoon commander knocked up the nearest house, but the occupants denied all knowledge of who owned the garages. Someone forced the lock off the first one and Lance-Corporal Rowledge opened the door. The floor was covered with assorted rubbish.

"Wait, can you smell anything?" We all sniffed. No one could smell anything suspicious, so Bill opened the second door. There was a blasting ear-splitting roar as the bomb exploded and we were hurled bodily backwards for several feet into the road. A pall of smoke and dust rose from the remains of the garage and various parts of my body began to hurt.'

In this explosion Major Johnson was severely injured. He was evacuated to England and was later replaced as Company Commander, though he subsequently recovered. The Battalion flew back to Germany in late November after an eventful and successful tour during which they found 32 assorted weapons, more than 6,000 rounds of ammunition, 32 grenades and 463lb of explosives. Nine hits on gunmen were claimed, one of whom later died of his wounds. The Battalion had one rifleman killed (Lance-Corporal Card) and 18 wounded.

On 10 September three young soldiers in the Argyll and Sutherland Highlanders were killed in County Tyrone when a 500lb bomb was detonated under their Saracen Armoured Personnel Carrier. The bomb had been hidden in a culvert beside a small border road near Dungannon. The force of the explosion was large enough to throw the vehicle and its occupants off the road and over a hedge and to create a 20ft crater. Four others were injured in the explosion.

As time went on the pattern of events remained much the same: shooting incidents, bomb explosions and bomb scares, protest marches, stone throwing, ambushes and IRA funerals. These funerals soon became a relatively common sight in the Belfast ghettos: the coffin, draped with the Republican flag, carried by solemn young men, the cortege of men in black berets and dark glasses, the shots fired over the grave, the swallowing up by the crowd of the firing-party and their weapons, and the funeral oration by an IRA official, urging more young men to rise and continue the fight against oppression. It became a ritual for the Army too; the Security Forces were not permitted to attempt to capture the firing-party while they were in the act of firing. It would have meant storming into the midst of the crowd with hundreds of soldiers and arresting and searching every person present – clearly unacceptable in PR terms. So it became a surveillance opera-

Top right: An early example of how technology has been brought to bear to solve some of the special problems posed by urban terrorism. In narrow streets, it is often impossible to determine the origin of a sniper attack. Codenamed 'Claribel', the boxes on the side of this 'Pig' house small radars that between them calculate the point of origin of a bullet's flight. **Below right:** A long-range photograph of an IRA funeral in Belfast. Such photographs are used by the security forces to help compile lists of IRA members and to check the whereabouts of known terrorists. The marchers wear the usual IRA 'uniform' of beret and dark glasses.

tion: long-range cameras, a helicopter monitoring the progress of the cortege, soldiers and RUC keeping a discreet distance, but watching and waiting for a gunman to put a foot wrong.

In mid October, however, there was a significant change. The militant Protestants in the Ballymacarrat area of East Belfast rioted, probably in a misguided attempt to show Westminster and the IRA that they were a force to be reckoned with. In fact it did their cause no good at all as they diverted part of the Army's attention away from the IRA and encouraged the Catholics to look towards the IRA for protection from the Protestants. The rioting was extremely violent and the Life Guards, in whose area it was, had to be reinforced by two Companies of Green Jackets.

In November the first recorded use by the IRA of an RPG-7 rocket launcher took place in an attack on Belleek RUC station in County Fermanagh near the border with the Republic. The police station had been strengthened by a contingent of men from the 16th/5th Lancers.

Below: Anti-rocket netting and steel shutters on the windows of the Springfield Road police station in Belfast. The netting is to detonate a rocket away from the fabric of the building and ensure minimum damage. Defences are being updated to protect against vertical attack by IRA home-made mortars.

The RPG-7 rocket crashed into the police station killing one police-man. A 16th/5th Lancer Sergeant rushed to man the 0.30in Browning machine-gun in the turret of a Saracen Armoured Personnel Carrier (APC) parked in the yard outside the station. He opened fire on the IRA position on a wooded hillside opposite the police station and just across the border. A second soldier engaged the terrorists with a GPMG. It transpired that five gunmen had opened fire on the police station using a machine-gun and rifles, but when the Irish Police reached their firing position the men had gone, and there were no traces of any hits on the terrorists. Before the year was out there were further RPG-7 attacks in Crossmaglen, Londonderry and Lurgan. The RPG-7 is of Soviet origin, but it is also made in Czechoslovakia etc. It is a well-tried and, if used properly, highly effective rocket launcher with an armour-piercing capability. There is no suggestion that these weapons were supplied by either the Soviet Union or Czechoslovakia. It is almost certain that they came from Libya.

Even though the level of terrorism remained disturbingly high for the remainder of 1972, the Security Forces had, during the year made several initiatives which would in time bear dividends. That autumn, to combat sectarian murders, the RUC formed the Special Patrol Group (SPG) for saturation patrolling and the identification and arrest of known terrorists. The SPG proved to be a major step along the road to re-establishing the police as the bulwark of the forces of law and order. Saturation patrolling was merely the concentration of police resources in one area in order to so dominate it that the opportunities for violent crime were reduced.

In September, the Darlington Conference, an attempt by the Heath Government to find a negotiated settlement to the political impasse in Ulster, had proposed a single Chamber for Stormont and proportional representation. Regrettably only three of the seven political parties in Northern Ireland attended the Conference. An agreement to set up an Executive (the Ulster equivalent of the British Cabinet) headed by Mr Faulkner was reached on 21 November. Elections were held the follow-ing June to establish the new Assembly of 78 members, and London-derry installed its first Catholic mayor for 50 years.

So ended the most violent year in the present Emergency. There were more bombings, more shootings, more soldiers killed, more terrorists killed and more civilian casualties than in any other year: 103 soldiers, 26 UDR, 17 RUC, 223 civilians, 95 Republican terrorists and three Loyalist terrorists. More than 27 tons of explosives and 1,264 weapons were recovered. Many Irishmen could not believe that it had come to this. The despair of the majority of the people was pitiful to behold.

6
THE POWER OF THE LOYALISTS,
1973–1974

The year 1973 saw a perceptible shift in emphasis in Ulster. In 1968–69 the Civil Rights Movement had made its mark, and 1969–70 saw the start of serious communal violence. The period 1971 to 1972 marked the beginning and continuation of a terrorist campaign by the Provisional IRA. In 1973–74 the Security Forces started to contain the terrorist offensive but, more significantly, there was a Protestant backlash.

Early in 1973, Lieutenant-General Sir Harry Tuzo was replaced by Sir Frank King as GOC, and Major-General Robert Ford by Major-General Peter Leng as Commander Land Forces (CLF). This was another year of explosions, sectarian violence and shootings though the statistics show that only about half as many people were killed by violence as during 1972. Serious crime as a whole was reduced by about 10 per cent and the crime detection rate rose substantially.

22 Light Air Defence Regiment undertook a 4-month tour in Londonderry, looking after the Bogside and Waterloo areas of the city from 15 March to 7 July 1973. Major Michael Kearon commanded 42 Light Air Defence Battery which was deployed in the Waterloo area of Londonderry on 20 June. At 0955 hours a GPO van arrived at one of the battery's vehicle check-points adjacent to the General Post Office. It was found to contain a very large car bomb. The bombers had used the so called 'proxy' technique whereby they intimidate (usually by holding the victim's family hostage under threat of death) an individual to drive a car bomb to a target and leave it there. It was quickly established that the bomb had been in the van for 25 minutes and that the terrorists had given only 30 minutes' initial warning before the bomb was due to explode.

On learning that the driver had refused to move the vehicle to a safer place, Major Kearon arrived at the check-point at 0958 hours. Without hesitation he climbed into the van and drove it 800 metres along the quayside and then pushed it into the River Foyle. Two minutes later, at 1004 hours, the van exploded under water causing negligible damage.

Left: The aftermath of serious rioting in the Falls Road, Belfast, in 1973.

The Ammunition Technical Officer later assessed the bomb as containing about 200lb of explosive.

The incident had started some 40 minutes earlier when armed terrorists held up the van and loaded the bomb into the back. They held another postal worker hostage and ordered the driver to take the van to the main Post Office in the City Centre and abandon it. Gunners at the 42 Battery check-point just short of the Post Office were particularly alert and sniffed the telltale smell of marzipan, so characteristic of gelignite, whereupon the driver admitted there was a bomb in the van. For this extraordinary act of gallantry Major Kearon was awarded the MBE. The citation read:

There is no doubt that this extremely cool and courageous act by Major Kearon prevented a very considerable number of casualties to both civilians and to members of the Security Forces, besides preventing serious blast damage to many municipal buildings, including the BBC station, in the immediate area. Moreover, what would inevitably have been publicized as an IRA coup was turned by his action into a morale-raising success for the Security Forces. Throughout this exploit Major Kearon acted with speed, decision, and with the utmost resolution. His determination to protect the lives and property of the local community and his total disregard for his own personal safety, despite his knowledge of the desperate risk that he was running, are deserving of the highest praise.

Left: A photograph of a smiling Mike Kearon taken the day after his heroic action in Londonderry. (Note the microphone of his Pye Pocketphone attached to the collar of his flak jacket.)

It is perhaps worth dwelling on this unselfish act of bravery a little longer by quoting from some of the hundreds of letters that were sent to Major Kearon after the event. They are indicative of the upswell of sympathy felt by many members of the general public for Major Kearon in particular, but also for all young men serving the Crown in Ulster. It is not possible to reproduce real names for security reasons:

Dear Major Kearon,
Once they wore shining armour . . . This thought persists as yet another week of viciousness, murder and savagery draws to its close in this unhappy country and my mental shutter comes down on the mayhem, but I am left with an inspiring memory. Most of us dream of that one pure moment in life when a chance to show the nature of one's 'true grit' presents itself. Just how many, I wonder, would react in the selfless and courageous way that you did.
My admiration and thanks go to you all, all the other brave young men who do a job so willingly. May you, and all of them, return safely to your homes and families and remember us not too unkindly in the years ahead and please believe that, for the most part, all we want is to get on with our life. Some madness has descended on our land – it must pass.

Yours sincerely,
Dorothy – (Mrs)

Dear Major Kearon,
Every day the ordinary people of our beloved province depend for our very existence on the Security Forces. To see you standing smiling in the newspaper picture gives me hope that some time soon this awful nightmare will be over. God bless you all.

Mr M.M.

Sir,
My mummy, sisters and I would like to add our congratulations to those you have already received for the very brave action you participated in today without thought for your own safety. Perhaps your motto is 'Serve first, self afterwards'. We all trust that the Powers that be will advise Her Gracious Majesty to reward you openly, it will have been well earned.
May we use this opportunity to thank you all for coming to guard us, also for the courtesy we have received from all ranks on our every day comings and goings.
We trust that our Heavenly Father who doeth all things well will keep you all in his loving care and keeping and walk with you each day. You are all ever in our thoughts and prayers and we sincerely hope that this terrible time will pass from us and you will be all rejoined with your loved ones.

God bless you, Sir, so very brave
Sincerely, An Ordinary Family

Never was so much owed by so many to so few.

And there were hundreds more.* Emotional they may be, but in the strained environment of Northern Ireland it is perhaps understandable. Cries from the heart these letters certainly are. They are from the bulk of the decent folk of Northern Ireland.

The sequel to the story is perhaps not so attractive. The Post Office workers staged a sit-down strike because they considered Major Kearon had endangered the lives of about 100 Post Office workers by driving the van along the quayside. You can never please everybody . . .

*Major Kearon kindly showed all his 'fan mail' to the author.

Hitherto, the IRA had avoided attacking Service families until on 9 August 1973 they detonated a 400lb bomb outside the married families' quarters at Alexander Road, Lisenelly. Miraculously only three women were injured. Such was the outcry at this cowardly attack on women and children that there have been no further IRA attacks on married quarters.

Such indiscriminate bombing and shooting has made considerable demands on the Royal Army Medical Corps. Typical of the high standards of life-saving medicine practised by members of the RAMC in operational situations was the action of Sergeant Bill Watt at Crossmaglen, South Armagh. On 27 October 1973, a bomb exploded near the RUC station there, inflicting multiple injuries on a private soldier. Sergeant Watt, attached to the infantry battalion on duty there, was first on the scene, and discovered that the injured man could neither speak nor breathe. Watt knew at once what to do. Using a disposable scalpel from his jacket pocket, and fashioning a tube out of a syringe casing, he performed a makeshift tracheotomy – and the soldier was breathing again. But there was still a two-hour helicopter flight to Musgrave Park Hospital, during which the casualty was conscious all the time, and the tube kept falling out of his neck. Throughout the journey, Watt stayed by his side, replacing the tube with another syringe casing to keep the airway clear.

By that December, the soldier had overcome the serious injuries to his larynx sufficiently to be able to speak again, although only in a whisper; and two years later he was married, with Bill Watt as his Best Man. Watt was subsequently awarded the British Empire Medal.

All RAMC sergeants in the field are briefed on how to perform a tracheotomy in an emergency. In Northern Ireland, regimental and RAMC medical orderlies carry first-aid satchels containing field dressings of various sizes and types to suit gunshot, blast and burn wounds of different degrees of seriousness. Morphine is carried at the supervising doctor's discretion. If, for instance, the orderly is operating with troops in Belfast or Londonderry within thirty minutes from the point of wounding to hospital, it is more efficient to administer morphine intravenously on arrival at hospital than intramuscularly on the streets (which takes longer to work). However, if he is operating with a close-observation platoon in the countryside, morphine will almost certainly be carried. In the case of Sergeant Watt, clearly his supervising doctor had authorized the carrying and use of a scalpel; and, being stationed in a permanent base, Watt had more than the usual contents of a medical satchel at his disposal.

The tragic events of the Emergency in Northern Ireland have resulted in thousands of deaths and injuries. One of the by-products of this state of affairs has been the improvement in the techniques for treating gunshot and blast wounds. Unlike conventional warfare, in which a casualty may have to survive on the battlefield for several hours until he can be evacuated through the military medical chain, which may also take time, in Northern Ireland casualties are usually in a large civilian hospital within 30 minutes. In the Falklands War it took up to five hours to get a casualty into a helicopter, and perhaps up to seven or eight hours before he was on the operating-table. Consequently, the emphasis had to be on self-help; every soldier in 2 Para was taught to administer a saline drip either intravenously or, in an emergency, anally. This technique saved countless lives. In Northern Ireland it is not necessary; soldiers are taught to get casualties to hospital as soon as possible, by ambulance or helicopter. Most serious casualties are taken to the Royal Victoria Hospital in Belfast, known to military and civilians alike as the RVH. The feats of surgery performed at this hospital are legendary, and the lessons learned in the repair of gunshot and blast wounds have been exported throughout the world. Because hospitals are so near, the traditional chain of aid posts, dressing stations and field hospitals has not been implemented in Ulster. Regimental Medical Officers (RMOs) accompany their battalions to Northern Ireland, but seldom get involved in the treating of gunshot wounds; by the time they are on the scene of an incident the casualty is usually on the way to the RVH. The RMOs are of course involved in everyday medicine and in keeping the battalion healthy.

3 RGJ undertook a planned tour of Belfast from 27 July to 29 November 1973. Battalion HQ was housed in the Springfield Road police station; A Company found themselves in the old Administrative Annexe of the Royal Victoria Hospital and were responsible for the Iveagh, Beechmount, Cavendish and Collins districts; they were also responsible for guarding the Royal Victoria Hospital which included preventing attacks on injured soldiers and the escape of IRA prisoners under treatment. B Company was housed in the North Howard Street Mill whence they looked after the Clonard, a Republican stronghold, and the Protestant fringe of the Lower Shankill. R Company were in MacRory Park, a camp completely constructed of 'Portakabins', and were responsible for the Rodney, St James and across the Falls Road to the Westrock and Whiterock. S Company was based in Vere Foster School and Henry Taggart Hall and looked after the notorious Ballymurphy Estate, New Barnsley and the Moyard area. The administrative elements of HQ Company were based in an old mill in Ligoniel in the north-west outskirts of Belfast. Finally, A Company 1st Light Infantry (1 LI), which was under command 3 RGJ, occupied Blackmountain School in the Protestant Highfield and Springmartin Estates.

3 RGJ area of responsibility conveniently covered most of the territory terrorized by the 2nd Provisional 'Battalion' of the IRA. This organization, until shortly before the arrival of 3 RGJ, had numbered about eight officers and thirty or more volunteers, but attrition by successive British regiments over the preceding months had steadily reduced its numbers to a few high-ranking officers and low-grade juvenile volunteers. Such a process of attrition had, of course, to be achieved by exclusively legal means, but there were still enough snipers, gunmen and bombers to make life unpleasant. 3 RGJ's first incident occurred on the afternoon of 28 July when a foot patrol was fired at by more than one gunman from a range of about a hundred yards. A burst of automatic low-velocity fire and several high-velocity shots missed the patrol, but went through the glass entrance door of some pensioners' flats. A few days later in New Barnsley an S Company patrol from the Anti-Tank Platoon noticed a young woman with a somewhat curious gait. On closer examination her discomfort was found to be caused by a .303in sniper rifle complete with telescopic sight. Two days later the familiar marzipan-like smell of explosive led another patrol to search a derelict house where they uncovered one rifle, a revolver, assorted ammunition and a quantity of explosives. This seemed to open the floodgates so that by the last week in August various finds netted eighteen weapons including a Soviet-manufactured RPG-7 rocket launcher and 2,600 rounds of assorted ammunition.

Then, on the last day of August, 3 RGJ shot the infamous PIRA terrorist, Jim Bryson. It is worth examining this incident in some detail. Bryson, who came from a fiercely Republican family, had acquired a reputation with the RUC for bullying and brawling during his youth. He grew into a squat, broad-shouldered evil-looking man, who readily joined the IRA when the troubles started in 1969, in order to indulge his homicidal tendencies. During the escalation of the insurrection in Belfast in 1971, Bryson developed into a cunning and ruthless terrorist. He operated mainly in the Ballymurphy area where his crude leadership and shooting exploits made him into something of a cult hero. In June 1972 he took command of the Ballymurphy Provisional Company, ruling it and the people of the Ballymurphy by a system of terror which demanded and received universal obedience. He was also extremely active himself and is believed to have murdered a number of soldiers and policemen with his Armalite rifle fitted with a telescopic sight. He was arrested in November 1972, but escaped from the Crumlin Road Court House in March 1973. He fled to Eire, but was asked by the Provisional Brigade Staff to return to the Ballymurphy in August to help redress the balance against the Official IRA whose influence had been growing in the area. He immediately started to terrorize the local Official IRA men who decided that Bryson would have to be executed. Such was the degree of mutual distrust among the IRA in the Ballymurphy on 31 August.

On the morning of the same day, an S Company corporal and a rifleman climbed stealthily into the attic of a flat directly overlooking a circle of open ground, surrounded by council houses, known as 'the Bullring'. Missing roof tiles afforded them a good view of 'the Bullring' and the roads leading off it. This was part of a pattern of three or four Observation Posts (OPs) which S Company maintained for collecting tactical Intelligence and general surveillance over the area. Soldiers would stay in the OPs for several days on end whereupon, if the position had not been compromised, they would be relieved by another team.

At 1830 hours that evening it was the corporal's turn on duty. He had seen nothing of interest all day and was bored. He noticed an olive-green Hillman Hunter approaching 'the Bullring'. Suddenly to his astonishment he saw three rifles sticking out of the car's windows before the car drove off out of sight. He reported on his radio to Company HQ all he had seen. Moments later another OP reported on the radio net that the car was continuing to cruise around the area followed by a red van. It subsequently transpired that what in fact was happening was that Bryson, accompanied by three notorious PIRA terrorists: Paddy Mulvenna, ex-adjutant and commander of the Ballymurphy Company, 'Bimbo' O'Rawe and Frank Duffy, were driving around the Ballymurphy, partly to demonstrate their disregard for the Army and partly to humiliate the Officials.

The Hillman followed by the red van reappeared in 'the Bullring', drove slowly around it and then stopped at a junction some fifty yards beyond. The occupants got out and Bryson began to direct them to ambush positions. The corporal carefully moved one of the roof tiles to one side so as to get a better view and to give himself a fire position. He inadvertently dislodged a tile which clattered down to the ground and alerted the ambush party, one of whom fired in the general direction of the OP. The corporal immediately fired four rounds although he could scarcely aim from his cramped position. He was forced to pull his rifle in when it developed a stoppage, and this enabled Bryson and his gang to escape. When the corporal looked again, the road was empty. Their position now compromised, the corporal and the rifleman set about enlarging the hole by kicking more tiles out. The corporal stuck his head out to try and get a better view and withdrew it sharply as two rounds hit the roof. Glimpsing a gunman, he fired three rapid rounds but missed.

Thinking that the gunmen were now making good their escape both soldiers hurriedly prepared to leave their OP. As they were doing so, the corporal was amazed to see the Hillman returning to the same junction. Ironically, Bryson had become confused by the same problem that had faced so many British soldiers in Belfast, that of determining where the fire had come from. In built-up areas it is virtually impossible to tell from which direction a shot is fired, the 'crack and thump' of a high-velocity round echoing and re-echoing off the walls of

the tightly-knit Belfast streets. Bryson, thinking he was driving into danger had thrown his car into a wild U-turn. As they came back into view, passed the OP and drove away from it, the corporal fired at the accelerating Hillman. The first rounds hit O'Rawe in the shoulder and catapulted him from the back seat into the front of the car. Then a 7.62mm round entered the back of Bryson's neck. As he slumped forward the car careered into the small front garden of 99 Ballymurphy Road. The two soldiers watched the car crash some two hundred yards

Left: A typical view from an Army sangar. Although the view from the corporal's OP in the case of the Bryson shooting would have been similar, it was of course a covert OP. A sentry in a sangar would normally be on guard for a period of two hours and would have a telephone link to his base headquarters.

away, and jumped down from the OP in the attic to the flat below where they took up fire positions to cover the car.

Mulvenna was the first to recover; he flung open the door of the car and rolled to the ground from where he engaged the OP with his Armalite. Duffy also began to fire from the back of the car with an MI carbine. Mulvenna then decided to make a run for it. As he did so the corporal fired three shots, two of which hit, and Mulvenna died instantly. The next to go was Bimbo O'Rawe who, though wounded, was still clutching a Garand rifle as he ran towards the door of 99 Ballymurphy Road. Again the corporal fired three shots, hitting O'Rawe as he pitched forward inside the house. He then turned his attention to Duffy who was firing wildly as he sprinted away down the road. The corporal fired but missed.

When S Company patrols arrived they found Mulvenna dead, Bryson unconscious and O'Rawe badly wounded. Bryson died three weeks later. In the follow-up, thirteen rifles and pistols and large quantities of ammunition and explosives were found. The perseverence, alertness and good shooting of S Company had rid Ulster of three heartless murderers. In all, that August, six gunmen were killed bringing the total number of terrorists put out of action in one way or another to 2,265, including 195 Protestants. In Belfast the three Provisional battalions ceased to exist. In their place the Provisionals created small 'Active Service Units' (ASUs) based on the Communist 'cell' system, whereby members would be known only to others in the same unit, and whose commanders would be directly responsible to the Belfast Commander, Ivor Bell. Ironically, the Provisionals were convinced that Bryson had been eliminated by the Officials; of course, no one had

---

Results
Statistics for the 3 RGJ tour of Belfast, 27 July to 29 November 1973

Casualties:		Submachine-guns	3
IRA killed	2	Rocket launchers	1
Wounded	1[1]	Pistols	18
3 RGJ killed	0	Miscellaneous (air rifles, etc.)	6
Wounded	0[2]	Total weapons	51
Serious Criminal Charges:		Ammunition	10,069 rounds
Arms/ammunition and explosives	41	Explosives	105lb
Attempted murder, membership IRA	22	Nail, blast, petrol, mortar bombs,	
Leading to Interim Custody Orders	25	RPG-7 rockets	10
Minor Criminal Charges:		*Shooting Incidents*:	
Rioting, assault	132	At the Battalion	272
		By the Battalion	244
Finds:			
Rifles	23	[1] Plus 1 possible. [2] Hospitalized.	

Results
Statistics for 40 Royal Marine Commando tours, 14 June to 18 October 1972 and 15 June to 17 October 1973

	1972	1973		1972	1973
Shooting incidents	280	25	*Own Casualties:*		
Rounds fired	602	40	Killed	3	Nil
Baton Rounds[1] fired	989	145	Injured	17	Nil
Explosions over 5lb	53	23			
Bomb hoaxes	193	280	*Finds:*		
			Weapons	52	40
Hits claimed by 40 Cdo:			Ammunition		
Definite	21	Nil	(rounds)	7,403	4,228
Possible	30	Nil	Explosives	765lb	320lb
Civilian casualties in area			Arrests	382	308
of responsibility:			Released	335	194
Killed	21	5	Detained	10	24
Injured	193	12	Charged	37	90

[1] The baton round (or 'plastic bullet') was developed to deter individual petrol bombers or stone-throwing rioters at ranges up to about 65 yards. When used at longer ranges a direct shot and not a ricochet off the ground is recommended to ensure velocity and accuracy. Severe shock and bruising are the maximum injuries likely to be sustained. If fired at too close a range, severe injury is possible. There have been one or two controversial cases of this happening and death has resulted. An outcry against the use of baton rounds has inevitably resulted. However, the RUC and Army must have a riot-control weapon available, and baton rounds are far more selective than CS gas. They have proved invaluable in dispersing riots.

seen from where the shots had come. Soldiers only appeared on the scene after the event. It suited the Army to perpetuate the myth.

The remainder of the 3 RGJ tour was equally eventful. There were more shootings and several bomb explosions, including one car bomb of some 450lb of explosive which slightly injured two Green Jacket soldiers. An A Company patrol wounded a sniper who habitually shot at sentries in McRory Park base from the City Cemetery. Blood trails confirmed the hit. Finally, on 28 November, the Battalion returned to England. Compared to many of the tours of 1971–72, it had been quiet. But it was very typical of the countless tours that have now been undertaken by every major unit in the British Army; four months of continuous activity, of 18-hour days, of constant patrolling and unrelenting tension; nights spent in cramped accommodation in bunk beds, or perhaps days and nights on end in an OP in a derelict building; the very real danger from bullet and bomb; the hatred of bigots but also the gratitude of the vast majority. Four months of this and the strain would show.

The year 1973 is perhaps best summed up by a comparison of the statistics of 40 Royal Marine Commando for their 1972 and 1973 tours. Those figures are typical of other units' results during 1972 and 1973, and illustrate the dramatic results achieved by the Security Forces during the period. While the IRA was still very much a force to be reckoned with, great advances were made by the Army and the RUC.

In 1974, the tour of 1st Regiment Royal Horse Artillery (1 RHA), commanded by Lieutenant-Colonel John Learmont,* was perhaps one of the more notable undertaken by a Royal Artillery Regiment in Ulster. 1 RHA were based in two locations – the Grand Central Hotel in the City Centre, which was completely taken over by the Army, and in a modern camp to the east of the River Lagan in Ballymacarrett, some two miles away. Those in the Grand Central Hotel were fully

*Now Major-General Learmont, Commander Artillery, 1st (British) Corps in BAOR.

The Royal Artillery

The Royal Regiment of Artillery have provided artillery support for the British Army since 1716. Their heavy-calibre weapons-close-support field guns, air-defence missiles and nuclear capable guns and missiles give vital support to the Field Army. During this century artillery has been a battle-winning asset. During the more mobile operations of the Second World War artillery was used with great effect to change the course of the battle. During the many post-war 'brush fire' campaigns, artillery has been used to flush terrorists out of hiding. In the Borneo war of 1962–6, single 105mm Pack Howitzers were used to provide harassing fire on to the border region, thus disrupting Indonesian infiltration. In the Falklands Campaign the British ability to command and control their scarce artillery resources rather better than the Argentinians was a war-winning factor. Such is the traditional role of the Royal Artillery.

Gunners have been used in the infantry role in many of Britain's post-war campaigns, but never to the same extent as in Ulster. For the past twenty-five years Gunner regiments have put their guns 'into mothballs' and trained hard to learn the different skills of the infantryman. This has been necessary because there are simply not enough infantry to take on the Northern Ireland problem single-handed as well as meet the many other responsibilities of the infantry worldwide: the maintenance of thirteen infantry battalions in the British Army of the Rhine until 1992; of the Hong Kong, Cyprus, Gibraltar, Belize, Brunei and Falkland garrisons (totalling eight battalions); of the UK contribution to the Allied Command Europe (ACE) Mobile Force to the NATO flanks in Norway in the north or to Greece and Turkey in the south; of the United Kingdom Mobile Force (Land) assigned to reinforce Denmark; of 5 Infantry Brigade (the Strategic Reserve ready to go anywhere in the world at a moment's notice); of the UK's UN contribution in Cyprus, and the maintenance of the Spearhead battalion kept permanently at 24 hours' or less notice to react to an emergency anywhere in the world, and finally the maintenance of sufficient battalions to defend the United Kingdom. In these circumstances the Royal Artillery and, indeed, the Royal Armoured Corps and Royal Engineers had to become 'instant infantrymen' in Ulster. In 1995 there are fewer commitments but there are also fewer infantry battalions.

As a result of the improvement in the security situation, however, the troop level in Northern Ireland was reduced sufficiently by 1981 to allow the infantry to undertake infantry tasks unaided. 39 Field Regiment was the last Gunner Regiment to serve in Northern Ireland in the infantry role. They left Fermanagh on 11 April 1981. Artillery batteries, meanwhile, continue to help guard the Maze Prison as well as fulfilling other static duty tasks. The Gunner motto is 'Ubique' ('Everywhere'). They have lived up to it in Ulster.

Right: The Grand Central Hotel in Belfast, occupied by 1 RHA in 1974. Note the anti-missile netting.

committed to the protection of the heart of Belfast from the bombers and incendiary-device carriers. In Ballymacarrett the attrition of the IRA was the main aim. Ballymacarrett is the only Catholic area east of the River Lagan and 1 RHA were constantly dealing with problems on the interface between the Catholic and Protestant areas.

The tour which began on 7 March 1974 started – literally – with a bang. Three hours after the Regiment took command, a 'proxy' bomber (a driver under duress) drove his van to the Grand Central Hotel and reported to the guard that there was a bomb on board. Two hours later, despite the efforts of the bomb-disposal experts, the van exploded with what was later estimated to be 300lb of explosives inside it. It was a great credit to the Regiment that no civilian or military casualties resulted from such a massive bomb.

The 13th saw another tragic event when three 1 RHA soldiers were shot down by two gunmen from the porch of a church just across the road from their position. One soldier, Gunner David Farrington, died instantly and the other two were wounded, one seriously. This shooting incident was all the more revolting in that the terrorists used a church from which to commit murder.

March continued to be a busy month, the Regiment dealing with nearly 200 bomb hoaxes and thirteen bombs. Again, the Grand Central Hotel suffered at the hands of the proxy bombers on 28 March when all the repairs and husbandry of the previous 21 days were undone in seconds. The Regiment was offered alternative accommodation, but the Commanding Officer, Lieutenant-Colonel John Learmont, in an Order Of The Day, praised his men for their efforts in preventing a major disaster, stated that the Regiment had a job to do in Belfast and that they would do that job based on the Grand Central despite the best efforts of the IRA. Needless to say the soldiers responded magnificently and redoubled their efforts to clean up the mess yet again.

April saw the start of the 'marching season'. Meanwhile, in Ballymacarrett really hard ground-work was beginning to show dividends. Several wanted men were arrested. May was even more successful: the number of bombs decreased as the month progressed, with a period of three weeks with no bombs in the city itself. One of the most wanted men in Belfast was arrested after a swoop by the Regiment on a public

Below: Security forces survey the aftermath of a car bomb in Hamil Street in 1973.

house, and the largest bomb ever to be planted in Northern Ireland (1,100lb) was defuzed after thirteen hours. On the same day, however, the historic Smithfield market, housing 100 shops and stalls, was burned to the ground by incendiary bombs.

The Heath administration had called the Sunningdale Conference in December 1973 between the eleven designate members of the Northern Ireland Executive and eight members of Prime Minister Liam Cosgrave's Dublin Cabinet. Unfortunately the possibility of reaching an agreement on power-sharing was torpedoed by a proposal to form a Council of Ireland to further the concept of the 'Irish Dimension'. Power-sharing really meant proportional representation, that is to say each community would be represented both in the Assembly and the Executive according to their numbers. Thus power would be shared by both communities which is virtually impossible in the British 'first past the post' system designed for a homogeneous community. The Council of Ireland idea was proposed by the Dublin Government and supported by the Social Democratic and Labour Party (SDLP) in Ulster. The idea was to institute a non-Executive Forum for an exchange of views.

The Protestant majority was just not prepared to accept a proposition which might prejudice their independence from the Republic. To a chorus of PIRA bomb outrages in the shopping centres of the main towns, and determined Protestant opposition, the power-sharing idea slowly collapsed. Of the twelve Northern Irish MPs elected to Westminster in the February 1974 General Election, eleven were opposed to the Sunningdale Agreement, which had set up a coalition government in Ulster. In the Province, the Loyalist splinter groups grew closer to the paramilitary UVF and the UDA. In a joint statement on 26 April they demanded the abolition of the Northern Ireland Executive and the Council of Ireland, the establishment of a Regional Legislature and double the number of MPs at Westminster. The Protestant militants emphasized their demands by attacks south of the border in Dublin and County Monaghan. The final blow was the general strike (of which more later) called by the Ulster Workers' Council (UWC) in May. This was supported by the three Loyalist splinter parties, the UVF and the UDA and with the sympathy of the Protestant majority. Before looking at the part played by the Army in the UWC strike, it is worth briefly mentioning how the Protestant paramilitary organizations achieved such an increase in power and influence.

The third attempt at Home Rule for Ireland was made in 1912. Resistance in Ulster was led by a Dublin lawyer, Edward Carson. 'We must be prepared', he told a rally of 50,000 Orangemen in Belfast, 'the morning Home Rule passes, ourselves to become responsible for the

Above: A military policeman armed with a 9mm Sterling submachine-gun searches a van at one of the Army check-points in the Lower Ormeau Road district of Belfast as part of a wider anti-terrorist operation in the city centre on 1 April 1974. Note the presence of a military policewoman in order that female pedestrians and drivers can be searched. The later and longer, all-strengthened-perspex version of the riot shield is seen strapped to the side of the Humber 1-ton 'pig'. (Press Association)

government of the Protestant Province of Ulster.' In the summer of 1912, magistrates licensed Orange Lodges to drill and train what amounted to private armies. By the end of 1912 these bodies were drawn together into a unified UVF which grew to be 90,000 strong. In April 1914, the UVF arms organizer, Major Frederick Crawford, landed at Larne Harbour a cargo of no less than 35,000 rifles and 3,000,000 rounds of ammunition, all of which had been purchased in Germany. Many of these rifles remain in illegal use today.

Carson, after some hesitation, put the UVF into Kitchener's Army in 1914. In July of 1916 it was virtually wiped out in the mud of the Somme. In 1920 Lloyd George approved the reform of the rump of the UVF as the Ulster Special Constabulary, categorized into the A, B and C Specials. The Specials were permitted to carry arms even when off duty and in plain clothes, a privilege which lasted until the dissolution

ASK
YOURSELF THIS QUESTION

When the battle has been finally won. Will I be able to stand and be counted amongst the men who won it?

MAKE SURE THE ANSWER IS
YES!

JOIN YOUR LOCAL UNIT OF THE

U.D.A.
YOUR COUNTRY NEEDS
YOU

Above: A typical propaganda poster encouraging young men to join the Protestant paramilitary UDA – note the intimidatory phraseology.

of the B Specials (the only one remaining of the three original categories) in 1969 and the formation of the UDR.

Since the Plantation, successive Protestant paramilitary organizations – the Planters Home Guards, the Volunteers of the 1780s, the Yeomen, the Peep O'Day Boys and the Orangemen of the 1790s, the Rifle Clubs and Young Ulster Movement of the late nineteenth century, the UVF of 1912 and their twentieth-century equivalents have all professed a fanatical devotion to the British Crown, the British Constitution and the British way of life. All of these organizations have been prepared to fight Britain to stay British!

By 1971 the UVF (see Chapter 2) almost ceased to exist as a co-ordinated force. In September of that year Charles Harding-Smith, a founder-member of the Woodvale Defence Association, took the initiative in bringing together various disparate Loyalist vigilante platoons under central co-ordination. He called this new organization the Ulster Defence Association (UDA), and it developed into the most influential and by far the largest Protestant paramilitary group. By October 1972 they felt themselves strong enough to take on the Army. After the accidental killing of a UDA volunteer by an Army Land Rover during serious rioting in Belfast, the UDA engaged in sustained gun battles with the Army all over Belfast on 11/12 October. Four civilians were killed and a large number of troops and police had to be treated for gunshot wounds. This was a misguided attempt by the UDA to demonstrate both to the IRA and the British Army that it was a force to be reckoned with.

The UDA continued to flex its muscles throughout 1973 so that by May 1974 the Loyalists felt strong enough to take on the British Government. On Tuesday 14 May, the Faulkner coalition defeated by 44 to 28 votes the Loyalist resolution to reject the Sunningdale Agreement (power-sharing and the Council of Ireland). However the hardline Protestant Establishment was not prepared to accept what they regarded as a dilution of the essentially Protestant and Loyalist nature of the government of Northern Ireland. The newly formed Ulster Workers Council (UWC) announced a strike of workers in power-stations. The UWC was headed by Harry Murray, the organization's self-styled Chairman. He was a shop steward at the Harland & Wolff shipyard in Belfast. The UWC demanded elections in Northern Ireland so that voters could express their views on the Sunningdale Agreement, adding that Faulkner's Unionists had betrayed pledges made before the 1973 Assembly Election. Faulkner led a 5-month-old coalition government at Stormont (Dec 1973–May 1984) consisting of Unionists, the Alliance Party and the Social Democratic and Labour Party. This period was the closest that Northern Ireland has come to a lasting political settlement since the beginning of the current troubles in 1969. It was the only period during which politicians representing both communities had together formed a coalition government in an attempt to find an acceptable form of representative government.

On Wednesday 15 May, intimidation by Protestant paramilitary volunteers forced thousands on their way to work in Belfast to return home. Immediately 40 per cent of the Province was deprived of electricity. Larne was temporarily cut off by the UDA. On 16 May there were 37 road-blocks around Belfast; shopkeepers were ordered to close by the UWC. Merlyn Rees, now Minister of State for Northern Ireland in the new Labour Government in London, warned the Loyalists at Westminster of the political consequences of the strike, and at the same time directed the Army to keep a low profile and not to provoke the Protestants. By Saturday 18 May, power blackouts were of six hours' duration. One hundred and fifty Army technicians arrived at Aldergrove Airport, prepared to take over the running of some power-stations, but on Sunday 19 May, after a secret reconnaissance of Bally-lumford power-station, the Army concluded that they would be unable to operate machinery without the help of senior staff. After a meeting at Chequers with Merlyn Rees, Harold Wilson declared a State of Emergency in the Province.

On Monday 20 May, there was massive intimidation by the UDA and 172 road-blocks around Belfast. The police were told to intervene only when life was at risk. The Army also, took no action against the UDA barricades. Food and milk shortages started to become apparent. Merlyn Rees met Lieutenant-General Sir Frank King at Stormont Castle and 500 more troops were ordered to the Province.

On Wednesday 22 May, the Army persuaded the UDA to take down barricades in the Sandy Row and Shankill areas of Belfast, but were understandably reluctant to become involved in strike breaking. By the Thursday the telephone system was beginning to collapse though the Post Office received a secret shipment of 50 mobile generators the same day. General King informed General Sir Peter Hunt, the Chief of the General Staff, that the Army could not cope with the power failure and Roy Mason, the Minister for Defence, told the Cabinet that the Army should not be used to break the strike. On the Friday Wilson held a Cabinet meeting and informed his Ministers of his determination not to give into the threats of the UWC. On Saturday 25 May, Harold Wilson spoke to the nation on the UWC strike:

As this holiday weekend begins, Northern Ireland faces the gravest crisis in her history. It is a crisis equally for all of us who live on this side of the water. What we are seeing in Northern Ireland is not just an industrial strike. It has nothing to do with wages. It has nothing to do with jobs – except to imperil jobs. It is a deliberate and calculated attempt to use every undemocratic and unparliamentary means for the purpose of bringing down the whole constitution of Northern Ireland so as to set up there a sectarian and undemocratic state, from which one-third of the people of Northern Ireland will be excluded. This is not – this has not been at any time over these past few difficult years – a Party matter in the House of Commons or in this country at all. Where the political wildcats of Northern Ireland seek to divide and embitter, all the major Parties in Britain have sought to heal and to unite. In the years before 1970 the then Conservative opposition supported the action the Labour Government took when we put the troops in, in a security role, and issued the Downing Street Declaration which gave the most specific guarantees to the people of Northern Ireland about their right to determine their own future. When Labour was in opposition we supported Mr Heath, Mr Whitelaw and later Mr Francis Pym, first when they suspended the old one-sided Stormont parliamentary system which had broken down, then when they devised a new constitution aimed at reconciliation and shared power in Northern Ireland and again in the initiatives they took to secure better relations between Ulster and the Irish Republic. On few constitutional issues in our history have we seen the full government party and the full opposition party voting together for such measures and carrying them with overwhelming majorities. Agreement was reached by the Northern Ireland Executive in the last few days on arrangements for a new and constructive relationship between North and South. It provides additional reassurance to those in the North who still feared that their way of life would give way to a new all-Ireland system threatening their religious and political beliefs. There is nothing to fear here and they know it.

What has been achieved in Northern Ireland these last two years provides a hope for its future. We are not going to see that set aside by thugs and bullies behaving as they did at Ballymena last night. We have made clear as a government, and we speak for the overwhelming majority of the House of Commons so recently elected, that we will not negotiate on constitutional or political matters in Northern Ireland with anyone who chooses to operate outside the established constitutional framework, with non-elected, self-appointed people who are systematically breaking the law and intimidating the people of Northern Ireland – their fellow citizens and our fellow citizens within the United Kingdom.

We stand by, as our predecessors stood by – and still stand by – the decision taken last year that the Northern Ireland Assembly and the Northern Ireland Executive provide the only basis for peace, the only basis for order and good government in Northern Ireland. Today the law is being set aside. British troops are being hampered in tasks which were already daunting and unprecedented within a nation supposed to be enjoying the benefits of peace. Those who are now challenging constitutional authority are denying the fundamental right of every man and woman – the right to work. They have decided, without having been elected by a single vote, who shall work in Northern Ireland and who shall not. By their action, children are prevented from going to school, essential services are in peril. The payment of social security benefits is reduced to chaos through interference with the methods of payment. By their use of force and intimidation they have condemned hundreds of thousands of workers to involuntary unemployment. What they do not realize – what I hope that they do not realize – is how far they may be imperilling the jobs of Northern Ireland for years to come, and this in a province where unemployment is traditionally one of the greatest social evils. We recognize that behind this situation lie many genuine and deeply held fears. I have to say that these fears are unfounded: that they are being deliberately fostered by people in search of power.

The people on this side of the water – British parents – have seen their sons vilified and spat upon and murdered. British taxpayers have seen their taxes they have poured out, almost without regard to cost – over £300 million a year this year, with the cost of the Army operation on top of that – going into Northern Ireland. They see property destroyed by evil violence and are asked to pick up the bill for rebuilding it. Yet people who benefit from all this, now viciously defy Westminster, purporting to act as though they were an elected government; people who spend their lives sponging on Westminster and British democracy and then systematically assault democratic methods. Who do these people think they are?

It is when we see the kind of arrogant, undemocratic behaviour now going on that the patience of citizens, parents, taxpayers becomes strained. Tonight I ask for the continued support of a long-suffering people in dealing with a situation in which the law is being set aside and essential services are being interrupted. It is our duty as the United Kingdom Parliament and the United Kingdom Government to ensure that minorities are protected, that those in greatest need are helped, that essential services are maintained, not by the condescension of a group of self-appointed persons operating outside the law, but by those who have been elected to ensure that these things shall be done.

The people of Northern Ireland and their democratically elected Assembly and Executive have the joint duty of seeing this thing through on the only basis on which true unity can be achieved – democratic elections, constitutional government and the spirit of tolerance and reconciliation. And in doing that they will have the support of the British Government, with our responsibilities within the United Kingdom and our responsibilities in world affairs, for law and order in Northern Ireland. We intend to see it through with them.

While Wilson was speaking, the Army moved into position near oil storage depots and petrol facilities. 1 RHA became the 'owners' of the only petrol station in Belfast city centre. On Sunday the Army formally

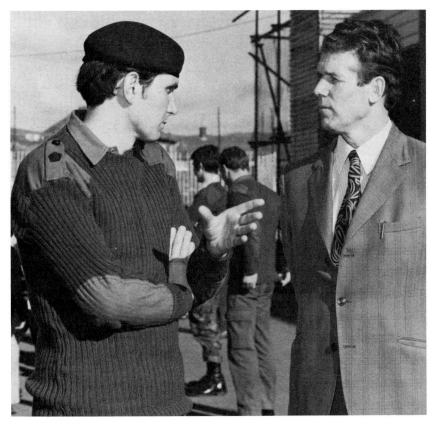

Above: The author talks to the headmaster of Blackmountain School in the Springmartin area of Belfast, where his Company was stationed in 1974.

told Rees that they could not operate the power-stations on their own; they were ordered to enter fuel storage facilities on Monday evening. William Craig, Vanguard leader, persuaded the paramilitary men in North Belfast not to fight the Army. At 5a.m. on Monday 27 May, the Army occupied petrol and oil installations in Belfast and Londonderry and 21 filling-stations throughout the Province in order to safeguard and maintain vital supplies. The UWC promptly called a total strike. The power-stations started their final run down as an electricity spokesman spoke of 'the point of no return'. Sewage facilities also started to break down causing serious pollution in rivers. The possibility of widespread contamination from sewage floods led to the setting up of field kitchens in some areas where the possibility of houses being evacuated existed. On Tuesday 28 May, Faulkner met his backbenchers and the Executive and resigned along with his Unionist Ministers. The Executive promptly collapsed. That evening the UWC celebrated victory on the Belfast streets. Faulkner had no alternative but to resign. The infrastructure of the State was collapsing around him and the people were not prepared to support power-sharing, the principle upon which he had staked his political future.

Upon the resignation of Mr Faulkner and his Unionists, the British Government had no alternative but to prorogue the Northern Ireland Assembly and to reimpose Direct Rule from Westminster which had ended only five months earlier on 31 December 1973. The failure of the Assembly was not only a reflection of the power of the Loyalists, but also of the deep-seated suspicions which existed between the two communities.

While Protestant violence subsided with the end of power-sharing, PIRA, whose operations in the towns were being thwarted by Security Forces successes, stepped up its terrorism on the border and opened a new campaign in England with bombs in London and Birmingham. Letter-bombs delivered to senior civil servants both in the Province and on the mainland, and the murder of members of the judiciary were further extensions of the guerilla campaign.

The 3rd Battalion The Royal Green Jackets started its third tour in Northern Ireland on 25 July 1975. The author commanded B Company 3 RGJ during this tour. (If the Green Jackets appear in this story to have won the war almost single-handed in Northern Ireland, the reader will perhaps forgive what is a natural bias, explained by personal experience in and close contact with the Royal Green Jackets.) It was a quiet tour. In the Catholic areas of Westrock, Whiterock, Falls Road, Rodney and St James's there were but four shooting incidents as against eight during the 3 RGJ tour of 1974 and 57 during their 1972 tour. The Battalion suffered only one casualty during their four months in Northern

Ireland: a Rifleman was wounded in the upper arm as he was patrolling in the Ballymurphy area. The most spectacular success of the tour occurred on 13 August: Lance-Corporal Stephen Pedrick noticed a van being driven rather erratically down Beechmount Avenue. It stalled as it turned left into Islandbawn Street. Pedrick, helpful as always, stopped for a chat with the driver who asked him for a push. Not to be outdone Pedrick invited him to open the back of the van. Inside was about 700lb of mixed explosives. The driver and his mate, none other than the IRA Belfast Brigade Explosives Officer, were taken to Spring-field Road Police Station.

Only two days later, acting on information, Corporal Bob West visited Healey's Funeral Parlour in Springfield Avenue. This very re-spectable establishment was housing about 650lb of mixed explosives. On 22 October, Battalion HQ received a telephone call to search a car in Hughes' Bakery on the Springfield Road. Corporal Paul Summer and his section found three mortars with 28 bombs, three other weapons, a large quantity of detonators and ammunition and most of the other accessories needed for bomb-making. Later, a Royal Engineers search team found a large quantity of explosive material and a further haul of detonators. This was a great achievement and resulted from the close co-operation between Intelligence agencies, 3 RGJ Battalion HQ and the sections on the ground.

Perhaps the most surprising side of the tour, however, was that the Battalion's Protestant areas were less quiet than expected. B Company, which had been allocated what was potentially the quietest slice of the Battalion area, decided to throw a few pebbles into the seemingly calm pond of the Protestant Highfield, Springmartin and Glencairn Estates – something previous battalions had not bothered to do, preferring not to disturb the *status quo*. During its four months in this largely Protestant area, B Company were shot at and there were several sec-tarian murders and bomb attacks; nevertheless the Company un-covered more arms and ammunition from Protestant houses than any Company before it. On 15 October, the UDA, annoyed by a succession of arms and ammunition finds and subsequent arrests, staged a major demonstration and show of strength in the area. B Company ignored it and the affair fizzled out. The only damage suffered was to the Com-pany Commander who was hit by an egg thrown by an irate Protestant housewife. B Company also had several contacts with IRA gunmen in its small Catholic area, the Collins, just off the Springfield Road. 3 RGJ returned to Shoeburyness in Essex on 1 November. Their successes had been due largely to inquisitive patrolling.

At Christmas 1974, PIRA called a ceasefire while a new Marxist splinter group formed the Irish Republican Socialist Party (IRSP) under

Army strength in Northern Ireland, 1969–74

1969	3,000	January 1972	14,218	January 1974	15,702
July 1970	11,243	July 1972	21,688[1]	May 1974	17,000[2]
January 1971	7,742	January 1973	16,854	November 1974	14,217

[1] Operation 'Motorman'. [2] UWC Strike.

Bernadette Devlin, and its military wing, the Irish National Liberation Army (INLA), under Seamus Costello, dedicated to forcing a British military withdrawal from Northern Ireland. The end of 1974 marked the end of a phase for the Army in the Northern Ireland campaign. Phase 1 had been the problem of the Civil Rights Movement and the Communal Violence of 1967–69. Phase 2 had been the Army intervention on a large scale, and the Temporary Peace, 1969–70. Phase 3 had been the PIRA offensive and its campaign against the Security Forces and the Protestants, 1970-71. Phase 4 had been the Failure of the Whitehall initiative and the deepening of the conflict, 1972–74. Army force levels had reflected these phases. For five years, the Army had borne the brunt. Towards the end of 1974, the process to reinstate the primacy of the RUC was initiated.

Above: A haul of IRA milk-churn bombs discovered in transit on the back of a lorry and disguised under the pile of earth. Beer kegs and milk churns have provided convenient containers for the construction of large, usually culvert, bombs.

Left: A typical Company base occupied by the 2nd Battalion, The Light Infantry, showing sandbagged sangars and barbed-wire defences. Note that windows and doorways have been filled with breeze-blocks, leaving sufficient room for firing ports. **Below:** Soldiers secure an LZ while helicopters fly-in supplies to the Crossmaglen base. Crossmaglen is supplied virtually exclusively by air, since the demands on manpower and the logistic effort to mount a road convoy into such an isolated base would be prohibitive.

Results
32 Light Regiment (now 32 Guided Weapons Regiment) undertook a 4-month tour in the Ardoyne and New Lodge area of Belfast from 9 October 1974 to 4 February 1975. The statistics for the tour are typical of many other tours and are reproduced below:

Shootings:

At Security Forces	183
By Security Forces	
SLR	76
Baton Rounds	446
CS gas	6

Explosions (nail, blast, petrol bombs): 24
Finds:

Weapons	23
Ammunition	3,060 rounds
Explosives	1,829lb
Nail, blast, petrol, mortar bombs	28

Searches:

Occupied houses	3,296
Unoccupied houses and derelicts	2,790
Cars	103,380

Arrests (not subsequently released):

Interim Custody Orders	26
Charged with serious criminal/terrorist offences	13
Charged with minor offences	12

Casualties (wounded):

Own troops	1
IRA	2[1]

Incidents:[2]   518

[1] Unconfirmed. [2] Including shootings, riots, armed robberies, bombs, finds, murders, kneecappings.

Below: Helicopter landing sites have been improved dramatically over the years. This picture shows a more recent supply run by a Wessex helicopter into a modern, better-protected helicopter landing site.

7

SECTARIAN VIOLENCE AND THE PEACE MOVEMENT, 1975–1976

Early 1975 saw the following battalions deployed in Belfast:

1st Queen's	Feb–May 1975, New Lodge and Ardoyne
1st King's Own Royal Border Regiment	Dec 1974–Apr 1975, Falls, Divis, Sandy Row, Unity, Shankill
1st Royal Welch Fusiliers	Mar–Jun 1975, Ballymurphy, Springfield, Whiterock
1st Royal Regiment of Wales	Dec 1973–May 1975, Holywood (Resident Battalion)
2nd Royal Green Jackets	Dec 1974–Mar 1975, Ballymurphy, Springfield, Whiterock.
40 Commando	Feb–Jun 1975, Andersonstown, Suffolk, Twinbrook.

3rd Royal Anglian was succeeded in Londonderry in March 1975 by 2nd Light Infantry; 1st Royal Green Jackets were on a rural tour in South Armagh centred on Bessbrook from December 1974 to April 1975 and finally, 1st Queen's Lancashire Regiment were the Resident Battalion at Ballykinler.

2nd Royal Green Jackets (2 RGJ) had taken over from 3 RGJ in November 1974 and were responsible for the Beechmount, Whiterock, Ballymurphy and Protestant Highfield Estate; Major Michael Festing commanded A Company in the Ballymurphy. One of the more remarkable changes in attitude among the more moderate people of the Ballymurphy area stemmed from Major Festing's attendance at Mass at Corpus Christi Church, in the middle of the Ballymurphy, on Christmas Eve. Festing came from a staunchly Roman Catholic, Northumberland family. His father was Field Marshal Sir Francis Festing, GCB, KBE, DSO, DL, Chief of the Imperial General Staff, 1958–61. The subsequent regular attendance of three or more uniformed members of A Company, who would walk across the area every Sunday morning to attend Mass, clearly encouraged some moderates and made it more difficult for extremists to whip up feeling against the Security Forces. During the Christmas 'ceasefire' called by PIRA, the Commanding Officer 2 RGJ, Lieutenant-Colonel David Ramsbotham,* spent many

*Now Major-General Ramsbotham, Commander of the 3rd Armoured Division in BAOR.

hours discussing the all too familiar problems of Northern Ireland with local church and community leaders. Often, what they said privately to him differed wildly from their publicly expressed opinions for the benefit of the media. Whether these exchanges of views had any effect on the hardline IRA men is doubtful, but they provided a fascinating and useful insight into local affairs and a good background when framing the outline of operations.

Army officers in Northern Ireland, particularly in the early 1970s, wielded enormous potential and actual influence and power. In some areas the Army became the *de facto* civil authority. A company commander would receive a stream of delegations from the local community and would be expected to advise on a wide variety of subjects: on the cleaning of the area, on fire precautions, the maintenance of street lighting, on the legality of vigilante groups, the need for and legality of various clubs, on the provision of recreation facilities, on the safe passage of Protestant workers through Catholic areas and vice versa, and on many other subjects. Intimidated families, forced to move by threats, would often rely on military transport to move their household goods. The life of one such family, resident in the Protestant Highfield Estate in Belfast, became intolerable in 1974. The husband, serving a prison sentence for possession of arms, was suspected by the UDA hierarchy of providing information to the Security Forces. His wife and two children, living on social security, were constantly intimidated and threatened and one attempt was made to burn their house down. Terrified, the woman asked the local Company Commander to provide a guard for the house. This was done, but clearly could not be an open-ended commitment. In the end, the family was moved at their own request to Belfast Docks by the Army and put on the ferry to Liverpool. They now live in England.

It says something for the calibre of the middle management of the Army (majors of 32–36 years of age commanding companies) that they cope so well in such demanding circumstances. Young non-commissioned officers (NCOs) have also come out of the Northern Ireland Emergency particularly well. These young corporals, often only 21 or 22 years of age, lead the section patrols on the streets and in the country. Apart from radio contact with their Company HQ they are alone and have to make instant decisions in testing circumstances on the ground. It is an enormous responsibility. Patrols operate under limitations which are the inevitable and natural result of internal

Left: A young Marine NCO leads a foot patrol in west Belfast. The microphone on his Pye Pocketphone is clearly visible outside his flak jacket, and he is wearing the black leather gloves specially developed for the urban environment in Northern Ireland; they provide padded protection when adopting firing positions on hard paved or brick areas. Note that he is also wearing Northern Ireland high-ankle patrol boots, which give more support to the ankles on a hard surface than did the standard-issue Army DMS boots. These were the forerunners of the high ankle boots now in general issue to the British Army.

security operations in an open democratic society. The soldier quite
rightly operates within the constraints of the common law. Each
soldier carries a small yellow card laying down the principles of
minimum force and which, among other things, forbids soldiers to
open fire except in cases in which a person is seen to be using a firearm or carrying a firearm which he is about to use. Thus young soldiers
find themselves in situations in which, heavily armed and trained
for aggressive action, they have to withstand obscenities, showers
of bricks and bottles thrown by hooligans, frequently little more than

children. They have met the challenge with a degree of self-restraint and self-discipline that does them and the Army credit.

In May 1975, the Labour Government introduced another political initiative with elections and a Constitutional Convention to seek a way out of the impasse, but the Protestant majority continued to reject any formula which included power-sharing, or any institutional link with the Irish Republic. Their stance was based firmly on the 1920 Government of Ireland Act. So the violence continued throughout 1975. Terrorist activity during their 'ceasefire' was conveniently

Left: Soldiers debus from a Land Rover mobile patrol to set up an instant VCP, thus achieving the maximum degree of surprise. Patrol commanders sometimes carried a 9mm Sterling SMG in order to leave their hands free to attend to other responsibilities, such as map reading or speaking on the radio; the heavy and bulky 7.62mm SLR, although providing much better protection, did tend to get in the way. **Above:** A similar mobile patrol dismounting to check a vehicle in the late 1980s. Note the changes in uniform and weapons, and the armoured Land Rover.

ascribed by PIRA to splinter groups outside their control. The Miami Showband killings, a UVF atrocity, attracted worldwide attention and sectarian killings resumed in earnest. In August, the UVF stopped a van containing members of a popular Irish dance band, the Miami Showband, and lined them up along the side of the road while a member of the terrorist gang planted a bomb in the back of the vehicle. This promptly exploded, killing him and another UVF man. The remaining members of the gang machine-gunned the musicians, killing most of them. The RUC arrested several suspects and two were later successfully charged.

Civilian deaths for 1975 totalled 196. Internment ended in 1975, the last of the internees being freed in December. Although, in the words of a former GOC Northern Ireland, 'Imprisonment without trial is better than murder without trial,' the measure had served, in the long term, to strengthen the bonds between PIRA and the Catholic population. As members of the UDA and UVF were also interned, similar sympathetic links were forged between them and the more extreme Loyalists. Internment had never been a satisfactory tool and it was introduced reluctantly by the Conservative Administration in 1971. Though it received the support of the Labour Party, they were keen to do away with the practice as soon as security considerations permitted. The formidable publicity in Europe and the United States outweighed most other considerations.

The year 1976 opened with the deployment of the Special Air Service (SAS) to help counter the rising number of sectarian murders, particularly in South Armagh, and to check the growing effectiveness of PIRA Active Service Units (ASUs) in the border area. The SAS have served in the Province ever since, and their special surveillance techniques and ability to survive in the open in all types of weather for long periods have contributed to the reduction of violence.

The Army, understandably, is not too forthcoming about the operations of the SAS, but it is no secret that they operate covertly in order to gain as much Intelligence on the IRA as possible. When the IRA started to operate in smaller ASUs, the structure of which was based on the Communist cell system, it became more difficult to identify, locate and destroy these terrorist units. ASUs operate independently and often in ignorance of other ASUs. IRA security therefore improved. The SAS are expert in countering tightly knit terrorist organizations, and were an ideal organization to take on the new-look IRA. Although it is not possible to cite specific examples, the SAS in Northern Ireland

Right: A soldier from 7 RHA uses a post-box as convenient cover from fire during a patrol in West Belfast. The parachute helmet and smock reflect the airborne role of 7 RHA. Note his riot baton handle protruding from the breast pocket of his flak jacket and the fact that he is wearing general-issue Army DMS boots and puttees. These were subsequently replaced by Northern Ireland patrol boots (see page 111).

have had some notable successes – both in gathering vital information and in direct offensive operations against the IRA.

In February 1976, the Constitutional Convention was reconvened only to demonstrate that the two sides were as far apart as ever. With the rejection of devolution the Convention was dissolved. A month later Harold Wilson met the Irish Premier, Liam Cosgrave; they agreed that there was no alternative to Direct Rule until the political parties in Northern Ireland agreed to some form of partnership and participation. In September, a further initiative by the new Secretary of State for Northern Ireland, Mr Roy Mason, to promote an interim plan for the transfer of some powers from Westminster, foundered on the same rocks of intransigence which wrecked the Convention.

In April 1976, PIRA began its attack on prison staff. When the 'Special Category status' which had been accorded to terrorist prisoners was withdrawn, some of them had chosen, as a protest, to live 'on the blanket', that is wear only a prison blanket for clothing. This campaign was later extended in 1978 to include the deliberate fouling of prison accommodation with human faeces, and became known as the 'dirty protest'. The campaign against prison staff was in retaliation for the categorization of terrorist prisoners as criminals rather than political detainees.

'Special Category' status had been accorded to both IRA and Protestant paramilitary internees by William Whitelaw, the Conservative Secretary of State for Northern Ireland in 1971. Prisoners were moved to The Maze Prison (formerly Long Kesh) shortly after internment began in 1971, housed in Nissen huts where they were free to wear their own clothes, freely associate with members of their own organizations, and control the running of compounds. These privileges led to the belief that paramilitary prisoners were 'prisoners of war'. In March 1976, the Labour Government, embarrassed by the 'Special Category', rescinded the privileges for anyone convicted after that date. No other Western democracy has afforded special status to terrorists. Whitelaw's decision, while probably well intended, only courted additional handicaps for many prisoners in the long term and complications for the authorities.

It was on 10 August 1976 in Andersonstown in Belfast that a Land Rover patrol of the King's Own Royal Border Regiment gave chase to a Ford Cortina carrying two gunmen who were escaping from a shooting incident in which they had opened fire on troops of the same regiment minutes earlier. As the Land Rover chased the car, an Armalite was seen to be pointed rearwards from a window of the car. The patrol fired four shots, seconds later the car swerved out of control, mounted the pavement and ran down a mother and her three children. The mother was injured and the three Maguire children were killed. As the patrol drew up at the scene of the accident one of the gunmen attempted to fire. He was shot and wounded. The driver was found to be already dead of gunshot wounds. It was as a result of this horrific incident that the Northern Ireland Peace Movement was formed by Mairead Corrigan and Betty Williams, the former an aunt of the dead children. Though the organization is now moribund, it played an important part for nearly two years in uniting moderate men and women of both communities in a demonstration of their revulsion of the continuing violence. Members of the Peace Movement were intimidated and harassed which only encouraged them to continue their work. The gradual return to near normal life in Northern Ireland in recent years undoubtedly owes much to these two brave women and to the movement which they started, not to mention the tragic sacrifice of Mr and Mrs Maguire's children. In October 1977 Mairead Corrigan and Betty Williams were awarded the Nobel Prize for Peace.

There is no doubt that the Peace Movement resulted in a drop in support for the terrorist organizations. This, and the growing success of the Security Forces, caused PIRA to set up a 'think-tank' at the end of 1976 to analyze the reasons for their growing decline and to recommend a new strategy and an organization to execute it. It reported to the 'Army Council' of PIRA in early 1977 with a recommendation to reorganize for a long war strategy, one which PIRA should be able to sustain for ten years or more. In a nutshell the new PIRA policy was as follows:

1. Took account of the growing war weariness of the Northern Ireland population and the unpopularity of PIRA.

2. Decided to pursue its ends by ruthless means which would require a smaller organization less dependent on popular Catholic support.

3. If sufficient damage could be inflicted on the Northern Irish economy, the British public might be induced to persuade the Westminster Government that the cost of maintaining the Union was too high.

4. By extending the campaign to attack British targets in Europe, international pressure might be brought to bear on the British Government.

5. A well-directed campaign of violence in the Province might provoke a Loyalist reaction which would reduce public support for the Protestants in Northern Ireland, making it easier for the British electorate to abandon them.

In short, the new PIRA policy was to force a British withdrawal by a long-term destabilization campaign to make Northern Ireland an unpopular issue in Great Britain. To achieve this it was decided that PIRA should be regrouped into two organizations: first, a clandestine organization composed of small active service units (ASUs), each of between three and five individuals. The traditional hierarchy of companies, battalions and brigades was to be eliminated gradually. Control was to be exercised by a new Northern Ireland Command HQ. Secondly, an overt organization based on the old hierarchical structure which would concentrate on political propaganda, penetration of the trades unions and the promotion of popular policies on housing and the eradication or reduction of unemployment. The Provisional Sinn Fein was to be pushed in a more radical direction to outbid the support of the Official Sinn Fein and IRA. The problem facing the authors of this new programme was that its radical and Marxist proponents were out of sympathy with its traditional Catholic supporters. Nevertheless, with the change in the insurgents' methods the struggle entered a sharper and more dangerous phase.

Essentially, the IRA's all-out attempt to destabilize the State had failed to produce the expected dramatic results as quickly as they had hoped. Until 1977, the IRA's tactics had been to use every means at their disposal – whatever the consequences – to force a British withdrawal. When that policy failed and indeed became self-defeating, they changed to what they saw as a more selective, effective and realistic long-term policy.

A preview of the type of campaign which PIRA was to open in the late 1970s was heralded by the assassination of the British Ambassador in Dublin, Mr Christopher Ewart-Biggs, on 21 July 1976. During the following year these attacks spread to BAOR, but were soon abandoned because they aroused more hostility than support. In early 1979 Sir Richard Sykes, the British Ambassador at the Hague, was assassinated and a Belgian banker was shot dead, possibly in mistake for the British Ambassador to NATO. There has been some speculation as to the source of these atrocities. Both PIRA and INLA, in conjunction with foreign terrorist organizations, have claimed responsibility. Sporadic links have been maintained with Libya, the PLO and, more permanently, with sympathizers in the USA, to obtain arms. There are reports that the PLO agreed to break their links with PIRA in return for recognition by the Dublin Government.

NORAID is a fund-raising organization in the USA which has provided millions of dollars over the years ostensibly to aid the 'victims of British imperialism in Northern Ireland', but in fact there is evidence to show that much of this money has been used to purchase weapons, ammunition and explosives for use by the IRA. President Reagan has recently condemned the activities of NORAID, and appealed to Irish Americans not to contribute to the deaths of Irishmen North and South of the border.

The year also saw the start of a rearmament programme by the IRA, not so much in terms of quantity but in quality; indeed, total weapon holdings were much reduced over the decade 1972–82. Weapons types also changed, with more variety and a greater concentration of more sophisticated weapons from 1976 onwards, the majority of them financed and supplied by supporters and illegal arms dealers in the United States.

Below: A typical weapons haul resulting from a planned search on 23 December 1981 at Combrain Street, Belfast, including two Martini-Henry rifles, three Steyr rifles, a cut-down M1 carbine, a .22 rifle, a Belgian FN rifle, a Webley revolver, various telescopic sights and a home-made submachine-gun.

The most popular weapon with IRA gunmen was the .223 AR15 or Armalite. It was light to carry, relatively small, therefore easy to conceal, as well as being an extremely accurate and effective rifle. The Armalite is manufactured in the United States and virtually all the IRA's Armalites are thought to have been smuggled into Ireland from the USA. They come probably via European ports such as Rotterdam and Le Havre, thence in container trucks by ferry either direct to Ireland or via England. In some instances they have been transferred to smaller vessels off the west coast of Ireland and quietly slipped ashore in fishing and other small boats. One such vessel was intercepted by the Irish Navy in 1984 and a sizeable haul of arms and ammunition was prevented from reaching the IRA.

The M-60 machine-gun, again of US origin, is the most prestigious weapon that the IRA have managed to obtain. The M-60 is the Standard US Army 7.62mm General-Purpose Machine-Gun (GPMG). It has a muzzle velocity of 2,800fps, a cyclic rate of fire of 550 rounds per minute, and an effective range of 875 yards (with bipod). In short, it is one of the most efficient machine-guns in existence. The IRA have never managed to obtain many, and the Army have captured most of these.

IRA weapons

Main weapon types

1970–75	1976–94
.223 AR15 (Armalite)	.223 AR15 (Armalite)
.223 AR18	.223 Ruger Mini 14
.30 M1 Carbine	7.62 Heckler & Koch G3
7.62 BM59/FAL	7.92 M43 Bolt Action
Garand .30 M1 Rifle	7.92 G43 Self-loading
	.303 SMLE/NO4 Self-loading
	.30 P17/03 Springfield

In addition, the IRA have had limited numbers of .30 and .50 Browning and M60 machine-guns at various stages. They also have had RPG-7 rocket launchers of Soviet origin, which they have used against armoured vehicles and police stations with limited success at various stages. These are regarded as prestige weapons.

It is by no means a comprehensive list of the IRA weaponry which has included BSA shotguns, AK 47 Assault rifles, Webley shotguns, AK 56 Assault rifles, Thompson submachine-guns, Woodmaster hunting rifles, 6.55mm AG semi-automatic rifles (Swedish Army), 7.62 NATO semi-automatic rifles, 8mm Swedish Carl Gustav M45 SMG, .455 and .38 pistols, Webley and 7.65 Mauser pistols and a variety of other weapon types.

Below: This ammunition find also included a crossbow and arrows – a favourite weapon of the UDA.

The RPG-7 is the standard rifle squad anti-tank weapon of the Warsaw Pact forces. It is a muzzle-loaded, shoulder-fired, recoilless weapon that can be reloaded. It fires a PG-7v HEAT rocket, 92mm long and weighing 2.2 kilograms, with a muzzle velocity of 328 feet per second. Within eleven yards of emergence from the muzzle, a rocket motor ignites and boosts the projectile's velocity to 985 feet per second. The warhead will penetrate 320mm of armour, that is, anything in use by the Army and RUC in Ulster.

Finally, of interest is the Garand .30 M1 Rifle. It was adopted as the Standard US Army rifle in 1932. Production began in 1936 and continued until the 1950s by which time about 5½ million had been made. The M1, the first self-loading rifle to be adopted as a standard weapon, was a particular favourite of the IRA during the early 1970s. Most of them originated in the USA.

In the early days, all these weapons were held and controlled by 'quartermasters' and were issued for use by selected gunmen. When the ASUs were formed in 1976, however, weapons became the property of these groups. They were hidden in occupied houses, with or without the knowledge of the occupants, in derelict buildings in towns and in the country, in hides below ground, in hedgerows, stone walls and

culverts. Many were and are kept south of the border, to be smuggled North for specific operations, but increasing co-operation between the Security Forces both north and south of the border, and weapon seizures by the Garda in the Republic have made this option less attractive.

Couriers are sometimes used to dispose of a weapon after a shooting. In Belfast in the early 1970s, a favourite IRA tactic was to hand a gun to a member of Cumann Na Bann (the women's section of the IRA) after a shooting. She would conceal it in her clothing or under a baby in a pram until it could be hidden in a safe house.

The year 1976 was a turning-point for the Army in Northern Ireland. The nature of the terrorist threat changed, which meant that the Army also had to adjust its tactics.

Above: A very substantial find of IRA weapons and ammunition. The mortars and mortar bombs illustrated are home-made IRA weapons that have been used on a number of occasions with varying degrees of success against security force bases. Other items include various calibres of ammunition, magazines, cordtex fuse wire and various types of explosive.

8
SOUTH ARMAGH: BANDIT COUNTRY

As the Army gained the upper hand in Belfast and Londonderry, by their attrition of the IRA, and denied safe havens to them, terrorists found it easier to operate from the Republic into the countryside just north of the border. South Armagh, a predominately Catholic area, was dubbed the 'Murder Triangle' and 'Bandit Country' by the Press. Fortunately, at an early stage in the campaign, the Army had established bases at Crossmaglen, Newtonhamilton, Forkhill, Bessbrook and some other border towns. The incidence of terrorism in South Armagh worsened in 1974 and 1975.

South Armagh is mainly open rolling country, a patchwork of farms interlaced with low stone walls; geographically all lines of communications run down towards Dundalk in the Irish Republic. The people are solidly Catholic. Smuggling, petty theft and violent persuasion were all traditional pastimes long before the start of the present emergency; the authorities in Dublin are held in as little regard as those in Belfast or Westminster. So by 1974, the Provisional IRA were beginning to wield enormous influence. Further north, a line of hills marks the natural, if not the political, boundary of the area and here, centred around the town of Newtonhamilton, Catholic domination begins to give way to Protestant settlements.

The border itself meanders through fields and hedgerows and it is difficult to know where it runs let alone guard it or block it in any way. The Army has always been the first to admit that the IRA can cross the border almost at will; it would take defences such as those which exist between East and West Germany to seal the border effectively. Clearly this is not a practical or desirable solution between two democratic and friendly states. Therefore, the only hope for the Army in a vast and rambling area is to keep such a close ear to the ground that they are able to be in the right place at the right time.

To the east the district town of Newry, isolated stronghold of the Official IRA, lies at the head of Carlingford Lough and behind it the mountains of Mourne rise into the sky in a setting of such beauty and tranquillity that the murder and destruction carried out almost daily become almost unbelievable. South Armagh was important because it was a traditional Republican stronghold. If the IRA could be defeated here, it would be a dramatic psychological victory for the Army.

The 1st Battalion The Duke of Edinburgh's Royal Regiment were responsible for the area from July 1973 to December 1974, as a resident battalion with its headquarters much farther north in Ballykinler. It was a measure of the worsening situation in South Armagh that the 1st Battalion The Royal Green Jackets (1 RGJ) were dispatched on a 4-month emergency tour, to be responsible specifically for South Armagh until April 1975. 1 RGJ's Tactical Headquarters, administrative elements and its Support Company were housed in an enormous nineteenth-century mill in the little village of Bessbrook, five miles west of Newry. A Company was divided between the former UDR Centre and the RUC station in Newry and was responsible for the town and its neighbourhood, a broad corridor down to the border with the Republic, containing the main road and railway line from Belfast to Dublin, and lastly, for Carlingford Lough and its northern shore. To help it in this latter task A Company had under command an aspiring gunboat – actually a Fleet tender – of the Royal Navy. B Company was based in Crossmaglen, with a platoon in the small village of Forkill, and was responsible for the bulk of the border county of South Armagh, while Support Company from Bessbrook, with the Mortar Platoon in Newtownhamilton, looked after the hinterland of the county. C Company was detached to come under command of the 9/12 Lancers and spent the tour in the Dungannon and Coalisland areas.

It was in many ways a frustrating tour for 1 RGJ. Soon after they arrived the IRA proclaimed its 'ceasefire'. This peace-that-was-no-peace lasted, except for one hectic period of two weeks, throughout their tour. Army operations were considerably inhibited by the restrictions on searching and interrogation which were imposed by government edict during the ceasefire, while the IRA were of course able to continue to operate on their own terms. The flow of Intelligence, on which counter-insurgency operations rely so heavily, was reduced by the restrictions to a trickle. But what else could the Government do? If the IRA offered a 'ceasefire' it had to be seen to be given a chance and the Army understood this.

In many ways South Armagh demanded less original thought from battalions. It was a battlefield in which patrols moved much as they would have done through the fields of Normandy in the summer of 1944. Excellent section tactics were the only defence against ambush,

Top right: A Green Jacket officer liaises with two members of the Eire Garda across the border. In recent years co-operation between security forces north and south of the border has improved dramatically. **Below right:** Members of B Company, 1 RGJ, return to the Crossmaglen base after a protracted patrol in the surrounding countryside. The use of camouflage cream is indicative of the fact that they have been involved in a surveillance operation.

the remotely detonated bomb, the booby trap and the sniper's bullet. Operations were based upon patrolling, mainly on foot, because vehicles on the narrow country lanes near the frontier were a sure invitation to an ambush. The battalions made extensive use of RAF Puma helicopters to lift patrols and picquets into position. The garrisons of Crossmaglen and Forkill were maintained exclusively by air. In addition battalions established Vehicle Check Points at random throughout the area and manned certain static road-blocks on a permanent basis.

When 1 RGJ left in April 1975 they were succeeded by the 1st Battalion The Green Howards who soldiered in South Armagh until August, when they were relieved by the 3rd Battalion The Royal Regiment of Fusiliers (3 RRF). Then, in view of the spate of sectarian murders in the area, the 1st Battalion The Light Infantry (1 LI) were flown to the Province on 6 September to reinforce 3 RRF. 1 LI were the Spearhead Battalion whose role it is to be ready to move anywhere in the world at 24 hours' notice to meet any emergency. The Army maintains such a battalion today. 1 LI spent one month in South Armagh and were then relieved by 42 Commando, also for one month. These reinforcements reduced the violence, but it is of course almost impossible for the Army to eradicate terrorism from South Armagh completely. It was particularly easy for terrorists from such towns as Dundalk, south of the border, to stage hit and run operations. In

January 1976 the SAS were also deployed in South Armagh and by means of special surveillance techniques have managed to keep a tight grip on the area.

It is perhaps worth studying one incident in South Armagh in some detail. It was an operational success for 3 PARA who completed a tour in South Armagh with Battalion HQ at Bessbrook from April to August 1976. One morning in mid June a routine patrol led by a Corporal called on a pub near the village of Belleek not far from Bessbrook. Normally the proprietress was friendly towards the Security Forces, but on this occasion she was not at all welcoming and appeared a little apprehensive. The pub was closed, but male voices could be heard beyond a door. The proprietress explained that her brother had come to visit her and suggested that the patrol should call again later. The patrol departed, but the Corporal decided to leave the road when out of sight of the pub and to circle round under cover to watch the building. Half an hour later three men left the pub. One was recognized as John Quinn, a PIRA suspect.

When the patrol returned to base it was quickly established that the proprietress had no brothers and that John Quinn, who had not been seen in the neighbourhood for some time, was thought to have been undergoing clandestine military training in the Republic. It was therefore decided to watch the pub. Two small patrols each consisting of four men were dropped off from vehicles in order to establish

Two photographs of troops working in typical South Armagh country-side. In the picture on the opposite page, note that the second member of the patrol is covering the left flank while the remainder advance. In the picture on the right, the leading soldier carries a GPMG, which is used in circumstances where long-range fire may be required.

Observation Posts (OPs) near the pub and to photograph and identify PIRA terrorists who were now known to frequent it. One patrol was to establish the OP to watch the pub while the other was to watch the countryside to the north and to the east in order to warn the patrol leader, a Staff Sergeant, of anyone approaching his OP. It was also in direct radio contact with Battalion Tactical HQ at Bessbrook. Four days later the Staff Sergeant suspected that his OP close to the pub had been spotted by a man entering the pub. Shortly afterwards a small boy came out of the pub, crossed the road and made straight for the derelict house. The Staff Sergeant concluded that the security of his OP had been compromised and evacuated the position promptly. Later, when the Staff Sergeant and his Lance-Corporal had temporarily left the

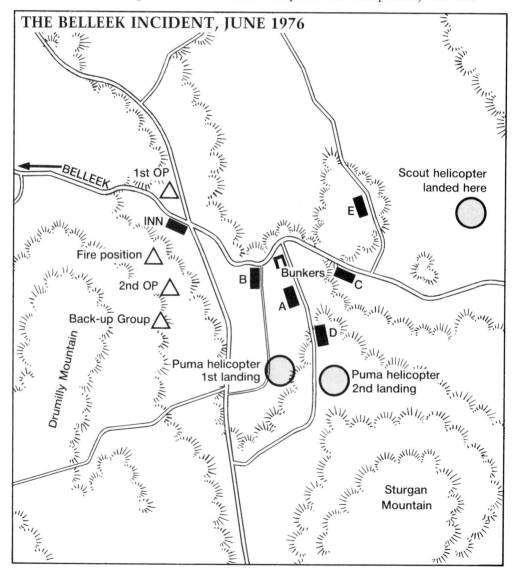

THE BELLEEK INCIDENT, JUNE 1976

radio-operator and the gunner in order to reconnoitre a new OP with a better view of the pub, they paused at a gap in the hedge which gave an excellent view of the surrounding countryside. They noticed a dark-blue car pull up at House 'A'. Four armed men wearing white hoods got out. It was 9.40p.m. and the car had been hijacked earlier that evening from a car dealer's showroom. The two NCOs watched as the four men made their way carefully along the hedgerows to House 'B'. The gunmen stopped outside the house, spoke to the occupants and then moved, two of them just south of the house and two a short distance to the east, where there were some concrete bunkers. Now that the terrorists had paused for a moment the Staff Sergeant had to make some quick decisions; he had been caught off balance. He was temporarily out of touch with his OP parties, the extra fire-power of his two light machine-guns (LMGs) and his communications back to base. The range, 500 yards, was too great for the lance-corporal's rifle to be used to any real effect. Without rapid reinforcement the gunmen would probably make good their escape to the east if fired on. The patrol commander resolved to report the situation to Battalion Tactical HQ as quickly as possible and then to concentrate his men and their firepower in the excellent position overlooking the gunmen in order to pin them down.

He left the lance-corporal to observe the gunmen, instructing him to open fire only if they started moving away. The Staff Sergeant moved back through the bushes to his OP position 50 metres up the hill. From there he relayed the situation to Battalion HQ through his supporting OP up the hill and ordered the latter to join him. Collecting all his men he set out to rejoin the lance-corporal. Before he could reach him the lance-corporal opened fire. He had held the gunmen in his sights for only a few minutes, but for what must have seemed an age to him. Fearing that his sergeant would not return with the patrol in time and thinking that the gunmen were going to disappear he fired at about 9.55p.m., fifteen minutes after they had got out of the car. He missed. The terrorists took cover in the bunker area and returned fire. Their bullets were striking the ground around the lance-corporal with a fair degree of accuracy as the rest of the patrol took up fire positions beside him. The concentrated fire-power of the whole patrol, two LMGs and five rifles soon forced the gunmen to seek cover or retreat. One was pinned down in the area of the bunkers where eventually he was lost to view. The other three withdrew eastwards, two of them slowly and using all available cover towards House 'C' which they reached some twenty minutes later. The other man ran fast across an open field. One of the LMG gunners chased him across the field with tracer, elevating the gun until he hit him. The gunman was seen to stagger and drop to his knees. He managed to crawl, through a hedge near House 'A' and escaped while the gunner was changing his magazine.

As soon as the Staff Sergeant's report reached Battalion HQ, four men were 'scrambled' in a Scout helicopter, and the Company Commander of Patrol Company in a Gazelle helicopter. Another eight men under a Platoon Commander were bundled into a large Puma helicopter. The Company Commander issued orders on the radio as the force flew into the operational area. On arrival in the twilight at about 10.15p.m., the Company Commander remained airborne to direct the action from his Gazelle. He ordered the Scout to land behind a knoll just north of the road, about 400 metres east of the bungalow at 'C' and to close on the building from the east to block off the gunmen's escape northwards or eastwards. When the Puma arrived it was told to land south-west of the house near House 'D', to prevent escape to the south and to deal with the gunmen. As the men from the Puma moved in, all the escape routes from House 'C' were covered by fire from the OP patrol on the hillside and the two helicopter forces without endangering one another's safety.

Meanwhile, the gunmen had barricaded the door of the bungalow and closed the curtains. One of the gunmen, John Quinn, got in touch with the RUC on the telephone offering to surrender to them in preference to the Army. When the men from the Puma helicopter had surrounded the bungalow its commander called on the gunmen to surrender. They refused. The subaltern, not knowing if the gunmen were holding the inhabitants of the cottage hostage, crept up to a window, smashed the glass with the butt of his rifle, fired three or four rounds up through the roof and repeated his demand. The two gunmen, John Quinn and Raymond McCreesh, came out without their weapons. A search of the house revealed an Armalite and a Garand with 150 and 119 rounds respectively. The latter was damaged and could only be reloaded with difficulty.

Meanwhile, the Scout and the Puma returned to Bessbrook to lift in a second platoon. As they were arriving the Company Commander in his Gazelle spotted a man moving across the fields from the vicinity of House 'A' towards House 'D'. He did not see him go in, but ordered the Puma to land its men from the new platoon just to the south of House 'D'. The troops were told to search it, its outhouses and the surrounding area. Nothing was found. Meanwhile the Scout remained airborne with a reserve of four men.

It was now 11.30p.m. and almost dark. The Company Commander continued to direct operations from his Gazelle using its Nightsun, and the Scout's to illuminate the ground. Nightsun is a lightweight, highpower searchlight, originally developed in the USA for use on helicopters. It is capable of providing 50 × bright moonlight at 1,100 yards for a 110 yards diameter beam. It can be equipped with a special infra-red filter so that at night a terrorist will not know that the beam is directed at him. Still keeping the reserve of four men airborne in the Scout, he ordered the rest of the newly arrived platoon at House 'D' to search House 'A'. There, the wounded gunman's Sten was found, loaded and cocked, lying on the road near the drive; in the tin shed they found the Peugeot, its doors open, the heater on and two empty 9mm cartridge cases inside the car.

Houses 'A' and 'B' and the bunkers were occupied and mobile operations ceased until first light. Early the following morning two search teams including two search dogs and a tracker dog were flown in to

Above: A sniffer dog trained in the detection of explosives. Dogs are an invaluable asset in enhancing the capability of RE search teams in the hunt for hidden explosives. Alsatians are usually used as guard dogs; labradors are more usually used as tracker and sniffer dogs. (MOD)

search the areas of Houses 'A' and 'B' and the bunkers. In the thick bushes round the bunkers, an 18-year-old gunman, Daniel McGuiness, was found asleep clutching his Armalite. He was carrying 141 rounds. It was his first mission.

Later in the day, the tracker dog found a positive track leading from the bunkers to House 'F' just over 2,000 metres to the south-east. There it subsequently transpired a car had been hijacked by an armed man at about 5.50 a.m. This was almost certainly used to evacuate Malachy McParland who was admitted to hospital in Dundalk in Eire that day with three bullet wounds in his back.

The three captured gunmen received 14-year prison sentences. What they had been planning is not certain, but they may have come to the area with the intention of attacking the original OP near the pub which the Staff Sergeant had feared had been compromised, or they may have been planning to ambush a routine Security Forces patrol. It was almost certainly not a sectarian murder since only one or two gunmen would have been required.

Many lessons emerged from this operation. The chain of success began with the suspicions of an alert corporal on a routine patrol and the planned surveillance of the pub. The OP Commander sent to watch it moved in time to evade trouble and to turn the tables on his probable assailants. The rapid arrival of reinforcements and their efficient direction from an airborne command post captured three of the four terrorists directly involved and all their weapons. It was a well-planned and stage-managed operation at every level.

3 Para had a good tour. They were followed by 40 Commando from August to December 1976. During 1977 the 1st Battalion The Royal Highland Fusiliers (1 RHF), the 1st Battalion The Worcestershire and Sherwood Foresters (1 WFR) and the 1st Battalion The Queen's Lancashire Regiment (1 QLR) came and went from South Armagh. They were followed in 1978 by the 2nd Battalion The Royal Green Jackets (2 RGJ), the 1st Battalion The Parachute Regiment (1 Para) and 42 Commando. And so the succession of infantry battalions has gone on ever since. 1 RGJ completed a tour from March to July 1981. A fascinating account of Operation 'Vehement' during that tour is repro-duced on page 259.

Top left: The many unauthorized border crossings afford an easy vehicle escape route for IRA terrorists into the Republic. The photograph shows an attempt to crater one of these crossings north-west of Crossmaglen by 9 Independent Squadron, RE, thus rendering it impassable. Enraged local farmers often fill in the resulting craters, only to have them blown up again by the Army in a continuing tit-for-tat process. **Below left:** Hijacked vehicles, possibly containing bombs, have been used by the IRA to block a main road from South Armagh into the Republic. Whether the vehicles actually contain explosives or not is relatively unimportant: security forces are compelled to mount a major clearance operation to find out. The IRA thus achieve their purpose in causing major disruption and delay.

South Armagh was relatively quiet in the mid-1980s. But the Security Force base in Crossmaglen was always a target, either the base itself or the soldiers patrolling from it. One method of ambushing foot patrols was to hide an explosive device, usually remotely controlled, in a wall or culvert and detonate it as the patrol passed. One such device was discovered on 21 February 1987 at Coolderry, near Crossmaglen, when a suspicious wire led to an IED hidden in a van. The bomb disposal officer subsequently discovered a 'ring main' of detonating cord connecting six bags containing 135kg of explosive. The same month, a joint RUC and military patrol were about to commence a routine clearance operation 4 kilometres east of Belleek when they became suspicious of a trailer by the roadside. The area was cordoned off at 10.05 a.m.. At 11.28 a.m., a bomb in the trailer exploded. Because the patrol had been alert and suspicious, they had forced the operator to detonate his bomb remotely and make a quick exit. There were no security force casualties. The device was found to have consisted of a trailer loaded with six beer kegs and two fertilizer bags containing 350kg of explosive. Only part of the booster charge had exploded.

The previous January, the IRA had attacked the Crossmaglen base with three Mk 10A home-made mortars. Two rounds overshot the base by approximately 20 metres and the third broke up on impact without exploding within the base perimeter. Forty minutes after the first attack a second salvo was fired, but the two rounds which landed in the base were also blinds. The baseplate consisted of two racks of large Mark 10A mortar tubes mounted on a trailer behind a tractor parked about 250 metres from the base. Fortunately no one was hurt in this incident, but it is illustrative of the many mortar attacks made on Security Force bases in the 1980s. Eight days later four mortar rounds were fired at a Permanent Vehicle Check Point (PVCP) at Fathom near Newry.

On 25 April 1987, Lord Chief Justice Gibson and his wife were driving in their car along the A1 south of Newry in South Armagh when an explosive device left in a vehicle parked on the hard shoulder was detonated remotely as they were passing. Five other civilians were injured in the incident and Lord Chief Justice Gibson and his wife were killed. PIRA claimed responsibility.

On 19 July 1987, Lance-Corporal Hewitt of the 1st Battalion the Royal Green Jackets was shot dead while on a foot patrol in Belleek. He was hit in the head by one high-velocity round and died almost instantly. Expert IRA snipers had the advantage of surprise, local knowledge and local help. Such an attack mounted from a carefully chosen spot is almost impossible to prevent. The alternative is not to patrol the streets. In August 1987, shots were fired at soldiers from the 1st Battalion the Queen's Regiment who were manning the Observation Post (OP) on point 799 in South Armagh. A total of 63 rounds were returned by the OP and one hit was claimed. But it was not only the Army that was the target in Armagh: on 22 January 1990, Inspector Derek Monteith of the RUC was fatally wounded in the kitchen of his own home. Gunmen had fired 15–30 high-velocity rounds from his garden through the windows. The previous November Lance-Corporal Samuel Halligan of the UDR was ambushed shortly after leaving Drumadd Barracks in Armagh in his own car. He too was killed. And sometimes even more sophisticated attacks were launched. On 20 October 1989, an RUC patrol car was ambushed in the centre of Belleek. A high- sided tipper lorry overtook the police vehicle whereupon a 12.7mm heavy machine-gun mounted in the back of the lorry opened fire, as did other terrorists with 7.62mm and 5.56mm rifles. The armoured Sierra police vehicle was hit a total of 66 times. The driver, Constable Marshall, was fatally wounded and the vehicle caught fire. The other RUC officer in the car was seriously wounded.

South Armagh remained consistently dangerous into the nineties. Incidents occurred on a regular basis. A few examples will suffice to illustrate the intensity of the war in this county. At 5.52 p.m. on Friday 28 September 1992, a single high-velocity shot was fired at a patrol of the 2nd Battalion the Light Infantry in Crossmaglen. Private Turner was struck in the chest by a .50 bullet which passed through his flak jacket and killed him instantly. The round was fired from a heavy calibre high-powered US-manufactured sniping rifle that no flak jacket could possibly be proof against. This weapon was used several times in the early 1990s and was probably operated by the same IRA gunman who chose his target and his firing position with considerable skill. A sniper in this kind of situation of course always has the advantage.

Mortar attacks on the Crossmaglen base continued unabated. There were attacks in 1993 on 4 February, 7 April and 11 July. The last occurred at 3 p.m. when a red Toyota Hiace van, which was used as the mortar baseplate, was driven to the back of a baker's shop only 60 metres from the perimeter fence. It contained one 'Mk 15' IRA mortar tube which was fired on a timer. The mortar bomb consisted of 70kg of home-made explosive, but although it exploded inside the base, it caused no casualties.

Sometimes the IRA were more devious. On 10 February 1994, a Mk 15 mortar was again fired at the Crossmaglen base. The bomb exploded within the base compound causing damage to a building but no casualties. The mortar baseplate, located within a blue Toyota Hiace van, was found. As it was being moved into the Crossmaglen base for further investigation, a second explosion occurred in the front of the vehicle, which was almost certainly remotely detonated and which seriously injured two soldiers. Right up to the cease-fire in August 1994 South Armagh remained a hotbed of terrorism.

Finally, mention should be made of North Armagh. Though it has not earned itself the same infamous reputation as South Armagh, battalions found it in many ways just as challenging. The North Armagh battalion is responsible for the northern and less wild half of County Armagh and the eastern end of County Tyrone – a total area of some four hundred and sixty square miles including 42 miles of border and forty-five crossing-points. The battalion is supported by elements of 2 UDR at Armagh and 8 UDR at Dungannon. While most of the area is a patchwork of small farms and orchards, it includes three sizeable built up areas – Armagh, Dungannon and Cookstown. Battalions in North Armagh were deployed with Battalion HQ and one company in Drumadd Barracks, Armagh, a company in Cookstown, a company in Middletown normally with a platoon detached to Keady, and a company in Dungannon with a platoon detached to Coalisland. During their 1979 tour 1 RGJ shot dead one IRA terrorist and wounded another after a gun battle in Keady. They discovered a 3,500lb culvert bomb before it was detonated and were involved in many other incidents. Two riflemen were wounded, but both were back with their battalions within a relatively short period of time.

As late as February 1993, snipers were still operating in North Armagh. On 25 February, a single high-velocity round was fired at but missed a patrol of the 2nd Battalion the Royal Anglian Regiment. And the Security Forces were still discovering large quantities of explosives in February 1994, only months before the cease-fire. On 16 February, 65lb of explosive and a quantity of equipment parts for Mk 15 mortars were uncovered by the Grenadier Guards three kilometres south-east of Cullavide.

Both South and North Armagh were from 1969 to 1994 particularly dangerous for the security forces. The county's proximity to the border and its predominantly Catholic population make it particularly vulnerable to violence. A Northern Ireland Tourist Board brochure describes Armagh as 'a city of saints in a garden of tempting apples'. The battalions have not seen too many saints in Armagh and were not much tempted by the apples.

9
THE ULSTER DEFENCE REGIMENT
(NOW THE ROYAL IRISH REGIMENT)

Early in 1983 a dinner was held at the Mansion House in London to launch an appeal for the Ulster Defence Regiment Benevolent Fund. At that dinner the Chief of the Defence Staff said: 'Thirteen years ago the Ulster Defence Regiment . . . joined the British Army's Order of Battle . . . Since those dark days what a remarkable record the Regiment has had . . . For thirteen years it has held its position in the front line and made an enormous contribution in the Province's slow but steady progress back to normality. No other Regiment in the British Army, since the time of the Napoleonic wars, can claim to have had such a long, sustained tour of active duty under such conditions. No Regiment has a better record of dedication and bravery.'

The UDR's origins date back to the earliest days of the current troubles in Ulster. In the light of the increasingly serious civil disorder in late 1968 and throughout 1969, the Wilson Government appointed Lord Hunt to head a commission on policing in Northern Ireland. One of the recommendations of the report, published in October 1969, was that responsibility for the protection of the border in particular and the province in general should pass from the RUC to the Army, and that a locally recruited, mainly part-time force, should be raised under the control of the GOC Northern Ireland. The formation of this new force, to be known as the Ulster Defence Regiment, began in January 1970. The first recruits were enlisted a month later, the Regiment was formed on 1 April and, uniquely, battalions took over their first operational tasks the same day. Initially seven battalions were raised, one for each of the six counties and the seventh in Belfast. Four months after their formation, as a result of a serious deterioration in the security situation, the Regiment was called out for the first time and remained on duty for ten days. Key-point guards were reinforced, vehicle check-points were set up and mobile patrols were mounted.

The Act of Parliament which authorized the formation of the UDR was passed on 18 December 1969 and defined the task of the Regiment as . . . to support the regular forces in Northern Ireland, should circumstances so require, in protecting the border and State against armed attack and sabotage'.

As a result of the upsurge in applications to enlist in the UDR, following the introduction of internment in August 1971, the decision was taken to raise a further four battalions: in January 1972, 8 UDR in Tyrone, 9 UDR in Antrim, 10 UDR in Belfast and, in September 1972, 11UDR in Craigavon. In 1985, 4, 5, 6 and 8 UDR were under the opertional command of 8 Brigade in Londonderry, and 1/9, 2, 3, 7/10 and 11 UDR under 39 Brigade in Belfast, four of the original eleven battalions having amalgamated into two.

On 1 July 1992, as part of the British Army's reduction in manpower exercise 'Options for Change', the UDR was re-named The Royal Irish Regiment (or RIR) and reduced to six battalions; 3 RIR under command of 3 Brigade, 4 and 5 RIR under command of 8 Brigade and 7, 8 and 9 RIR under command of 39 Brigade.

The strength of the UDR today is approximately 4,000 all ranks of which 10 per cent are Greenfinches – the female members of the Regiment. The Regiment is leaner than in 1972, but this is largely because of the weeding out of those who seldom if ever turned up for duty. It is also more efficient, fitter and younger. A recent survey showed the average age of the UDR soldier to be thirty-two. Compared with the Regular Army, this is still a considerably older average age. The vast majority of trained soldiers join their battalions between the ages of $17\frac{1}{2}$ and 18, and complete three or six years in the Regular Army. Some stay for nine or twelve years, leaving between the ages of 27 and 30. A small minority, most of whom become SNCOs and WOs, complete 22 years service. Thus only the officer corps (approximately 5 per cent of the total strength of the Army), who are entitled to serve until the age of 55, are likely to serve beyond the age of 40.

Apart from the eight days' intensive training given to a recruit on joining the RIR, each soldier must carry out at least twelve full days training a year including a minimum of three days at annual camp. Battalions train at Ballykinler in County Down, Magilligan in County Londonderry and, since spring 1976, Warcop in Cumbria. Officers attend courses at The Royal Military Academy, Sandhurst and all ranks attend courses at other Army schools such as the School of Infantry at Warminster and the School of Engineering at Chatham. Battalions are commanded by Regular officers and the Training Major, Quartermaster, RSM and a further six warrant officers or senior NCOs are also attached from Regular British Army units. Full-time RIR officers, many ex-regulars, are employed as adjutants and administrative officers. Battalion Seconds-in-Command and all company com-

Ulster Defence Regiment average age						
18–25 years		33.7%	35–44 years	21.9%	over 53 years	4.6%
26–34 years		28.7%	45–52 years	11.1%		

manders are part-time soldiers. More than 1,500 members are now full-time members of the Regiment, which gives the RIR a viable daytime capability. The Regiments have now been allocated their own Tactical Areas of Responsibility (TAOR). In early 1975, 9 UDR became the first battalion responsible for its own TAOR, an area covering South Armagh. 3 UDR followed in June 1976 when it assumed responsibility for East Down.

Today the RIR is primarily responsible for providing military support to the RUC over some 80 per cent of the Province, and battalion commanders are military advisers to the Chief Superintendents commanding police divisions. Within these TAORs they can and frequently do assume operational control of regular army companies or platoons. For instance, during a very intensive fortnight of operations following the mass escape from the Maze Prison in September 1983, 3 UDR had at various times under command elements of three regular battalions, as well as elements of the Royal Navy and RAF. This assumption of responsibility for their own TAORs has meant that all battalions must have a 24-hour capability, manning an operations room, patrolling and reacting to incidents. This increased operational capability was fully achieved in 1977 by an increase in the permanent cadre establishment, allowing battalions to recruit one or more full-

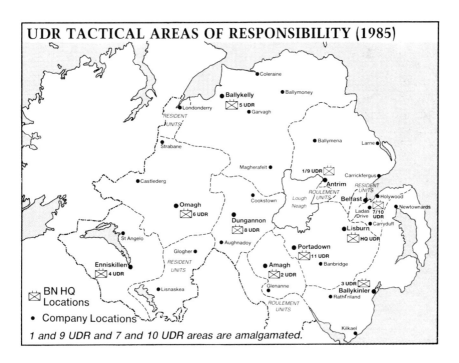

UDR TACTICAL AREAS OF RESPONSIBILITY (1985)

Coleraine
Ballykelly   Ballymoney
Londonderry   5 UDR
RESIDENT   Garvagh
UNITS
Strabane
Ballymena   Larne
Magherafelt   1/9 UDR
Castlederg   Antrim   RESIDENT
Carrickfergus   UNITS
ROULEMENT
Cookstown   Lough   UNITS   Belfast   Holywood
Omagh   Neagh   Newtownards
6 UDR   Ladas 7/10
Dungannon   /Drive UDR
8 UDR   Lisburn   Carryduff
St Angelo   HQ UDR
Aughnadoy   Portadown
Glogher   11 UDR
RESIDENT
Enniskillen   UNITS   Amagh   Banbridge
4 UDR   2 UDR
Glenanne   3 UDR
BN HQ   Lisnaskea   Ballykinler
Locations   Rath'riland
ROULEMENT
Company Locations   UNITS
Kilkael
1 and 9 UDR and 7 and 10 UDR areas are amalgamated.

time platoons. Until that time, the full-time soldiers had been employed for the most part on the security of company centres, and the Regiment was purely a part-time force. From 1977, a much greater emphasis was placed on the role and training of the permanent cadre soldiers. They are highly professional soldiers and as thoroughly trained for their internal security role as their Regular counterparts. Although it is no longer correct to think of the Royal Irish Regiment as a part-time force, these part-time soldiers still continue to play a vital role in relieving the permanent cadre from operational tasks by night and at weekends, and the fact is that, without their loyal volunteer service, battalions would not be able to fulfill their operational commitments.

In the twenty-five years of its history, the Royal Irish Regiment has achieved numerous successes. In one short Chapter it is only possible to give a few representative examples. On 5 February 1972, a section of 4 UDR was carrying out a foot patrol on a lonely road in the border area of Fermanagh when they saw an old and battered car coming towards them. The car stopped short of the patrol, three men got out, took something out of the boot and threw it over the hedge. The patrol ran

Right: An NCO briefs fellow members of the UDR prior to an operation. Notice the list of cars of interest to the left of the map. Such a list will have resulted from previous suspicious behaviour by certain car owners or previous incidents involving these cars. UDR members have access to a central computer holding details of all suspect cars in Ulster. (MOD)

forward and detained the men and, on searching behind the hedge, found an RPG-7 rocket launcher. This was the battalion's first major success, one of many to follow in the years to come.

In the early hours of a morning in May 1977, 1 UDR, at the request of the RUC, carried out a cordon and search operation on a number of houses close to the shores of Lough Neagh, and arrested six local men. Later the same day four companies carried out a planned search operation during which they found four well-covered hides containing: two RPG-7 rocket launchers, a rifle, a revolver, more than 200 rounds of ammunition and 50 feet of cordtex and a detonator.

On the night of 8 November 1982, a mobile patrol of 5 UDR was passing through Swatragh, a notoriously troublesome village in County Londonderry, when the rear vehicle came under fire. The patrol returned fire, deployed and fired illuminating rounds. A second mobile patrol was approaching the village when they saw the flares and deployed a foot patrol. A man was seen running across the road into a public house. The patrol carried out an immediate hot pursuit, cordoning off the area and searching the out-buildings. In one they found a much wanted terrorist, armed with a loaded 7.62 Heckler-Koch rifle. In

recognition of his vigorous reaction, the patrol commander was subsequently awarded the Queen's Gallantry Medal, and one of the section commanders a Mention in Despatches.

On the evening of 13 November 1982, 3 UDR received information that a car had been found abandoned close to the busy main road from Ballynahinch to Newcastle in County Down. The operations room placed the road out of bounds, and the following morning, while the battalion attended the Remembrance Sunday service in the cathedral in Downpatrick, other patrols carried out a clearance operation. The battalion's search dog, Oliver, indicated at a culvert running under the main road. On looking inside, the patrol commander saw four beer kegs and a milk churn; a command wire was located running to a nearby derelict house. During a prolonged clearance operation, spread over the next 72 hours, the Ammunition Technical Officer (ATO) neutralized a massive landmine consisting of some 500lb of explosives. It seems probable that the Provisional IRA had hoped to detonate it under vehicles carrying UDR men to a Remembrance Sunday service.

In May 1984, a search team from 6 UDR, accompanied by the Battalions's search dog, was tasked with searching an empty farmhouse in a lonely area of County Tyrone. Almost immediately the dog indicated

Right: UDR soldiers are trained to operate in both Army and RAF helicopters. In this case they are seen emplaning into an RAF Wessex helicopter. They are clearly engaged in rural operations, as the last member of the patrol is carrying an A41 radio set only suitable for use in a non-urban environment.

in the corner of a septic tank close to the house. Underneath was a cunningly covered hide from which emanated a strong smell of explosives. Over the next two days the ATO, covered by soldiers of the Battalion, recovered from this hide some 3,800lb of home-made explosives made up into 66 separate devices. It was the largest single find of explosives ever made in the Province.

Off-duty UDR soldiers were always terribly vulnerable. One of the many tragic examples of their murder took place on 25 September 1988. Private McKinney of 2 UDR was arriving home after midnight, having completed a tour of duty at Drumadd Barracks, Armagh, when he was ambushed by two gunmen who fired at least 40 rounds at him from close range. He was killed instantly. It was impossible to guard against such an attack which underlines the courage of countless UDR and RIR men and women who faced this mortal danger.

On Thursday 28 June 1992, a Wessex helicopter pilot noticed three men acting suspiciously in the area of a stream bed near Cappagh. Having picked up a six-man team from 8 UDR, the helicopter gave chase to a cream Ford Escort van, the driver of which was cornered in a house where he was arrested. In the follow-up an AK 47 assault rifle and two GPMGs were found as well as mortar parts and bomb-making equipment.

No account of the UDR/RIR is complete without some reference to the women members, the Greenfinches, who are fully integrated members of their Battalions. Originally formed in August 1973 to provide patrols with the capability to search women, they now fulfil most of the roles of the men, except that they are not permitted to carry arms. They drive vehicles on patrols, man operation rooms and Intelligence cells and take part in searches for arms and explosives as well as relieving men in such administrative tasks as cooking, clerical work and store-keeping. That they share the same risks as the men was tragically illustrated in July 1984 when a Greenfinch corporal was one of two members of a foot patrol killed when a landmine exploded under the road, detonated from across the border in Donegal.

The RIR does, of course, have some limitations. The part-time element suffers, because of its very nature, from lack of training, but to some extent this is made up by enthusiasm and hard work. Moreover, although the Regiment recruits from all sections of the community, the very high proportion of Protestants in the Regiment (97 per cent) is damaging in propaganda terms.

The advantages, however, far outweigh the disadvantages. The Regiment is widely deployed throughout Northern Ireland, so there is an opportunity for all members of the community to join and contribute to local security. The deployment of the RIR provides an infra-structure for security operations all over the Province. Many members of the Regiment are strongly motivated and dedicated people. Many part-timers have reported for duty on two or three nights a week since the Regiment was formed, in addition to carrying out their civilian jobs and bringing up families. There is a great depth of local knowledge available in the Regiment. The Battalion Intelligence cell and the small, company-level Intelligence cells ensure that this potential is fully exploited. The RIR contributes some 200 soldiers and servicewomen every day and night of the year to active security force operations, with a greater contribution at weekends. The increasing size and experience of the permanent cadre, coupled with increased training, is leading to the creation of a well-organized and efficient full-time element in the RIR, whose operations can be of a more sophisticated nature than those carried out by the part-time soldiers. Having said this, RIR soldiers may not be used for riot and crowd control They may not patrol the staunchly Catholic areas of Belfast and Londonderry, except with and under the command of a Regular unit.

Right: A UDR patrol demonstrates the principle of 'always having one leg on the ground'. Note that, while two members of the patrol are moving, one has his rifle in the shoulder, covering the patrol to the rear, and another is crouching in a fire position covering forward.

They may not take part in covert or plain clothes operations and they are not permitted to screen suspects. Therefore the UDR is very carefully controlled and, since it is predominately a Protestant force, it is important that it should be seen to be.

By August 1994, fatal casualties totalled more than 200, the majority incurred when off duty. That the Regiment refuses to be intimidated by this cowardly IRA tactic and that recruiting remains buoyant is a measure of the courage and steadfastness of the soldiers of the RIR. Their contribution to the offensive against terrorism in Northern Ireland has been critical. As long as so many Ulstermen and women are prepared to serve their country so unstintingly the IRA cannot win.

Left: Private Scott of 4 UDR on sentry duty at his barracks perimeter. Note that the UDR was one of the first units in the British Army to be issued the SA80 rifle in the late 1980s.

10
A CHANGE IN TACTICS

In 1977, a further initiative was set in motion by the Government at Westminster when the Secretary of State for Northern Ireland launched a new policy to re-establish the primacy of the RUC. The priority task for the Army was to be the elimination of terrorism with the aim of restoring the RUC to their normal policing role throughout the Province. The Army's level of involvement was to be reduced accordingly. By then it was possible to classify areas as Black, Grey or White: Black denoting constant terrorist activity, Grey infrequent terrorist activity and a partial return to normality, and White indicating no indigenous terrorist activity. In the White areas, where the terrorist threat did not warrant the permanent presence of soldiers, the RUC could carry out their normal policing role. In the Grey areas, where there was still a significant, if sporadic, threat from the terrorists, the RUC would need some military support. Only in the Black areas, where the terrorists continued to pose a dangerous threat, such as the border fringe of South Armagh and small areas in Belfast, would the RUC need a permanent, high-profile military presence. The next three years saw the gradual success of the new policy as the areas in which normal policing was resumed steadily increased, and the presence and strength of the Army slowly diminished.

The success of the Security Forces in bringing PIRA terrorists to justice, the breaking up of its command organizations and suppression of terrorist activity in the main towns, combined with greatly reduced support for terrorism, led to the major reorganization of the IRA, described in Chapter 7. The IRA became a smaller, more radical organization, based on 3–5-man cells. They aimed to conduct a long-term campaign, calculated to focus political, economic and diplomatic pressure on the UK Government. Despite this, the Secretary of State determined to press on with his new 'Way Ahead' policy. Under this, the role of the RUC would be to establish and maintain law and order throughout the Province, using Army support wherever and whenever necessary. The Army was specifically enjoined to support the RUC with the military strength and specialist skills, not found in a police force, to counter organized revolutionary terrorists.

The Secretary of State for Northern Ireland was to be responsible for the direction of security policy. A Security Co-ordinating Committee, under the chairmanship of the Chief Constable in consultation with the GOC, was to report to the Secretary of State. An Operational Policy Committee, attended by the Deputy Chief Constable (Operations) and the Commander Land Forces (CLF), reported to the Chief Constable and GOC. There were also joint committees at Regional level, attended by Regional Assistant Constables and Brigade Commanders and at Divisional level attended by RUC Divisional Commanders and Battalion Commanding Officers. Later in 1979 an overall Security Co-ordinator was appointed.

Detailed military tasks fell into two categories: first, the Army was to counter the paramilitary terrorist threat. They were to do this by suppressing terrorist movement and activities, by catching terrorists red-handed and by arrests made at the request of the police and by a deterrent presence. Secondly, the Army was to give the police the protection they needed to carry out their normal activities. Military operations in these two categories were to fall into the following types: Framework operations, reactive operations, specialist operations, covert operations and static tasks.

Framework operations are the planned overt operations by which the Army obtains a detailed knowledge and feel for an area. They include routine patrolling on foot, in vehicles and by helicopter, to suppress terrorist activity; spot-checks and searches of vehicles; reassurance of the populace at large by a physical presence after an incident; keeping in touch with members of the community going about their daily business, as well as keeping an eye on suspected terrorists and their associates; stopping and questioning suspicious persons and lastly, holding reserves always ready to react to the unforeseen.

Reactive operations are quite simply those operations which require an immediate reaction by the Army to terrorist incidents, also pre-planned reactions to specific information or Intelligence, and contingency plans to cover such events as demonstrations and marches.

Specialist operations require the provision of support to the police in bomb-disposal, air reconnaissance, specialist air and ground photography, and specialist search techniques provided by the Royal Engineer search teams.

Covert operations involve the building up of evidence of terrorist organizations and activities, using specialist surveillance techniques leading to prosecution or red-handed arrest.

Lastly, static tasks include key-point guards (radio and TV masts, communications centres, dock facilities, airports, etc.), prison guards (HMP Maze and others), prisoner escorts, Belfast City Centre and other Town Centre Security, permanent vehicle check-points, RUC police station guards and Army base guards.

The legal powers of the Army in Northern Ireland were to remain unchanged. The provisions of the Northern Ireland (Emergency Provisions) Act were considered sufficient to allow the Army to operate independently of the police where normal policing was no longer possible.[*]

Such then was the change in direction which was instigated in 1977, partly as a result of the change in IRA tactics, but mostly because of the considerable progress made in the Province in restoring normality in many areas, and in reducing the incidence of terrorism in others.

The summer of 1977 saw another, but unsuccessful, Loyalist United Unionist Action Council (UUAC) call for a general strike after elections introduced power-sharing in 23 out of 26 councils. The aim was to force the Westminster Government to return to a strict observance of the 1920 Act. Nevertheless, it caused widespread disruption. Hundreds of cases of intimidation by the UUAC were reported and Larne Harbour was closed for several days. The Spearhead Battalion was flown in from the mainland and all the battalions of the UDR were called out. The Security Forces removed 730 Protestant barricades. The collapse of the strike marked the beginning of a decrease in the influence of Protestant extremist organizations, but PIRA was by no means beaten. The first obvious result of their reorganization was the renewed bombing campaign which reached a climax in early 1978 with the La Mon Restaurant disaster. This outrage, in which twelve innocent civilians were killed and more maimed, so appalled public opinion that even the ruthless leadership of PIRA had to suspend bombing for a short period. The La Mon Hotel is situated in a Belfast suburb. The Provisionals later claimed that their warning to clear the building was heeded too late. Realizing that their supporters were shocked by this bombing of innocent men and women enjoying a night out, the Provisionals publicly apologized for the loss of life. Public indignation did not affect Provisional tactics for very long and, after a short lull which was long enough for people to forget the 'accident', the Provisionals were back in action bombing stores, shops and areas where civilians gathered.

The vicious, inter-sectarian violence continued unabated throughout 1977. Tit-for-tat killings and maimings by the Provisionals and the Protestant paramilitary groups, and the rival warfare between the Provisionals and the Officials tended to account for an increasing proportion of the total casualties, the more the Security Forces got on top of the situation. Two days in May 1977 illustrate the extent of inter-sectarian strife in Ulster. On 10 May, a Protestant bus driver was

[*] The legal status of the Army in Northern Ireland is discussed in depth by Robin Evelegh in his book, *Peacekeeping in a Democratic Society*.

shot dead at the wheel of his bus in Belfast. Later the same day the body of a Catholic was found in the garden of a derelict house in Belfast. On 12 May, Mr Douglas Deering, who owned a small supermarket in Rosslea, County Fermanagh and who was a local Justice of the Peace, was shot dead at work. He was a Protestant. The same day terrorists fired four shots at a petrol tanker driver who was driving his vehicle through East Belfast – fortunately they missed. During two days in July 1977, four members of the OIRA were shot by PIRA assassination squads and a further sixteen people were seriously injured in gun battles or assassination attempts. Two of these were boys aged thirteen and fifteen, one of whom had been 'kneecapped' while the other had gunshot wounds to the chest. Where murder is considered inappropriate by the punishment squads, 'kneecapping' is popular: it consists of shooting the victim in the back of the knee in such a way as to cripple him either permanently or temporarily depending on the degree of skill used in administering the punishment. Such is the mentality of the men of violence in Northern Ireland.

One action involving 45 Commando during their June–October 1977 Belfast tour is fairly typical of many and is worth consideration in some detail. On Friday 12 August at 1210 hours, a high-velocity shot was fired at a mobile patrol in a Land Rover in Gransha Park in the Turf Lodge area of Belfast by a gunman in a fire position believed to be in Norglen Gardens. The round went through the windscreen and passed through the side of Lance-Corporal Thorpe's head, fortunately causing no permanent injury, and then through the windscreen of the following Land Rover. At 1330 hours, during the follow-up, one high-velocity shot was fired at a group of Marines forming part of a cordon which had been set up as a result of the original shooting in an attempt to prevent the escape of the gunman. Marine Bewley was hit in the chest and later died in Musgrave Park Hospital. During the 'hot pursuit' resulting from this shooting, two .455 Webley pistols, one loaded, together with 159 assorted live rounds and two transceiver radios were found.

Later during the follow-up, at 1358 hours, a blast bomb estimated to have contained 1–2lb of explosive was thrown at a Military Police team in Norglen Parade. Lance-Corporal Lock, RMP received serious injuries to his right foot and Lance-Corporal Hobbs, RMP multiple lacerations to both legs.

Left: An example of IRA 'justice' – the Provisionals have always seen themselves as both judge and jury of the Catholic community. In this instance, the victim has been tarred and feathered, probably for a relatively minor offence such a stealing from a fellow Catholic. More serious crimes result in either 'kneecapping' or summary execution.

At 1511 hours another high-velocity shot was fired into Norglen Parade by a gunman believed to be in the Whiterock area. The shot went through a window of a flat near the Marines in the cordon, but fortunately hit no one. At 1533 hours a small crowd tried to barricade the south end of Norglen Parade with a vehicle. Two baton rounds were fired to clear a path for access for an RMP Team. At 1545 hours yet another high-velocity shot was fired at the cordon, this time from the direction of New Barnsley. Again there were no casualties. During the follow-up at 1624 hours, one Webley Scott 12 bore sawn-off shot-gun, some shotgun cartridges and an imitation Thompson machine-gun were found in Norglen Parade. An RMP Team on the way to deal with the shotgun find was heavily stoned, and sharpened metal pickets were thrown by a crowd of youths, one of these 'spears' actually pene-trating the Macrolon armour of the Land Rover and slightly injuring the RMP sergeant who was forced to fire two 9mm shots over the heads of the yelling mob in order to extricate the team from a danger-ous situation.

At 1706 hours, a low-velocity shot was fired at the Marines in the cordon in Norglen Parade by a gunman believed to be in the Whiterock Road area. Shortly afterwards two men were arrested at a vehicle check-point on suspicion of carrying out the shooting. Finally, at 1740 hours, three to five shots were fired at the cordon in Ardmonagh Parade, again from the Whiterock. Fire was returned and by 1830 hours all troops had withdrawn from the Turf Lodge area. During the six hours that the Marines of X, Y and Z Companies of 45 Commando had spent in the Turf Lodge area, they fired a total of 62 baton rounds and searched 108 houses. They found some illegal arms and ammunition and arrested a few suspects. Arguably they aggravated the situation by their presence and they probably alienated some innocent families by their house searches, but what else could they do? Shot at continu-ally for nearly six hours, with one of their number killed and more wounded, they persisted bravely and resolutely to uphold the law. Each incident as it occurred was investigated calmly and coolly by a Royal Military Police team. The cordon was maintained with great courage and tenacity in order that the law might function properly – that shootings be investigated, photographs at the scene be taken, weapons be recovered and searches be undertaken. The point has to be made that if a shooting incident takes place, it has to be investigated in a proper manner. To allow that principle to be overtaken by the flurry of events is to give in to terrorism and to recognize, albeit implicitly, that the normal process of law and order has broken down and that a state

Left: Marines of 45 Commando on patrol in the Turf Lodge area of Belfast during September 1977.
Inset: A member of 1st Battalion The Royal Hampshire Regiment chats with a local child in London-derry during their 1991 tour.

of war exists. The price paid by the Marines for their persistence during the Battle of Turf Lodge on the 12 August 1977 was one Marine killed and one Royal Corps of Transport driver attached to Z Company 45 Commando wounded. In addition, a Royal Military Police lance-corporal was wounded.

On 16 October 1977 more than a hundred SKS/AK-47 Assault Rifles and a quantity of rocket launchers and ammunition destined for Northern Ireland was seized at Schipol Airport, Amsterdam. This was one of a series of major interceptions of large quantities of arms on their way to Eire or Northern Ireland. 250 Assault Rifles, 243 revolvers, 500 grenades, 100 landmines and a large quantity of ammunition had been seized on 28 March 1973, on board the MV *Claudia*. In 1984 an even larger consignment was intercepted by the Irish Navy following an international operation involving various US, British and Irish agencies. The arms shipment had originated from the United States where it had been loaded aboard a sea-going trawler which crossed the Atlantic and made a rendezvous with a small coastal fishing boat out-side Irish territorial waters off the west coast of Eire. It was intercepted by the Irish Navy as it entered territorial waters.

In November 1977 Lieutenant-General Sir David House was re-placed as GOC Northern Ireland by Lieutenant-General, Sir Tim Creasey. Creasey was chosen to oversee the 'Way Ahead' policy and in particular the gradual handing back of responsibility for security to the RUC.

The 2nd Battalion of the Green Jackets has served with distinction in Ulster on seven separate occasions, its most recent tour commencing in October 1985. Its December 1977 to April 1978 tour will long be remembered by the Battalion, mainly because of the tragic death in action of its Commanding Officer, Lieutenant-Colonel Iain Corden-Lloyd, OBE, MC.

The Battalion deployed to Crossmaglen, Forkill, Newry, Newtown-hamilton and Bessbrook. Within days of arrival a patrol from B Com-pany based in Crossmaglen, and led by Sergeant Bennett, was blown up and shot at from across the border. The Patrol Commander's radio-operator was lifted off his feet by the force of the explosion and deposi-ted some way back along the track but, unperturbed, he grabbed his radio and calmly sent back detailed reports which enabled a rapid follow-up to be mounted. Sergeant Bennet received severe head in-juries as a result of which he was later invalided from the Army.

A week later, C Company at Forkhill suffered an IRA mortar attack. Fortunately most of the living accommodation was empty at the time and the IRA's aim was not good, so there were only minor casualties. The aftermath of the attack could have ended in disaster. The firing

A series of photographs depicting the aftermath of the mortar attack on the Forkill base. **Top:** the flat-bed lorry with its improvised mortar tubes having discharged their bombs from a site on a nearby housing estate. **Above left:** The commanding officer gives an interview to a BBC TV camera team, describing the mortar attack. **Above right:** As he is giving the interview, a booby trap is set off by two RUC policemen examining the lorry, and the CO rushes to their assistance. **Right:** One of the policemen lies severely injured in the road.

platform for the attack, a flat-bed lorry, exploded as it was being driven away by the RUC. The lorry had been booby trapped by a very cleverly hidden device which even the Ammunition Technical Officer (ATO) had failed to detect. Fortunately the two policemen were not too seriously injured.

February was a black month. During a follow-up operation after the Close Observation Platoon (COP) had had a contact in the border area, the Commanding Officer's helicopter crashed while taking evasive action under fire. Lieutenant-Colonel Corden-Lloyd was killed and the COP Commander, Captain Philip Schofield, and the pilot were badly injured. The loss of Iain Corden-Lloyd was of course a tragedy for his family and friends, and the Green Jackets and the Army lost one of their most promising young Commanding Officers who many say was destined for much greater things. It was a tragedy that could have been the undoing of a lesser battalion, but life had to go on. The Second-in-Command assumed command and the Battalion continued to conduct operations. As if one death were not enough, Rifleman Nicholas Smith was killed near Crossmaglen a few weeks later while removing a booby-trapped Irish tricolour from a telegraph pole.

Above: The remains of the Gazelle helicopter after the crash in which Lieutenant-Colonel Ian Corden-Lloyd was killed while flying to support his troops engaged in operations against the IRA in South Armagh.

The Battalion continued to dominate their area to the end of their tour, with the result that very little happened. Consequently there was a feeling among some people that the tour had not been a success. From the purely statistical point of view this may have been the case, but statistics do not tell the whole story. The fact is that 2 RGJ dominated the area to such an extent that the IRA were consistently frustrated in their plans. It was a quiet tour and in many ways typical of most tours since 1978 – such is the extent to which the Army has since then kept the lid on the security situation.

The main technical innovations of PIRA in 1978 were the increased use of remote-controlled bombs which enabled them to destroy targets in greater safety and with more precision, and a new method of making explosives from fertilizers. Clearly this made life more difficult for the Security Forces despite restrictions on the sale of sodium chloride-based weed-killers, and control in the import and movement of explosives. Two of the most infamous remote-controlled bombings were the attack on 10 October 1981 on a bus filled with Guardsmen returning from Guard Duty at the Tower of London, and the attack on 20 July 1982 on the Green Jackets' Band playing lunchtime music in Regent's Park. Also, the Warrenpoint attack on 27 August 1979 was a classic command-detonated or radio-controlled bomb attack. The bomb was detonated from a position across Carlingford Lough in the Irish Republic. In the case of the two London bombings, the terrorists are thought to have been within sight of their targets when they activated the bombs. Clearly radio-controlled bombs have made the Army's task immeasurably more difficult. The jamming of radio frequencies is difficult because of not knowing which frequencies to jam. The search for a counter to this threat continues. In the meantime, the IRA now have a much more effective bombing capacity.

The year also saw the first use by PIRA of the US-manufactured M-60, a highly sophisticated and very effective modern machine-gun. On 1 March, Lance-Corporal Bulmer of 2 LI was leading a four-man patrol along Cliftonpark Avenue near the North Lodge area of Belfast. It was a mixed patrol with two soldiers of 2 LI and two soldiers from 40 Field Regiment Royal Artillery. 2 LI were Province Reserve Battalion and were being made familiar with the area by 40 Field Regiment whose area it was. Gunner Shepperd was hit and mortally wounded. The patrol returned fire and put eight rounds through the window from which the M-60 had been fired. However, the two terrorists involved in the attack managed to escape using a van parked behind the house which they had taken over. Two members of PIRA were later convicted of murdering Gunner Shepperd. The incident highlights the difficulties faced by the Security Forces patrolling in an urban area.

Every window is a potential ambush point. Firing positions are carefully selected houses, either occupied or derelict. An escape route is carefully reconnoitred and a vehicle placed so as to provide a means of escape. A designated carrier, often a member of Cumman Na Bann (the women's section of PIRA), is sometimes employed to remove the weapon. The only counter to an urban ambush of this nature is by multiple patrolling or saturation patrolling, that is to put sufficient patrols on the ground so that, if the ambush is sprung, the escape route of the terrorist is threatened by another patrol.

The year 1979 saw an upsurge in attacks against the Security Forces, particularly against off-duty UDR soldiers. PIRA appreciated their importance as the eyes and ears of the Security Forces, and their value in supporting the RUC. Remotely-detonated bombs caused nearly thirty per cent of Security Force deaths in an IRA campaign against the Army which concentrated on rural and border areas. In Belfast and other towns the victims were mostly civilians, selected from among wellknown businessmen, policemen and prison warders. For the first time prominent figures were singled out for attack in the United Kingdom and on the mainland of Europe. Mr Airey Neave, MP, a firm opponent of terrorism in Northern Ireland and a close adviser to Prime Minister Margaret Thatcher, was killed in a car bomb attack at Westminster in April. The Irish National Liberation Army (INLA) claimed responsibility. INLA is an organization based in Dublin where it picks up recruits expelled from the Provisionals. There is little to distinguish this organization from PIRA. Its aims are similar, but its membership is more select; if it is possible to be more extremist than PIRA, then it is marginally so.

The twin atrocities of the assassination of Earl Mountbatten at Mullaghmore in the Republic of Ireland, and the Warren Point massacre occurred on 27 August. Lord Louis Mountbatten, the 79-year-old uncle of the Queen, his 14-year-old grandson, Nicolas Knatchbull, and the 16-year-old boatman, Paul Maxwell, were killed when terrorists detonated a bomb on his boat *Shadow V*. The Dowager Lady Brabourne aged 82 died the next day. Approximately 50lb of explosives were hidden in a space under the boat's floorboards and were probably detonated remotely from a vantage point on the shore. On 23 November 1979 Thomas MacMahon was found guilty of the murder of Lord Mountbatten by a special criminal court in Dublin.

Late in the afternoon of 27 August, a convoy of three vehicles was travelling from Ballykinler Barracks, County Down to Newry with men of 2 Para on board. At 4.30 p.m. they approached a trailer loaded with hay and straw bales parked in a lay-by at a place called Narrow Water, where Carlingford Lough is only a couple of hundred yards wide

Above: Warrenpoint – the site of the first bomb, to the left of the main road in a lay-by, can clearly be seen. The remains of the blasted 4-ton truck hit by the explosion lie on the central reservation. The site of the second bomb was adjacent to the main gates of the castle, visible to the right of the main road.

and where it separates Ulster from the Republic. As the rear 4-ton truck of the three vehicle convoy passed the trailer there was a large explosion. An estimated 500lb of explosives had been placed in milk-churns which had been hidden in the hay and straw bales and deto-nated by men in the Republic using remote control. A nearby Army patrol in the town of Warrenpoint reported the explosion. Meanwhile the IRA gunmen in the Republic opened fire on the remaining vehicles. During this exchange a young English tourist was hit and killed. Two Land Rovers from 2 Para, on patrol in Warrenpoint, sped to the scene. At Bessbrook in County Armagh the 1st Battalion the Queen's Own Highlanders put an airborne reaction force on standby, but held it back until their Commanding Officer had evaluated the situation himself.

The Battalion had started a 20-month residential tour only the previous month. Lieutenant-Colonel David Blair, with his radio-operator, Lance-Corporal Victor McLeod, landed in a Gazelle heli-copter in a field behind a lodge with gates leading to a large house. Behind these gates and the associated wall, the surviving paratroopers had taken cover and were returning fire at the gunmen across the Lough. Doctors had also landed in a Wessex helicopter and were tend-ing the wounded. It was 4.59p.m. when Lieutenant-Colonel Blair ran over to talk to the Para Officer in Command, Major Furseman, and the Wessex with wounded in it commenced its take-off. At that moment a 1,000lb device, placed in the lodge gates, exploded and killed twelve men including Lieutenant-Colonel Blair, and seriously wounded two others. So close was Blair to the explosion that his remains were never found. The Wessex helicopter was damaged but not irreparably. In all, eighteen soldiers, mostly Paras, were killed at Warren Point. It was the worst single incident in the present emergency.

After the event, Prime Minister Margaret Thatcher visited the Army in the Province on several occasions and always made her support for the Security Forces' efforts very clear. It is said that she has an affinity with military men; this may be so, but she certainly expects the same degree of efficiency from them as she demands elsewhere. Senior officers have learned to get their briefings correct in every detail and have to be prepared to be cross-questioned minutely.

Despite Mullaghmore and Warrenpoint, 1980 saw a continuation of the shift of the initiative back to the Security Forces. The Bennett Report on police interrogation methods, which had been published in March 1979, following a critical Amnesty International Report in June 1978, exonerated the RUC and did much for the morale of its CID and Special Branch. Having said this, the Report substantiated some of the findings of the Amnesty International Report of June 1978 that some ill-treatment of prisoners had taken place. However, the Bennett Report also stated firmly: 'Our own examination of medical evidence reveals cases in which injuries, whatever their precise cause, were not self-inflicted and were sustained in police custody.' It recommended among other things, the installation of closed-circuit TV cameras in all interview rooms used for interrogation. While the vast majority of the RUC are an efficient and impartial police force, it is inevitable that in an all-Protestant force there have been some exceptions. Recently there have been some disturbing revelations about the connections between a few policemen and members of Loyalist gangs. In the spring of 1980, two RUC men, Sergeant John Weir and Constable William McCaughey, were charged and convicted of murdering a Catholic shopkeeper in June 1977 in revenge for an attack by the Provisional IRA, and in collaboration with the UVF.

With the encouragement of Mr Haughey's Dublin Government, the Security Forces in the Republic increased their counter-terrorist operations considerably, as a result of Anglo-Irish inter-government talks initiated by the murder of Mountbatten. The year also saw several arrests and munitions finds south of the Border which undoubtedly hampered terrorist operations. After a bad year in 1979, because of the eighteen deaths at Warrenpoint, 1980 saw a substantial decline in Security Forces deaths.

Towards the end of 1980, PIRA embarked upon the first of its hunger-strikes in the prisons at The Maze and Armagh, aimed at restoring political status for convicted terrorists. PIRA supported the strike with a brief bombing campaign in London, but, the hunger-strike crumbled in December. In January 1981, Protestant extremists shot some of the organizers of the hunger-strike and PIRA retaliated by murdering Sir Norman Strange and his son and burning their house in County Tyrone. Towards the end of the month PIRA resumed its campaign of destroying commercial targets in the towns of Northern Ireland.

At the end of 1980, the strength of PIRA was estimated to be between 300 and 400 members, with about 1,000 active supporters who provided safe houses, transport and other facilities. The hard-core strength was about a third of the active strength of 1972, but the reduction probably reflected deliberate policy as much as the effects of attrition. Thus by the end of 1980 startling advances had been made by the Security Forces. The level of violence had been reduced drastically since the early and mid 1970s. But PIRA still operated effectively. Many could be forgiven for wondering if the end would ever be in sight.

Above: The IRA introduced the technique of using home-made mortars deployed on the back of lorries or inside vans in the early 1980s. The various marks of this home-made weapon have proved consistently inaccurate and relatively ineffective. Nevertheless they have provided the IRA with a 'stand-off' method of attacking military targets – and even 10 Downing Street from a 'baseplate' in Whitehall in February 1991, and later Heathrow Airport.

Left: A general view of the
town square in Crossmaglen.
On the left is the so-called
Baruki sangar, named after
Corporal Baruki of the Parachute Regiment, who was killed
by a bicycle bomb on the site of
the sangar. It is permanently
manned by soldiers from the
Crossmaglen base and is used
to monitor everyday routine in
the town. The statue shown in
the inset is located at the far
end of the square; it was
erected by the IRA in memory of
their members who have died in
the cause of 'Irish freedom'.
The other inset shows the
typically cramped living
accommodation for soldiers in
the Crossmaglen base. Bunks
are constructed in three tiers,
and packed close together.
Living in these conditions for
months on end is not conducive
to either rest or privacy.

Left: A typical IRA poster appealing for the continued support of the Catholic community. Below: An example of one of the many posters issued by the security forces providing advice to the ordinary citizen on ways of frustrating sectarian gunmen.

11
EQUILIBRIUM, 1981–1983

In March 1981, yet another initiative by the Secretary of State for Northern Ireland, Mr Atkins, to explore devolution and power-sharing, was rejected. In the same month, the 'dirty protest' at the Maze and Armagh prisons ended, but a second, better-organized and more serious hunger-strike started. The campaign against the abolition of political status for IRA prisoners was supported by a well-orchestrated propaganda campaign at home and abroad aimed at placing the British Government under severe pressure. Capitalizing on the image of martyrdom, the first hunger-striker, Bobby Sands, won the seat for Fermanagh and South Tyrone on 10 April in an emotional by-election. When he died on 5 May, support for the hunger-strike reached its peak, both in Ireland and abroad, particularly among the Irish-American

supporters in the United States. According to a return submitted to the Department of Justice, the Northern Aid Committee (NORAID) collected $250,000 from sympathizers in six months. The hunger-strike developed into a contest of political will between the British Government and Provisional Sinn Fein. PIRA backed the campaign outside the Maze with 64 murders, 20 of them members of the Security Forces. During the summer ten hunger-strikers died and a further seven withdrew. The Government's determination paid off. Support for the hunger-strike declined. Under pressure from the Catholic Church and relatives, and realizing that further deaths would be fruitless, PIRA recognized defeat and called off the hunger-strike on 3 October. The Government had won a significant victory and could afford to introduce prison reforms without giving way on the crucial question of political status. On the debit side, PIRA succeeded in worsening relations between the Government and the Catholics and sharpening the strife between the two communities.

The level of violence in Northern Ireland during the six months from October 1981 to March 1982 continued to be high, with an increase in sectarian killings following the end of the hunger-strike on October 3. There were signs that PIRA intended to launch a campaign of assassinations and bombings to provoke a Protestant backlash aimed at reinstating its self-appointed role as the protector of the Catholic minority. During the autumn the Provisionals claimed responsibility for a series of murders, especially in the border area, and later renewed its bombing campaign on the mainland. Extremist Protestant paramilitary groups, in particular the Ulster Freedom Fighters (UFF), an illegal group operating under the aegis of the UDA, claimed responsibility for several murders which they alleged were in response to the PIRA campaign during the hunger-strike which had taken 64 lives. The murder of the Reverend Robert Bradford, the Official Unionist Party (OUP) MP for Belfast South, by PIRA in November 1981 caused particular anger in the Protestant community and was followed by demonstrations by Protestant paramilitary organizations in Belfast and Londonderry.

Meanwhile, the Army continued with normal operations. 45 Commando stopped a van at a check-point in Shaws Road in Belfast and found 250–300lb of home-made explosives in the back. This led to a further 1,400lb in an ingenious hide in a disused furniture factory in Y Company's area. A complete list of the finds and of the other incidents during this tour is set out in the table.

During October and November 1981, PIRA claimed responsibility for five bomb attacks in London. The first explosion took place on 10 October 1981 close to Chelsea Barracks when a remote-control device was used to ambush a bus full of Irish Guardsmen returning from guard duty at the Tower of London. Two civilians were killed and 40 people, including 20 Guardsmen, were injured. Lieutenant-General Sir Steuart Pringle, Commandant General of the Royal Marines, was seriously injured when his booby-trapped car blew up outside his house in South London on 17 October. PIRA claimed responsibility for the bomb, the 'trembler' mechanism of which was similar to that used in the bomb which had killed Mr Airey Neave in 1979. Although Sir Steuart Pringle's right leg was subsequently amputated he resumed his full duties as head of the Royal Marines on 31 March 1982.

Then, on 26 October, Mr Kenneth Howarth, a Metropolitan Police bomb-disposal expert, was killed while attempting to defuze a bomb in a Wimpy bar in Oxford Street. Bombs were also found and defuzed in two Oxford Street department stores on the same day. PIRA claimed responsibility for an explosion on 13 November which seriously damaged the South London flat belonging to the Attorney-General, Sir Michael Havers. The final attack of this mainland bombing campaign took place on 23 November outside Woolwich Barracks in south-east London, when a booby-trapped toy pistol blew up injuring two women, both wives of soldiers. PIRA later claimed responsibility.

The Reverend Robert Bradford and Mr Kenneth Campbell, a social worker, were murdered on 14 November by PIRA gunmen. The murders were condemned forthrightly by both Mr Prior, Secretary of State for Northern Ireland, and the Prime Minister. Mr Paisley and two other OUP MPs were suspended from the House of Commons for five days after the Speaker had ruled that they were guilty of disorderly conduct and ignoring the authority of the Speaker.

Results
Royal Marines 1981 tour, Belfast

Arrested	500
Charged	Nearly 100
Houses searched	446
Cars searched	1,010
Finds	8 rifles, 6 pistols, 314 rounds of ammunition, 84 detonators, 16 bomb kits
Shooting incidents	By terrorists at 45 Commando, 131
	Fire returned by 45 Commando, 40
Bomb incidents	Actual, 10
	Hoaxes, 25
Baton rounds fired	308

These statistics are not untypical of all Royal Marine Commando tours. Indeed, in the early 1970s, all the figures were substantially higher. They represent a busy, dedicated and dangerous 4½ months in Northern Ireland.

After his suspension from the House, Mr Paisley announced that the Ulster Unionists would make the Province ungovernable and, he added, in the light of the Prime Minister's refusal to institute a third security force (i.e. in addition to the Army and the police) the Unionists would demonstrate that such a force was already in existence. On 23 November Unionist supporters in paramilitary uniform held a parade in Newtownards. Estimates of the numbers involved in the parade of this so-called 'Third Force' varied from 5,000 to 15,000. There was also considerable industrial disruption in Belfast. Mr Prior reiterated on 24 November that the British Government would not allow private armies to take over the work of the police and the Army. After some months little more was heard of the 'Third Force'.

Meanwhile the battalions continued the campaign of attrition against the IRA. Although 2 RGJ managed to find 35 illegal weapons, 3,615 rounds of ammunition, 27 grenades and 9lb of ammunition during their December 1981 to March 1982 tour in West Belfast, their tour and indeed the city as a whole was relatively quiet during that time. They found that since their last tour the RUC had taken the lead. The 'Way Ahead' policy was at last beginning to be seen to work. One of the surprising features of the tour was the extent of ordinary crime. In the 2 RGJ area of responsibility there were more than seventy armed robberies in the space of four months. Kneecappings and the occasional inter-sectarian murder occurred with depressing regularity. Tragically, the 2 RGJ tour was marred only two days before the Battalion was due to return to England when a mobile patrol was fired on close to the RUC Springfield Road police station and three riflemen were killed in a highly organized PIRA ambush involving an M-60 machine-gun. The bomb left at the firing-point and designed to catch the follow-up forces mercifully failed to detonate.

Corporal William Lindfield was in command of a mobile patrol which was taking an RAF Sergeant from Brigade HQ to the C Company base at North Howard Street Mill. The patrol mounted its two Macralon Land Rovers (Macralon is a form of blast resistant but not bullet-proof armour) inside the Springfield Road police station and drove out of the back gates. They turned right, and right again down Crocus Street back towards the Springfield Road. When the leading Land Rover, driven by Cpl Lindfield, was 50 yards down Crocus Street, all hell was let loose as automatic fire was brought to bear on it from very close range. Also in the Land Rover were Rifleman Daniel Holland, Rifleman Mark Mullen, a corporal from the Coldstream Guards (who were taking over from 2 RGJ) and the RAF sergeant. Cpl Lindfield, realizing that his vehicle had been hit, accelerated out of the killing zone as fast as he could. He drove across the Springfield Road, into a side-street where he stopped. Rifleman Holland had received gunshot wounds in the head and was unconscious; the RAF sergeant had also been shot in the head and was bleeding badly, although still conscious. The Guards L/Cpl, although he had been hit in the head by a ricochet, was able to look after the other wounded men. Cpl Lindfield rushed back across the Springfield Road with Rifleman Mullen to where the other Land Rover was standing in the killing zone.

Its driver, L/Cpl Darral Harwood, having seen the other Land Rover hit, had endeavoured to get himself and his crew out of the vehicle before they reached the killing zone. He had managed to fall out of the driver's door, dropping his rifle in the process, but his companions were unable to get out so quickly. Rifleman Anthony Rapley was hit in the back of the head and died instantly; Rifleman Malakos received gunshot wounds in the stomach, neck and jaw. Another Guardsman, who was unscathed, was in a state of shock as, by now, was Rifleman Mullen who had attempted to assist Rapley only to find that he was dead. L/Cpl Harwood dragged Rapley's body behind a car, leaving Cpl Lindfield to run under fire to the door of the house whence the enemy fire was coming. By now, reinforcements had arrived from the nearby Springfield Road police station; they had heard the firing and they were

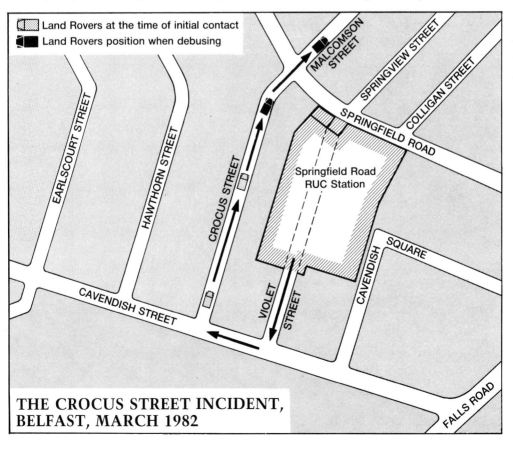

Land Rovers at the time of initial contact
Land Rovers position when debusing

MALCOMSON STREET
SPRINGVIEW STREET
COLLIGAN STREET
SPRINGFIELD ROAD
EARLSCOURT STREET
HAWTHORN STREET
CROCUS STREET
Springfield Road RUC Station
CAVENDISH SQUARE
VIOLET STREET
CAVENDISH STREET
FALLS ROAD

THE CROCUS STREET INCIDENT, BELFAST, MARCH 1982

able to prevent Lindfield from going any farther. For his gallantry Lindfield was awarded the Military Medal. The citation reads:

. . . In all his actions were beyond reproach and throughout he displayed a coolness, courage and professionalism of the very highest order and which was an outstanding example and inspiration to all around him. His actions won open praise from police and civilians who witnessed him and his grip of the situation was mainly instrumental in re-establishing order in a very confused and shocked situation with multiple casualties.

His prompt and correct actions at the moment of contact, with no consideration for his own personal safety undoubtedly saved further serious casualties, and his gallantry and aggressive reaction to enemy fire were in the highest traditions of the service. His professionalism, leadership and gallantry both during and after the incident have been exemplary and present the strongest case for official recognition with a high award.

In the incident, Rifleman Rapley was killed instantly, Rifleman Malakos died on the way to hospital, and Rifleman Holland died on the operating-table. The RAF Sergeant recovered from his wounds.

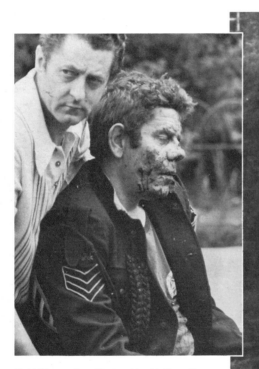

Right: The remains of the bandstand in Regent's Park on which the band of 1 RGJ were playing when the IRA exploded a large remote-controlled bomb on 20 July 1982. (Press Association) **Above:** Sergeant Michael Lewis being helped by a member of the public who had been listening to the band. Sergeant Lewis received severe injuries to his knee and back, which have caused him continuing pain since the event. He was awarded £24,000 compensation by the Criminal Injuries Compensation Board in May 1985. (Mike Moore)

On 20 July, shortly before one o'clock, a bomb exploded underneath the bandstand in Regent's Park, upon which the band of the 1st Battalion The Royal Green Jackets (1 RGJ) were playing. Six members of the band were killed instantly and one died of his wounds two weeks later. All the remaining bandsmen were injured. A few hours before, men of the Household Cavalry Mounted Squadron had been cut down by a car bomb as they rode through Hyde Park on their way to ceremonial duties in Whitehall. No one will ever forget the horrific Press photographs of men and horses lying stricken in the road. These incidents reminded the nation that the Army had for years been under threat not only in Northern Ireland but also in mainland Britain as well as in BAOR and elsewhere in Europe. That day was a sad one for the two regiments concerned. Other regiments returning victorious from

Above: A Marine searches a van in Belfast, July 1983, while a comrade stands guard. The Marine in the foreground is equipped with a 5.56mm Armalite rifle, a small pool of which are held for limited distribution. These relatively light-weight weapons are used for particular operations or, as in the case here, by patrol commanders. (MOD)

the Falklands Campaign were the first to send their commiserations.

Following the kidnapping of Mr Thomas Cochran, a part-time Sergeant in the UDR, by PIRA on 22 October, the UVF retaliated by kidnapping Mr Joseph Donegan, a Roman Catholic later the same day. On 24 October the UVF admitted responsibility for beating Mr Donegan to death. PIRA later claimed responsibility for killing Mr Cochran whose body was not found until 29 October. Then on 16 November Mr Lennie Murphy, reportedly the leader of the UVF, was shot in Belfast and later died in hospital.

Late on 6 December 1982, a bomb exploded without warning in a bar in Ballykelly, County Londonderry, killing a total of seventeen people, including eleven soldiers of the 1st Battalion the Cheshire Regiment and injuring more than 60 people. INLA immediately claimed responsibility for the bombing. This incident was one of the most callous and terrifying crimes in Ulster's tragic history. Mrs Thatcher said in the House of Commons on 7 December: 'The slaughter of innocent people is the product of evil and depraved minds, the act of callous and brutal men. No words can express our absolute revulsion and complete condemnation. However nothing will deflect the Government from its resolve to free Ulster of terrorism and to restore peace to Northern Ireland.'

The following May, the Government extended the period of Direct Rule from Westminster by a further twelve months. Perhaps the main development of 1983 was the series of so-called 'super-grass' trials. Informers, who were normally convicted or suspected of terrorist offences themselves, were generally offered immunity from prosecution, police protection, a cash sum and anonymous resettlement in the United Kingdom in exchange for discussing details of terrorist offences. The 'supergrass' system of obtaining prosecution material was supported by most Loyalist politicians, with the notable exception of the Reverend Ian Paisley. It was of course vehemently opposed by PIRA.

The 1st Battalion The Royal Highland Fusiliers (1 RHF), The Black Watch (1 BW), The 3rd Battalion The Royal Regiment of Fusiliers (3 RRF), the First Battalion The Royal Regiment of Wales (1 RRW), the 1st Battalion The Light Infantry (1 LI) were all in Belfast at some time during 1983. The 2nd Battalion the Queen's Regiment were in Londonderry. It was another year of sectarian violence and rioting for these battalions, though the statistics show an improvement. Serious disturbances took place on 12 July during the Protestant Orange Day March in Ballynahinch, twenty miles south of Belfast. More rioting occurred in the Bogside area of Londonderry on 15–17 July as tension increased after a series of attacks on both the Protestant and Catholic communities. Two RUC officers were shot dead in the city on 17 July.

A major breakout of Republican prisoners from the Maze Prison occurred on 25 September, when 38 inmates escaped, using guns and knives and by hijacking a lorry within the prison compound. By early 1985 sixteen of these escapers had not been recaptured. This incident was a major propaganda coup for the IRA and undid at a stroke much hard work by the Security Forces in putting these men behind bars. Despite this major setback the statistics show the continuing success by the Security Forces in securing convictions in 1983.

The year drew to a close with one of the nastiest attacks to date in Northern Ireland. On 20 November a group describing itself as the 'Catholic Reaction Force' fired on a congregation of about 60 people

Right: Total devastation in Bridge Street, Omagh City, after an IRA bomb attack. Severe parking restrictions have reduced the incidence of these car-bomb attacks in city centres.

Results
Overall statistics for 1983

	Charged	Convicted
Murder	75	14
Conspiracy to murder		7
Manslaughter		3
Explosives Offences	48	47
Firearms Offences	150	103

Most other statistics also showed a general improvement over 1982:

	1982	1983
Shooting incidents	547	424
Bombs	332	367
Bombs neutralized	113	101
Armed robberies	580	622
Amount stolen £	1,392,202	830,258
Deaths		
Civilian[1]	57	44
Army/UDR	28	15
RUC	12	19

[1] Including terrorists.

at the Mountain Lodge Pentecostal Gospel Hall at Darkley, County Armagh. During this attack, in which the terrorists used automatic weapons – one of which was later identified by police as having been used in INLA operations – three innocent worshippers were killed and seven more injured. The Catholic Reaction Force said in a Statement on 21 November that the attack was a 'token' retaliation for recent sectarian violence against Catholics in Armagh. All Army leave in the Province was cancelled and extra troops and police were drafted in to reinforce patrols in the area in an attempt to restore local confidence.

The year ended with the horror of the Harrods bombing in London on 17 December. Two police officers and three shoppers were killed and 91 persons, of whom thirteen were policemen, were injured. PIRA issued a statement on 18 December claiming responsibility for the

attack, but said that it had not been authorized by the organization's army council and asserted that there would be 'no repetition of this type of operation'. The Harrods bombing received wide Press coverage and comment and, following as it did the Regent's Park and Hyde Park bombs of 20 July 1982, it backfired against the IRA. Condemnation abroad was universal, but more important Security Forces and civilians alike, both in Northern Ireland and on the mainland, renewed their determination not to be intimidated by a terrorist organization.

The period from 1981 to 1983 saw some sort of equilibrium in Ulster. The statistics showed a decrease in violence; the IRA kept a relatively low profile. So, for different reasons, did the Army which by this stage had succeeded in putting the RUC back in a position of authority while, at the same time, taking a back seat themselves.

12
TACTICS AND TECHNIQUES

In Germany or mainland UK, Brigade and Divisional commanders command their formations as an entity. A brigade in Germany, for instance, consists of two mechanized infantry battalions and an armoured regiment (or two armoured regiments and one infantry battalion depending upon role and location), an artillery regiment, an engineer squadron and other supporting and administrative units. An armoured division normally consists of three brigades. A brigade or divisional commander in Germany actually takes his entire brigade or division out on manoeuvres on a reasonably regular basis. He actually commands it. In Ireland he does not, except in name, command a brigade. 39 Infantry Brigade is responsible for the Belfast area and 8 Infantry Brigade for the Londonderry area and from the late 1980s 3 Brigade for the Armagh area, and in turn each battalion in these brigades has its own area of responsibility. Even though the brigade commander 'commands' these battalions, the constituent battalions of the brigade seldom if ever act in concert as a brigade. In reality the brigadier co-ordinates and lays down the policy for several independent commands in his area.

Thus the business of the senior officer in Northern Ireland is different from the conventional situation. He is much more in the business of management and co-ordination than command. In accordance with government policy, senior police and army officers sit on various committees at local and regional level and originate and update policy on all security matters. Sensitive decisions on whether or not to authorize house searches on the basis of indefinite information or to crater border crossing-points despite local objections often have to be taken at brigade level or even at HQ Northern Ireland at Lisburn. Inevitably senior officers rely to a great extent upon their various experts, particularly those in the Intelligence world.

In order to keep in touch with their battalions on the ground they are likely to spend a great deal of their time visiting them, asking questions and delving into problems. The same applies to the more

Left: A morale-boosting visit by 'Miss Green Jacket'. Up-and-coming young models are often invited to visit troops in Northern Ireland, not only for morale-boosting purposes, but also to enhance their own careers.

senior commanders in Lisburn. Commander-in-Chief Northern Ireland is a Lieutenant-General and responsible to the MOD in London, but often in a crisis has had a direct line to No. 10 Downing Street. Commander Land Forces (CLF) is a Major-General and responsible for the day to day running of military affairs in Northern Ireland. Both these are operational commanders, regularly called upon to give military advice to politicians and civil servants and to take sensitive decisions on a range of security matters but, unlike a Major-General in Germany, who is a Divisional Commander, or a Lieutenant-General who commands 1st British Corps, he will not manoeuvre large formations of thousands of men and tracked vehicles about the battle-field.

Both are completely different, but in their own ways equally demanding forms of leadership.

The Ulster Emergency has done wonders for junior NCO leadership ability in the British Army. The young corporals and lance-corporals are put in charge of a 'brick' (a 4-man patrol) on the streets and are not only responsible for their own brick, but may be called upon to take difficult decisions in demanding circumstances. The middle management of the Army, the Majors commanding Companies, have also been tested. They have been responsible for literally running large areas of Belfast, and for deploying their Companies of approximately 100 men over a large area to keep the peace. Perhaps Battalion and Platoon Commanders have had fewer demands put upon them in the peculiar circumstances of Ulster; in conventional warfare it is they who would be the more severely tested. Consequently, it has not been possible to apply many of the lessons learned in Ulster to the Army's main purpose in life – the defence of Europe as a partner in NATO and contributing towards UN operations. Serving in Ulster does, however, prevent battalions from getting stale and enhances standards of leadership. Naturally, incorrect procedures can be learned in the Emergency conditions, and much time is spent 'unlearning' many of the techniques of urban IS operations on return to BAOR.

Northern Ireland is fast becoming a distraction from the Army's main responsibilities to NATO, and also in the few remaining colonies (the Falklands, Gibraltar and Hong Kong) and in those countries with which the UK has bilateral defence agreements (Belize, Cyprus and Brunei). The future in Northern Ireland lies with the increasing implementation

Top right: A Para section returning from a border patrol. **Below right:** Military patrols in rural areas still mount 'snap' vehicle checkpoints today.

of the 'Way Ahead' policy and the progressive handing back of responsibility for security to the RUC.

Tours of duty in Northern Ireland have become a way of life for most infantry soldiers. Men who have served for nine years or more have probably undertaken between three and six tours in the Province. Periods of enlistment in the Regular Army are for three, six or nine years, after which, soldiers may opt to serve up to a maximum of 22 years. Many longer-serving men have now been back to Northern Ireland either on numerous 4½- or 6-month roulement tours, or will have completed one residential 18-month tour there. Ironically, most infantrymen enjoy the Ulster experience; those who spend 18 months there find that they genuinely like being stationed in Ulster. Northern Ireland allowances mean that most of them are are better off – and much of Ulster is both beautiful and fascinating to visit. Men on 6-month tours live a hectic life which, after all, is what most men joined the Army for – taking part in real operations rather than endless training. In contrast to the general public's image of Ulster, most soldiers are keen to go on their first tour and, surprisingly, to return on subsequent tours. However, men who have completed more than three or four tours, do begin to regard the experience as something of a chore.

Patrolling

Patrolling in Northern Ireland has two main purposes: domination of the ground, so as to deny the enemy freedom of movement and, secondly, to get to know the area intimately in order to build up a detailed knowledge of the area and its inhabitants.

During the period from 1969 to 1971 patrolling was reactive rather than preventive. Battalions were having some difficulty in even keeping up with the pace of events; they were seldom able to take the initiative. As the years passed, patrolling maps were updated and the sheer volume of Intelligence on the inhabitants of the battalion or company's area of responsibility provided such a degree of back up that patrol commanders were able to put a name to most faces they passed in the street.

In Belfast or Londonderry, battalions were given an area of responsibility. In the early 1970s the West Belfast Battalion was responsible for the Falls, Whiterock, Springfield Road, Collins, Beechmount and Ballymurphy areas (all Catholic) as well as the Highfield, Springmartin, Glencairn and Village areas (all Protestant). In 1974 the author was responsible, as a Company Commander, for part of this area, namely the Collins, part of the Springfield Road as well as the Highfield, Springmartin and Glencairn estates. The total population of this area was approximately 25,000. The area included two large factories, a wood-yard, a home for mentally handicapped children, a slice of Blackmountain itself – a large hill on the edge of Belfast – and the interfaces between the Catholic Ballymurphy and the Protestant Highfield estates and the Protestant Springmartin and Catholic Collins. The requirement was to dominate the area and to learn as much about it as possible in four and a half months.

So as not to have to start from scratch, each battalion sent an advance party to Northern Ireland some weeks before the arrival of the main body of the battalion. This consisted of the commanding officer, company commanders, platoon and section commanders, who would tramp the ground with patrols from the battalion they were relieving. Thus by the time the battalion's second-in-command, the company seconds-in-command and the platoon sergeants brought over the bulk of the men, the commanders had made themselves familiar with the ground. The Battalion Intelligence Officer had preceded the advance party by several weeks, so that he could assimilate the accumulated knowledge of the Intelligence Officer of the battalion being relieved. This system of relief took some years to develop and has now been refined to a drill. During the early years, however, battalions were rushed out at little or no notice as both the Government and the military merely reacted to events.

The whole system is designed to maximize knowledge of a battalion or company area in the short 6-month roulement tour. These constraints do not apply to the same extent to a 2-year tour as part of the garrison.

Whatever the length of tour, proper preparation and training for a Northern Ireland tour is, of course, absolutely vital. In the early years training was haphazard. For a start, few were absolutely certain what to train for. Now there is a well-oiled training machine, which puts every battalion through a standard Northern Ireland training package, including intensive patrolling, either urban or rural depending upon battalion location, riot-control techniques, shooting at fleeting targets, first aid, powers of and procedures for arrest, orders for opening fire, IRA bomb and weapon recognition and capabilities, IRA techniques, capabilities and organization as well as training in the use of various items of internal security equipment. Soldiers now go to Northern Ireland well-prepared and trained.

It is important that patrolling be co-ordinated. A haphazard system is unlikely to produce results nor will it dominate the area. Conversely a predictable and repetitive plan, however well co-ordinated, can be used by the enemy to mount ambushes. A Company Commander will therefore try to achieve a balance between these two sometimes conflicting requirements.

As a general rule there will always be someone on the ground 24 hours a day. This was certainly the case at the height of the troubles in the early and mid 1970s, though it was not always the case in the 1990s when the Army's role was more reactive. That presence need not be obvious. It could be, and often is during the early hours of the morning, a static presence in the form of covert OPs. A well-sited OP can often dominate large areas of a Company area. Indeed the OP need not be covert. It may be on top of an obvious block of flats and its presence may be well known. If this is the case it will of course have to be well guarded and defended.

It is patrolling, however, on foot or in vehicles, that actually dominates an area. The physical presence of soldiers prevents the enemy from preparing or planning an illegal activity. Having said this, the IRA would argue that the presence of soldiers on the streets is provocative and the catalyst for their terrorist activities. But the rule of law cannot be maintained without regular visits from those upholding the law. Those who physically attack the representatives of law and order on the streets have no defence in law. These patrols must be seen regularly on the streets to give confidence to the local population. This can be achieved by foot or vehicle patrols. In some respects the latter have a high profile and are easier and safer to mount.

The best method of securing information and of really getting to know an area, however, is on foot. The majority of patrols in an urban area must always be on foot. The Company Commander must therefore plan a matrix of vehicle and foot patrols which cover the entire Company area 24 hours a day in an irregular and unpredictable pattern, in such a way that no patrol is ever left unsupported by another patrol. Into this pattern he will work the odd static OP. Thus all patrols are mutually supported. Indeed some are 'multiple' from the outset; that is to say two or more patrols will cover a grid of side streets working in parallel in a co-ordinated manner and in radio contact. In this way they will discourage an ambush by possibly cutting off escape routes.

All patrols will be given a task or tasks by the Company Commander. These may include:

1. Setting up a Vehicle Check Point (VCP) on a particular road for a particular period.

2. Updating house occupancy in a particular road or street.

3. Visiting a factory at opening or closing times. *

4. A security visit to a sub post office or garage, both favourite targets for robberies.

*The author provided a patrol every working day outside Mackie's Factory in West Belfast, when he was a Company Commander late in 1974, at the beginning and end of the day shift in order to prevent a sectarian attack against the exclusively Protestant workforce.

5. Visiting a particular family which may have been the subject of sectarian threats.

6. Looking for suitable sites for future OPs.

7. Searching derelicts, etc., for hidden arms.

8. Monitoring a parade or funeral.

and many other tasks.

The plan must be constantly updated and checked to ensure that one is a step ahead of the enemy. Above all, patrol commanders must be debriefed by the Company Commander after each patrol. Only in that way can the Intelligence 'jigsaw' be kept up to date. The most significant snippet may be of value at a later date, for instance that a new family has moved into a particular house.

The patrol commander, his briefing complete, leads his four-man patrol to the sandbagged bunker by the entrance to the base. Pointing their rifles into the bunker they cock their weapons and run zigzagging out of the gate. They are instantly 'on patrol' away from the comparative safety of the company base where, even if they can be mortared, they at least cannot be shot at.

As the patrol commander leads his patrol into the area he has been told to investigate he will be conscious of several things: perhaps most importantly of all he will be looking into every window and doorway, every street corner and hedgerow for a possible telltale sign of an ambush – something glinting in the sun, an open window, a curtain moving, something that could be construed as a signal by perhaps boys to a waiting gunman or bomber. He will also be responsible for keeping his patrol together, watching each man and ensuring he is carrying out his allotted task. Thirdly he will be navigating: however familiar he and his patrol are with the ground he does have to be aware all the time of precisely where he is – in the event of a contact he must be able to report instantly over the radio where he is and in which street. Next, as patrol commander he will be responsible for communicating over his radio with Company headquarters and with other patrols out on the ground supporting him or working with him. Lastly and most important of all he will be carrying out whatever the patrol task is: as patrol commander it will be he who has to fill in a written patrol report after the patrol. It will be he who carries out identity checks or checks the occupants of vehicles at a VCP. In short the pressure will be on the JNCO all the time. The chances are that he is a young 23-year-old corporal who has been in the Army for five years. This may be his first or second Northern Ireland tour. The responsibility, by any yardstick, is unusually great.

In order to be selected as a JNCO, a Rifleman will be recommended by his Company Commander to attend an annual JNCO's cadre run by his battalion. Assuming he passes this testing 6- or 8-week course he will be promoted to Lance-Corporal. Assuming again that he performs well for two or three years as a Lance-Corporal he will become eligible for promotion to full Corporal. He is of course more experienced at this stage. If considered good enough he will then be sent on one or both of two courses: a JNCO's Skill at Arms course at the School of Infantry at Warminster, which will teach him the art of instructing soldiers in the various Infantry weapons, and secondly the JNCO's Tactical course at the Tactical Wing of the School of Infantry at Brecon, where he will learn to command soldiers in operational situations. However he will be trained almost exclusively for conventional warfare in North-west

Europe. He will only concentrate on the urban terrorist situation during the weeks immediately prior to an operational tour in Northern Ireland.

This then is the young JNCO in command of a patrol. It is primarily his war in Northern Ireland.

Surveillance and Intelligence

Success in Northern Ireland is based upon accurate and comprehensive Intelligence. The Intelligence effort is organized by the Battalion Intelligence Officer, whose staff is specially augmented for a Northern Ireland tour and which will probably consist of a warrant officer, per-

Left: The presence of such OPs is public knowledge. Nevertheless, their value lies in the permanent blanket surveillance of a large urban area. More detailed local surveillance can be superimposed by additional, covert OPs. Here, Corporal Roger Soames of Aylesbury, Buckinghamshire, and Marine Thomas Taylor, of Accrington, both of 40 Commando, Royal Marines, keep watch from the newly established observation post on the roof of Artillery flats in the New Lodge area of Belfast on 1 August 1972. (Press Association) **Inset:** Today much more sophisticated equipment is used to identify long-range targets. This equipment is intended primarily for night-time photography and has an image intensifier gain of x150,000 and a binocular lens magnification of x3.5.

haps two senior NCOs and a number of junior NCOs and riflemen. They will gather their Intelligence from the following:

1. Patrol reports from the companies of the battalion on the ground.
2. Close liaison with the RUC and Special Branch.
3. Information provided by the Intelligence staff at Brigade Headquarters.
4. Their own contacts among the civil population within the battalion area of responsibility.

Intelligence is, of course, a continuous process. An incoming Intelligence Officer will inherit a great deal of data from his predecessor. He will, during his time, add to it and sift it. More important, he will cast a fresh eye on the same information and perhaps come up with a solution that had evaded his predecessor. The main tasks of the Intelligence Cell are:

– to build up and maintain an up-to-date and accurate 'rogues' gallery' of all the suspected IRA and other paramilitary activists and sympathizers in the battalion area.

– to pinpoint weapon and explosives hides.

– to provide the RUC with any relevant information that will produce the evidence necessary for an arrest.

– to collate any useful information that will enhance the battalion's operational capability.

In the early 1970s, emphasis was very much on overt patrolling. Later in the campaign it was public knowledge that there was greater emphasis on covert operations – which result in more preventive than reactive operations. In rural areas close observation platoons dug into hides for long periods, watched known border crossing points or known IRA houses and were able to steer other patrols on to the enemy if they could see them. In urban areas, observation posts were set up in derelict houses and on rooftops In one incident in the author's area of responsibility in the Collins district of Belfast, a platoon commander had set up an observation post in a derelict semi-detached house, with a good area of observation and field of fire looking down to the Springfield Road. After the OP had been in position for two days, a shot rang out from what sounded like the other side of the wall against which the three men in the OP were leaning. After extricating themselves from their cramped positions, they were just in time to see a gunman disappearing around a street corner 150 yards away. It transpired that the gunman had taken up a position very quietly several hours before, in the other of the two semi-detached houses, which was lived in, and had fired at a patrol on the Springfield Road which fortunately he missed. This is illustrative of the sort of cat and mouse game that was played in the backstreets of Belfast.

Search Techniques

The Royal Engineers are responsible for providing expert search teams in Northern Ireland, but they cannot possibly cover the whole Province. For this reason each battalion sends soldiers, usually from the Assault Pioneer Platoon,* to the School of Engineering at Chatham to attend a 'Search techniques' course prior to a Northern Ireland tour. They are taught search techniques, in both urban and rural environments. Team members are also taught how to disarm booby traps, as they are obviously more likely than most to be confronted with them while searching for arms, explosives and ammunition.

Search techniques in a rural environment largely involve having an eye for the ground. Clearly it is not possible to search large areas of countryside comprehensively. It is necessary to put oneself in the mind of the individual hiding the arms, ammunition or explosives. Normally anyone hiding something in the country will choose a suitable marker such as a lone tree or a particularly prominent track junction. Often a search in the vicinity of such a 'marker' has produced results. Farm outbuildings, manure or silage heaps and culverts are popular hiding-places.

* The Assault Pioneer Platoon (now sadly removed from the establishment of an infantry battalion) was responsible for minelaying/clearance and other related engineering work, and so were the natural candidates for this task.

Below: A Royal Engineer search team is briefed prior to a planned search operation.

In urban areas, clearly there are many more practical hiding places. Any attic, floorboard or the inside of a false wall can accommodate an illegal weapons cache. It is not possible to search every house on an estate in a systematic manner. First, it would cause such a storm of protest that it would be counter-productive in PR terms. Second, in order to prevent material being smuggled out at one end of the estate while the other end was being searched, it would require so many soldiers to cordon and monitor the estate as to render the prospect a non-starter. Third, it would probably be more effective to use some or all of the soldiers in some other way. Thus searches are normally only undertaken on receipt of specific Intelligence. Then permission has to be sought (and is not always granted) from Brigade Headquarters, before a search of a private house is sanctioned. Unless in 'hot pursuit' after a shooting incident, even a Battalion Commander may not authorize entry into or a search of, a private residence. If, as a result of specific information, permission is granted for a search of a house, the householder will be informed that his house is going to be searched and he will be invited to accompany the search-party during their search. If it is necessary to cause any damage such as lifting floorboards, the damage is always repaired by special teams. The householder will be asked to sign a form saying that no damage has been caused or, if it has, that it has been or will be repaired. Obviously searching houses causes resentment which is why it is only undertaken if there is positive Intelligence that weapons are being concealed.

Search teams are equipped and trained to do their job as quickly and efficiently as they can, and to cause as little damage as possible. Apart from a range of mundane items such as jemmies, spades and screwdrivers, they are equipped with metal detectors, explosives 'sniffers', inspection mirrors and fluorescent hand lamps. Most explosives 'sniffers' will indicate the presence of gelignite, dynamite, nitroglycerine, nitro-benzine and some other types of explosives.

Bomb Disposal

Bomb disposal has developed as an art since the IRA started to use the bomb as a weapon widely in 1971. The British Army already had Explosive Ordnance Disposal (EOD) personnel before the present Emergency in Northern Ireland. They were mostly employed in disposing of Second World War German bombs. These teams, found from the Royal Army Ordnance Corps and Royal Engineers, have various disposal aids available to them. In particular, remotely-controlled vehicles capable of carrying and operating a variety of equipment necessary for the locating and disposal of dangerous objects have been developed. These vehicles enable the Ammunition Technical Officer

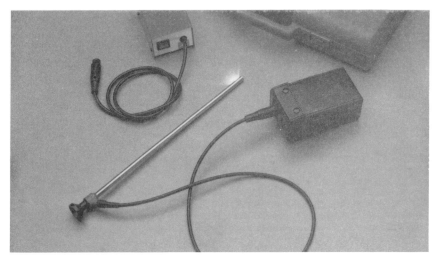

Above: An example of the very latest search equipment in the form of an endoscope, which provides the ability to look through walls, into small cavities and under floorboards for hidden weapons or explosives. **Below:** An explosives detector in operation in a shopping precinct in west Belfast during the early 1970s. Such equipment and its modern successors allow male soldiers to search females. (Pacemaker Press)

(ATO) to remain at a safe distance while he locates, identifies by TV camera, and monitors a suspected bomb. If he decides that the object is too dangerous to be approached, he can attempt to disarm or destroy it, using various aids on the vehicle.

In many instances, a manual approach is necessary, either to prevent blast damage or because forensic evidence is required. In such a case the ATO will wear an EOD Suit which is designed to give some protection against fragments, blast and flame during the disarming of small, improvised explosive devices (IEDs). It will also provide a measure of protection at greater range against larger 'devices'. If a manual approach is made the ATO will carry an inspection set consisting of

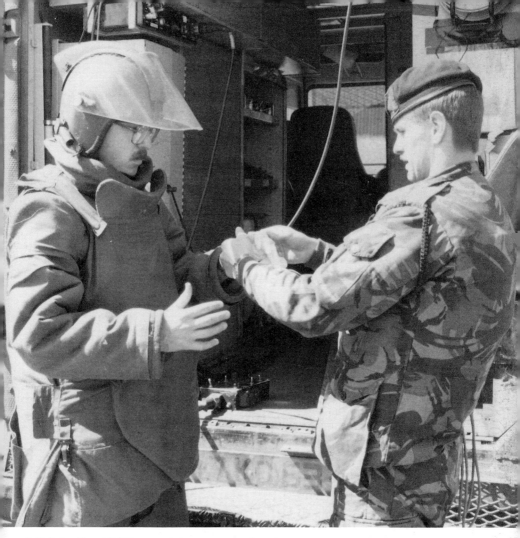

Left: Rather like a knight in armour being prepared by his squires before combat, an ammunition technical officer is seen here being kitted out prior to examining a suspected car bomb in the late 1970s. **Above:** one of his successors in the early 1990s goes through the same process.

light probes, extension rods, mirrors, magnets, lock viewers and hooks and line. All these components are made of nonferrous metals. Should a remote operation be possible, the Wheelbarrow Remote Bomb Disposal Equipment is used. The Wheelbarrow is a concept which first saw operational service in 1972. The vehicle is powered by two reversible electric motors running off two inboard 12V batteries. It has a range of 110 yards, limited only by the 18-way control cables through which commands are passed. Its mean endurance is two hours. Wheelbarrow, which has been progressively developed over the years, can now attack virtually any IED. If the ATO runs out of time, the vehicle is damaged rather than a man being killed.

Wheelbarrow, the British Army's mobile remote EOD system, which has been developed and refined since the early days of the Emergency, and which is in continuing use today. It has a wide variety of 'add-on' elements, so that the system can be adapted to deal with different types of target. Among its many attributes, Wheelbarrow has the ability to tackle petrol tankers (top left), a favourite target for IRA bombers. Among its other features are a closed-circuit television camera and monitor to allow remote surveillance, lights to illuminate the target and a shotgun to disrupt the firing mechanism of an explosive device. Over the years, the system has saved many bomb-disposal experts' lives, allowing, as it does, remote examination and neutralization of terrorist devices. The two pictures on the left show Wheelbarrow Mark VII in operation in the 1970s. The problem has hardly changed in the 1990s. On the right, two photographs of operations with its successor, Wheelbarrow Mark VIII, here dealing with a suspected bomb in the boot of a car. (MOD).

Equipment

IS situations throughout the world, but perhaps particularly in Northern Ireland, have spawned a whole new inventory of IS equipment. There seems to be no limit to the inventiveness and ingenuity of security forces and manufacturers to meet an increasingly sophisticated threat from the IRA. As a result, the IS equipment market throughout the world is dominated by British and US companies who have in many areas a virtual monopoly. The range of IS equipment includes armoured vehicles, water cannon, tear-gas grenades and launchers, baton rounds, explosives detectors, bomb-disposal equipment, body armour and shields, protection equipment, X-ray equipment, surveillance equipment and special communications equipment. In addition to his normal combat clothing, the British soldier in Ulster is equipped with a fragmentation vest or flak jacket to provide protection against blast fragments and low-velocity small arms fire, and an internal security combat helmet which gives a higher degree of ballistic protection than the normal Mk. 4 steel helmet.

In some countries the army is automatically called upon to deal with a riot. Elsewhere, as in the UK, the police are used and the Army is only called in as a last resort. Many countries have formed special so-called 'third force' organizations, specifically to deal with riots and other IS problems. Examples are the Compagnie Républicaine de Sécurité (CRS) in France and the Federal Border Guard in the Federal Republic of Germany. Had such an impartial and well-disciplined force

Left: A Mark VII Wheelbarrow mounted on a remote-control Eager Beaver. This system has been developed to bring all Wheelbarrow's features to bear on targets that would otherwise have been inaccessible.

Right: When troops were first deployed in Northern Ireland in 1969, their standard British Army helmets were not fitted with any form of visor. The SA12 visor illustrated here was soon adapted to fit on the helmet to provide protection against stones and other missiles during riots. (Also illustrated is the SA12 riot shield.)

Below left: The IS helmet was a basic answer to providing rudimentary protection, primarily for drivers.

Below right: The current internal security helmet fitted with a visor for riot control purposes in use in Northern Ireland today.

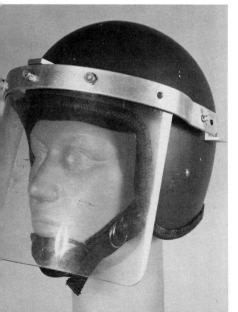

existed in Northern Ireland in 1969, would it have been necessary to call in the Army? The philosophy of the CRS in France is diametrically opposed to the British approach of minimum force. In France maximum force is used at an early stage to demonstrate to the rioter that the authorities mean business and to deter any further misbehaviour. The CRS put down the May 1968 student riots in Paris ruthlessly. The German police use much the same tactics. The British, on the other hand, have always used only the necessary degree of force to meet a given situation. They have escalated if necessary. There are arguments in terms of pure efficiency for both approaches. Perhaps the more excitable European temperament needs a tougher approach. The philosophy of 'minimum force' by both the British Army and police does however appear to work best in the United Kingdom.

Left: The latest patrolling technique in urban areas allows soldiers to 'travel light'. These members of a 1st Battalion The Royal Hampshire Regiment patrol in Londonderry are wearing their flak jackets under their combat clothing and are carrying ammunition for their SA80 rifles in their pockets.

Communications

In an urban IS situation it is not convenient or efficient to use conventional radio equipment. In 1969, when the British Army first deployed on the streets of Belfast and Londonderry, they brought with them their Larkspur A41 radio sets. It was fortunate that at that junction the IRA threat had not developed sufficiently for instant communications to be a prerequisite for at least adequate operations in an urban environment. The A41 was a disaster in and around buildings. Often it was necessary to fly a Sioux helicopter as an airborne relay station to ensure efficient communications. If the helicopter was shot at or ran out of fuel, soldiers on the ground often had to resort to the GPO telephone system!

Conventional military radio equipment is, by and large, too heavy, bulky and complex for use in the streets. More important, VHF radios are designed to operate most efficiently when there is a reasonable line of sight between radio stations. Buildings get in the way. It therefore became necessary in the early 1970s to introduce small so-called Pocketphone radios which operate in the VHF and Ultra High Frequency (UHF) bands via permanent rebroadcast stations. A purchase of hand-held Pocketphone UHF-type PF5-UH single-channel sets operating between 405 and 440 MHz or 440 and 470 MHz was made. These had a 15V rechargeable NiCd battery and gave up to 24 hours' operation. In a situation where troops are operating from static bases it is important that transmissions be scrambled or in cipher. Thus over the years the Army has been issued with off-the-shelf 'civilian' equipment which has provided efficient and simple communications between patrols on the ground and Company and Battalion Headquarters. In addition, the Army has the ability to detect and locate illicit transmitters.

Vehicles

Most armoured personnel carriers (APCs) today are tracked, and tracked vehicles are not suited to IS operations for a number of reasons. They are difficult and expensive to operate and maintain, they are noisy, they cause damage to roads and, most important of all, they are classed as 'tanks' by the layman. Use of tanks in an IS situation is often politically unacceptable and conjures up visions of Soviet tanks in the streets of Prague. Therefore most armoured IS vehicles are 4 × 4 wheeled vehicles, which afford protection from small arms fire up to 7.62mm ball. Most IS vehicles are provided with observation blocks and firing posts. Vulnerable points on the vehicle, such as the fuel tank and the radiator, must be given special protection and the vehicle must be so designed to allow rapid exit from and entry into the vehicle by the crew and passengers. IS armoured vehicles can be fitted with a variety of armaments including water cannon, tear-gas launchers and machine-guns. Some can even be electrified to prevent rioters climbing on to the vehicle. In addition to armoured vehicles, there are a number of other types of vehicle that are commonly used in IS situations: water-cannon vehicles, which may or may not be armoured, conventional 'soft skin' vehicles which have been covered in a form of appliqué lightweight armour as protection against blast and low-velocity rounds and lastly, armoured bulldozers for the removal of barricades.

In Northern Ireland the British Army for many years used the GKN Sankey AT-104 IS vehicle commonly known as the 'Pig' as its standard APC. This has been adapted in many different ways: one such adaptation known as the 'Flying Pig' can unfold large fenders from each flank so that, if parked in the middle of a road, the vehicle can block most of the road off, and afford protection against missiles thrown by rioters. The Daimler Ferret Scout car was used for both rural and urban pat-

Right: A British Army 'pig' deployed in Belfast. This version is commonly known as the 'flying pig' owing to the extendible fenders, which provide protection for troops on either side of the vehicle and allow them to block access to a narrow street. The picture depicts a Republican protest about the Queen's visit to Ulster in August 1977, and shows a march in the Falls Road area of Belfast organized by the Provisional Sinn Fein (the Provos' political wing). (Press Association)

rolling until quite recently in Northern Ireland. So also until recently was the Alvis Saracen APC, particularly as an armoured ambulance.

Patrolling in Northern Ireland is also carried out in Land Rovers. The British Army were forced to develop GRP and Macralon armour for standard Land Rovers in an attempt to provide some protection against blast, fire and acid bombs and low-velocity small arms fire. GRP is a form of fibreglass which is used to cover the body and roof of Land Rovers, while Macralon, a form of strengthened plastic, is used to cover windscreen and windows.

The RUC are equipped with the Hotspur Armoured Land Rover. This is the grey painted police vehicle so familiar on the streets of Belfast. It is equipped with 'add-on' 4.76mm Hotspur steel, and windscreen, side and rear windows are of 29mm laminated glass. Another Land Rover variant is the Shorland Mk. 3 armoured car, employed by the UDR. The origins of the Shorland Mk. 3 go back to the mid 1960s when the RUC asked Short Brothers to produce a light armoured vehicle suitable for IS and border patrol work. Shorts con-

Left: A two-vehicle Ferret patrol operating in an urban environment. This trusty and well-tried vehicle has been consistently used for patrolling and is preferable to the higher-profile tracked vehicles used by some other nations in IS situations.
Below: Another well-tried vehicle, the Alvis Saracen, was originally developed as the British Army's general war APC for use in north-west Europe. It has since been adapted for use in the APC role in Northern Ireland, and the ambulance version is still in use today. (MOD)

verted the long wheel base version of the Land Rover by reinforcing the suspension and axles to take the weight of the armour and by modifying the gear ratios. The armoured shell varies in thickness between 8.25mm and 11mm and can withstand 7.62mm ammunition at close range, while the windscreen can be quickly covered with an armoured shield fitted with vision slots. The Army has also used the Pyrene and Mercedes-Benz cannon as well as armoured bulldozers for barricade removal. Unlike other countries, water cannon use has been rare: as high-profile equipment, it is not used unless absolutely necessary. In the 1990s highly manoeuvrable armoured Land Rovers fulfil every task.

Helicopters

Helicopters have provided tactical mobility for the army in most campaigns since the Malayan emergency, but there has always been such a shortage of this asset that their use has not been a war-winning factor. Perhaps for the first time in Northern Ireland the Army has roughly the number of helicopters it can usefully employ. In the early 1970s, the Army was equipped with Sioux and Scout helicopters. The Sioux was of US design, but manufactured in Italy by Augusta. It was a very basic helicopter, an excellent workhorse and capable of carrying two or three passengers for observation and liaison purposes. The Scout was designed and manufactured by Westland Helicopters and limited numbers are still in use with the British Army today in certain theatres. It was a rugged helicopter, capable of carrying two crewmen and four soldiers in the rear compartment if the seats were removed and the soldiers sat on the floor facing outwards with their feet on the skids. Thus the Scout was suitable for the first so-called 'Eagle' patrols in which the machine swooped down in a country lane and dropped the four soldiers, who could mount an instant roadblock for a limited period. When they wanted to move on they would recall the helicopter which was loitering nearby.

The RAF supported the Army with twin-engined Wessex helicopters capable of carrying 12–16 troops, depending on range. They were held on standby, mostly in South Armagh, to move a Quick Reaction Force (QRF) at a moment's notice to a trouble-spot. They provided the Army with greater tactical flexibility in rural areas though they were of little relevance in Belfast or Londonderry.

Helicopters have remained remarkably immune to small arms' fire. Several have been hit over the years, and one or two have been forced to land pretty quickly because of damage, but none has been 'shot down'. The only fatalities have been through pilot error, and in the case of taking evasive action. It would be surprising if the IRA have not been trying for some time to obtain a Soviet-manufactured hand-held

An HU.15 Wessex transport helicopter lifting an ATO team with its vehicle and trailer into South Armagh in 1975. The Wessex, now replaced by the Puma, was an invaluable workhorse in Northern Ireland throughout the 1970s. Its twin engine configuration gave it tremendous durability and lift capacity.

Above: The Gazelle helicopter shown here is used for communications and surveillance purposes in Northern Ireland. **Below:** Men of a 1 RGJ Eagle patrol fly in to set up a snap VCP on a country road near Newry, 19 March 1975. While the soldiers approach a car, the helicopter takes off again and hovers overhead, ready to redeploy the patrol – in most circumstances it is safer for the helicopter to remain airborne, since it presents a vulnerable target while stationary on the ground.

surface-to-air missile system (SAM-7) for use against helicopters. So far they have not succeeded, though if they did, helicopters would merely have to fly at 'ground level' all the time instead of some of the time. If they flew at 50 feet and below, the SAM-7 operator would not have sufficient time to acquire his target, fire the missile and achieve lock-on with the infra-red heat-seeking system. Thus SAM-7 could cause inconvenience, but would not prevent helicopter operations.

Some of the bases in Armagh, particularly Crossmaglen, are dangerous and difficult to reach by road. If a large convoy is required to re-supply Crossmaglen the route has to be cleared and picqueted. Clearly the simplest method of routine supply and liasion is by helicopter and this is indeed the method normally used.

Finally and perhaps most importantly, helicopters are used in Northern Ireland for casualty evacuation. Many lives have been saved by flying grievously wounded soldiers direct to a hospital helipad – and in Northern Ireland all the main casualty hospitals have helipads.

In the mid and late 1970s the new generation of helicopters were introduced to Ulster. The Gazelle replaced the Sioux as the Army's communication, liaison and observation helicopter; the Lynx replaced the Scout as the utility helicopter and the Puma has replaced the Wessex as the RAF support helicopter. All these types have an enhanced payload and passenger-carrying capability.

13
1984–1994: TOWARDS A CEASE-FIRE

There was a marked increase in terrorist incidents during March 1984. William McConnel, an Assistant Governor at HMP Maze, was shot dead on 6 March by PIRA gunmen outside his home in East Belfast. His assailants had taken over the house opposite the night before. He was shot in the head at close range as he said goodbye to his wife and child the following morning. Two days later, Private David Montgomery, a part-time soldier in 11 UDR, was murdered by PIRA gunmen at his father's service station near Moira. He was singled out by two gunmen from among several people in the service station shop and shot twice in the head with a 9mm pistol. There were a number of shooting incidents between the 9th and 13th, in one of which an ex-UDR soldier died.

Also on 8 March, terrorists used an RPG-7 rocket launcher to engage soldiers travelling along the Springfield Road in an armoured vehicle. The weapon was fired at a range of some 30 metres from the front of a house in a side-street which had been taken over the night before. The rocket missed, but immobilized a coal lorry travelling in the opposite direction. The soldiers failed to recognize the attack for what it was and drove on. The terrorists' get-away car would not start and they were forced to abandon some of their equipment as they escaped on foot. Even the Emergency in Belfast has some elements of farce.

On 9 March the Loyalist Londonderry Action Committee staged a march across the Craigavon Bridge in protest at the proposed changing of the City Council's name to 'Derry' from 'Londonderry'. There were about 1,600 marchers and 650 bandsmen. After some clashes with the RUC, the protesters eventually returned East of the River Foyle after being addressed by the Reverend Ian Paisley – and other speakers – and dispersed. During the march the RUC were attacked with petrol bombs by about 100 Republican hooligans from the Bogside. Fourteen baton rounds were fired, there were four arrests, and injuries were sustained on both sides. The violence subsided, but flared up again that night when the RUC were again petrol-bombed by a crowd of about 60,

Top left: The Puma helicopter, the general support helicopter in use in Northern Ireland. **Left:** Graffiti abounds still in the urban areas of Northern Ireland. Although particular events, such as Bobby Sands' hunger strike, have influenced IRA graffiti propaganda, the theme has remained constant.

again from the Bogside. The police fired 32 baton rounds and made a number of arrests. The interesting thing about this series of events on 9 March 1984 was that the Army was not involved in any of them. The 'Way Ahead' policy, begun in 1977, which aimed to re-establish the primacy of the RUC, had clearly succeeded. A measure of its success was the extent to which PIRA turned their attention away from the Army and attacked RUC and UDR targets.

On 14 March, an attempt was made by the UFF on the life of Gerry Adams, MP. He and four Sinn Fein associates were in a car in Belfast City Centre when they were fired upon from another car. All but one of the men in Adams' car were hit but only one was seriously wounded. Adams himself was hit three times, but miraculously escaped serious injury. Two soldiers in plain clothes, who saw the shooting and who were engaged on another task at the time, gave chase and, together with an off-duty UDR soldier and a policeman, arrested the gunman after a short pursuit, and took possession of three pistols. One of the gunmen had accidentally shot himself in the hand.

A soldier escaped with temporary deafness and shock when a command-detonated bomb exploded close to him on the Whiterock Road, West Belfast, on 4 April. The main force of the explosion was deflected by a corrugated iron fence and a mound of earth in front of the device. Two men were arrested shortly afterwards by a military patrol as they climbed a wall out of the city cemetery; the firing-point had been inside the cemetery, about 100 metres away from the device on the end of a wire. What paid off here was the tactic of multiple mobile patrols adopted by the Army since the mid 1970s. If patrols of four men (or 'bricks' in the terminology of the soldier) operated in a grid pattern they afforded each other protection and mutual support. The idea was that a gunman's escape should be threatened by a patrol working say two streets away from another patrol; this was designed to deter him from opening fire in the first place, but if he did – probably because he had not detected the supporting patrol – the chance of an interception following an ambush was much greater. In this instance on the Whiterock the tactic was a classic success.

An incendiary device that was intended to engulf an RUC mobile patrol in a holocaust of flames failed to achieve the desired effect in Londonderry on 6 April. The explosion, which was accompanied by several high-velocity rounds, only resulted in a small fire in the road.

On 8 April, Mr Thomas Travers, a magistrate and incidentally, a Catholic, was wounded and his daughter was killed when they were shot by terrorists in Belfast while they were on their way home from church. The two gunmen approached them from behind and opened fire at close range. During their get-away the terrorists handed their weapons to a woman accomplice who was spotted by a passer-by and subsequently arrested by the RUC; two handguns and a wig were recovered from her. One can only assume that the motive for the killing, which went wrong, was to demonstrate that in the judgement of PIRA, it was not acceptable for Catholics to serve as magistrates.

On the same day, a soldier was slightly injured when a command-detonated device exploded three feet from him at a border crossing-point near Castlederg. Although the device contained some 44lb of explosive, for some reason the main force of the explosion was vertical. The command wire led to a firing-point in the Republic.

On 8 May, Private Johnston, a part-time soldier in 8 UDR, was shot dead as he arrived for work at the Drummglass Hospital outside Dungannon. Two terrorists, armed with a 5.56mm rifle and a shotgun, opened fire at close range as Private Johnston parked his car. The murder had been preceded by a house takeover. The householder's car was used by the terrorists to drive to and from the scene of the shooting. On 9 May, soldiers in West Belfast fired seven rounds at a joyrider who attempted to run down two of their number after failing to stop his car when ordered to do so at a road-block. He received minor injuries to his arm and was apprehended. This incident underlines the difficult decisions faced by soldiers each day. Should they open fire or not? In this case they were quite correct to do so because their lives were in danger.

On 12 May, Colour-Sergeant Hillen, a part-time soldier in 6 UDR, was shot and killed on his farm near Aughnacloy. The terrorists escaped across the border 500 yards away. The killing of UDR men, defenceless as they are when off duty, is of course a particularly despicable form of terrorism. By May, 6 UDR men had been killed during 1984. Increasing integration of UDR and Regular Army battalions was taking place at this time, not to 'beef up' the UDR – who were in no need of any such thing – but because UDR battalions were now judged to be perfectly capable of taking elements of regular battalions under command, a demonstration by the military hierarchy of their faith in the UDR. The Queen's Own Highlanders had one company under operational control of 4 UDR in May. In other areas, Regular battalions relieved UDR battalions or vice versa, showing that both were interchangeable. One company of the 1st Battalion The Devon and Dorset Regiment deployed into the 11 UDR Tactical Area of Responsibility (TAOR) from 4 to 12 May, while 11 UDR departed Northern Ireland for their summer camp. On 12 May, 2 UDR departed on summer camp and were relieved by one company of the 1st Battalion The Royal Highland Fusiliers. At this time the 1st Battalion The Royal Regiment of Fusiliers (1 RRF) were stationed at Ballykelly, 2

Queen's were in Londonderry and A Squadron of the 15/19 Hussars were relieving 156 Locating Battery Royal Artillery as the Prison Guard Force at HMP Maze.

It is perhaps also worth recounting in slightly more detail the events of one day earlier in May, to illustrate the succession of minor events in any 24-hour period which take up the majority of the time of infantry battalions in Northern Ireland today. In south-west Belfast in the 39 Brigade area on 4 May at 1100 hours, two gunmen entered the house of Mrs Rosin O'Neill at 24 Stewartstown Park. They told her they were members of INLA and that they intended to use the house for 'an operation'. During the next few hours some seven terrorists came and went, using Mrs O'Neill's Datsun and the Skoda car of a visiting friend when the Datsun developed a mechanical fault. At 1430 hours, a neighbour, Mrs Annie Marie Reid, called but got no reply. Fearing that the caller would be suspicious, two masked men entered Mrs Reid's house next door and occupied it until 1700 hours. At 1525 hours, a lorry carrying CO_2 gas cylinders arrived at No 24. The driver and his assistant were held while the terrorists prepared an explosive device. Mr O'Neill returned home just before 1700 hours and was also held.

At 1705 hours, the driver was told to take his lorry to the front gate of the Woodburn RUC Station. When he arrived he raised the alarm. The station was evacuated by the rear gate. During the evacuation three or four low-velocity rounds were fired from a nearby side-street at the area of the gate. About 200 locals were also evacuated from the danger area. During the setting up of traffic diversions to isolate the area, a further three or four rounds were fired at policemen. There were no casualties. At 1800 hours, an incendiary device on the lorry exploded setting the vehicle alight. The Fire Brigade extinguished the fire and at 1915 hours the area was declared clear. The lorry had contained twelve CO_2 gas cylinders, one of which had been doctored to effect a slow gas release. The cylinders were surrounded by six boxes of firelighters which were ignited by an electrical system. The explosion was a failure and caused no casualties. By Northern Ireland standards the affair was a minor event, but it had terrified and inconvenienced a lot of people, not least the O'Neill and Reid families and the 200 evacuees. The Army, RUC and fire brigade had been heavily involved. The incident illustrates the ability of the terrorists with relatively little effort to tie down large numbers of security forces for long periods of time and to intimidate innocent citizens. As in most of these cases, the hostages were released unharmed.

That same night there were a series of minor incidents throughout Belfast:

▷ At 2023 hours, a military patrol was stoned on Springhill Avenue in the Ballymurphy and fired one baton round to disperse its assailants.

▷ At 2027 hours, a bus was hijacked in Glen Road by a group of hooded youths. It was driven to Shaws Road and set on fire. The fire service attended, but withdrew when stoned. The bus was gutted. Shots were reported in the area.

▷ Rival gangs of youths fighting at Unity Flats were dispersed by the police at 2335 hours. One youth was slightly injured and seven arrests were made.

▷ At 2359 hours, a small blast bomb was thrown from a group of twenty hooligans at a military foot patrol in Doan Road. One baton round was fired to disperse the gang.

▷ At 0037 hours on 5 May, a taxi was hijacked in Upper Strandfield Street and was set alight with petrol bombs. It was gutted while the fire brigade were repelled with petrol bombs.

▷ A crowd of twenty youths threw stones and two petrol bombs at a

EOD vans deploy to deal with a suspected railway bomb.

joint RUC/Army patrol in Horn Drive. Three baton rounds were fired and the gang dispersed at 0045 hours.

▷   At 0125 hours, six petrol bombs were thrown at a RUC mobile patrol in Whiterock Road without causing any damage.

▷   At 0135 hours, a number of petrol bombs were thrown at New Barnsley RUC Station and a passing police mobile patrol by a group of about 30 hooligans. There were no casualties or damage. The military quick reaction force fired five baton rounds to disperse the gang.

▷   At 0157 hours, four petrol bombs were thrown at a military ambulance passing Kelly's Corner.

▷   At 0332 hours, three petrol bombs were thrown at a police mobile patrol in Hillman Street.

▷   Two buses were hijacked in the Monagh Road at 0528 hours and Crumlin Road at 0705 hours, and set alight. Both were gutted.

Such was a single night of May in Belfast in 1984. Further comment would be superfluous.

The lessons to be drawn from the statistics shown for 1–14 May 1984 are really threefold. First, the Emergency is, unfortunately, still with us. Second, casualties are much reduced though clearly it is quite unacceptable that these statistics should occur in 1984 in the United Kingdom. Third, by steady attrition and good police work the terrorists, criminals and hooligans are being brought to justice. Convictions are being achieved and, perhaps most important, the RUC are taking the lead.

May also saw the start of the Marching season which was marked by the traditional Republican and Loyalist Easter parades across the Province. The Republican events produced the usual hackneyed rhetoric, masked speakers and marchers in paramilitary garb. Shots were fired during one parade in Carrickmore, County Tyrone, but in general there were no significant clashes with the RUC. The Loyalist parades attracted a good turnout and featured the usual plethora of bands and bowler-hatted marchers. They also passed off without incident.

The summer of 1984 was relatively quiet. Towards the end of the year the pendulum of violence started to swing higher again. On 19 October, Gunner Timothy Utteridge was shot dead in an ambush in Turf Lodge, south-west Belfast. Another soldier was wounded. PIRA gunmen fired the rounds at the patrol from a range of about 100 yards. Again, the firing-point was in a house which had been taken over the night before. The gunmen, who had used two 5.56mm weapons, escaped in a stolen car which was later found abandoned in Andersonstown. Early the next morning, a soldier suffered a fractured skull and other injuries when he was knocked over by another stolen car in

Andersonstown. He had flagged the car down whereupon it had driven straight at him. Two other soldiers fired a total of four rounds at the car, but although it crashed soon afterwards, the driver escaped, apparently unscathed. On 28 October, a military patrol was ambushed by several gunmen in Londonderry. Thirty-three high-velocity rounds were fired at the patrol. They all missed. The terrorists escaped in a hijacked car. On 29 October, two gunmen were engaged by a joint RUC/Army patrol in Armagh. Although there were no confirmed hits, four suspects were arrested – three by the Garda (Irish police) in the Republic and one by the RUC.

It is perhaps of interest that the Royal Navy maintain an average of. four ships on operational duties in Northern Ireland, usually two on off-shore duties and two on patrol on inland loughs. During the period 16 to 29 October, naval boarding-parties stopped and searched 59 ships. Containers aboard ships are also usually searched. During the same period, RAF Support helicopters flew some 279 hours and Army Air Corps helicopters some 559 hours. Numerous air reconnaissance sorties were also flown.

These were some of the more notable occurrences in October 1984 in the Province. But pointless, sometimes petty, incidents of violence and intimidation are occurring most days in Ulster. A diary of events in Londonderry for 4 October 1984 is typical:

▷ At 0125 hours, the Ammunition Technical Officer (ATO) cleared a hoax IED from outside 21 Spencer Road, Waterside. It comprised four beer cans, two batteries, various pieces of wire and a watch-face.

▷ Between 1128 hours and 1256 hours, an anonymous caller, purporting to be 'IRA', made four hoax telephone calls to the RUC warning of seven bombs in Londonderry city centre, and one bomb in Prehen Park on the southern outskirts of the city.

▷ At 1145 hours, two masked men, one armed with a handgun, hijacked a DOE Land Rover from Central Drive, Creggan and drove it away. They returned with the vehicle five minutes later, told the driver that it contained a bomb, and ordered him to park it outside Fort George. He complied and then informed the RUC who declared it a hoax at 1220 hours. A beer keg and some wire had been placed on the vehicle.

▷ At 1200 hours, three armed and masked men hijacked a Toyota van in Lislane Drive, Creggan. The vehicle was driven to Central Drive, Creggan where a beer keg with wires attached was placed in it. The driver then complied with an order to park the van on the Craigavon Bridge. He alerted the RUC, who declared the vehicle a hoax at 1306 hours.

A fortnight in 1984
It is of interest that during the period 1 to 14 May 1984, the following incidents took place throughout the Province.

Shootings:		UDR wounded	0
Involving Security Forces	13	RUC killed	0
Not involving Security Forces	5	RUC wounded	15
Heard only	3	Civilians killed	2
		Civilians wounded	16
Bombings:			
Explosions	4	*Finds*:	
Bombs neutralized	3	Rifles	5
		Pistols	2
Incendiaries:		Explosives	760lb
Explosions	2		
Bombs neutralized	0	*RUC charges*:	
		Murder	3
Casualties:		Attempted murder	6
Regular Army killed	0	Firearms	5
Regular Army wounded	3	Armed robbery	4
UDR killed	2	Others	3

▷ At 1210 hours, two masked men, one armed with a handgun, hijacked a Water Services Bedford van in Rathlin Drive, Creggan. The driver was forced to drive to the Telstar Public House, Creggan, where another masked man appeared and a beer keg with wire attached was loaded on to the vehicle. The driver complied with instructions to park the van in Victoria Car Park, Guildhall Square and to warn the RUC. At 1247 hours the RUC declared the vehicle a hoax.

And in Belfast on the same day:

▷ At 2326 hours, an anonymous call to the telephone exchange warned of a bomb at the railway station in the Friendly Street area of the Markets, Central Belfast. ATO was tasked to a beer keg which was found lying against the railway station fence in Stewarts Street, Markets, which he declared a hoax at 0246 hours the following day.

As 1984 drew to a close the IRA nearly pulled off their attempt to kill the Prime Minister and several members of the Cabinet when they succeeded in breaching police security at the Grand Hotel, Brighton during the Conservative Party's annual conference. The Prime Minister herself narrowly escaped injury or death. A report published in January 1985 exonerated the Sussex police from any serious degree of blame, but recommended that police forces on the mainland receive special training from the Army and RUC in search and security techniques.

On Christmas Eve 1984, Dominic McGlinchey, one of the most notorious of IRA (and later INLA) terrorists was sentenced to life imprisonment for murdering the mother of a police officer. His luck had run out on St Patrick's Day, when he was caught visiting his two sons who had been spotted by the police in the Republic and put under surveillance. Inside the house, where McGlinchey was arrested and to which his sons had led the police, was found an arsenal of fourteen guns and 600 rounds of ammunition. Eighteen hours later he was in the hands of two RUC officers – the first person extradited from the South to Northern Ireland for terrorist offences. Previously all attempts at extradition for terrorist offences from the Republic to the United Kingdom had failed because the offences with which the criminals were charged had been adjudged 'political' rather than terrorist by the Irish judiciary. Extradition from one country to another is naturally a bilateral agreement and specifically excludes political offences in order to safeguard genuine political refugees. There are signs that the Irish authorities are now prepared to continue to extradite to Northern Ireland IRA terrorists wanted for murder in the United Kingdom, but arrested in the Republic.

Although only tried for the one offence, the RUC suspect that McGlinchey was involved in the construction and planting of at least 30 bombs, in twenty shootings and twelve armed robberies. In an interview in the *Sunday Tribune*, which McGlinchey later denied giving, he allegedly admitted involvement in about 30 murders, 200 bombings – including the Ballykelly discotheque bomb in which seventeen people died – and giving a gun to a person involved in the killing of three worshippers in a Pentecostal Church in South Armagh. Putting men like McGlinchey behind bars is perhaps the best hope for Ulster.

The Provisionals suffered serious losses during 1984, with twelve IRA men dying in terrorist attacks or being shot by their own organization as alleged informers. In one 18-day period in December, five IRA volunteers died while on missions to kill members of the security forces. Although the Army had its worst year for deaths since 1981, with nine soldiers dying, it was the locally recruited RUC and UDR who bore the brunt of terrorist violence: nineteen of their members were killed during 1984, many of them while off duty and unarmed.

At 0946 hours on 1 February 1985, Private James Graham, BEM, a part-time soldier in 4 UDR, arrived at Derrylin RC Primary School in the school bus to take the children to swimming classes. As he was parking a gunman fired about seven 5.56mm rounds at him from a range of only two metres. Then at least two gunmen entered the bus and fired a further eighteen 5.56mm and six 7.62mm rounds at Private

Graham killing him instantly. Two of his brothers, both part-time UDR soldiers, had already been murdered and James himself had survived a previous attack in October 1980. PIRA claimed responsibility for the murder.

In the early hours of the morning of 23 February a military patrol in 8 Infantry Brigade's area encountered three armed and masked terrorists in a field near Fountain Street, Strabane. Shots were fired and all three were killed. The dead men were identified as Charles Breslin (aged 21), Michael Devine (aged 23) and David Devine (aged only 17), the latter being brothers. The following weapons were found: one 7.62mm FN FAL SLR, one 5.56mm FN FNC rifle, one 5.56mm Ruger mini 14 rifle, all with loaded magazines; two home-made rifle-grenade projectors and two home-made grenades; two modified 12 bore shotgun car-

tridges designed to project grenades. This incident was a major success for the Security Forces and probably resulted from excellent Intelligence. Only a few days later, however, at about 1330 hours on 28 February two armed and masked men hijacked a flatbed lorry on a country road near Drumuckaval, Crossmaglen. The driver was held in a field until 1900 hours when he was released; he immediately contacted the RUC. At 1837 hours, the RUC police station at Newry came under mortar attack. One mortar round hit the canteen killing seven policemen and two policewomen. Eight other policemen and 25 civilians were injured.

The follow-up operation located the mortar baseplate on the back of the hijacked lorry in a car-park in Monaghan Street, 200 metres from the RUC station – the mortar was a home-made modified 9-tube 'Mark

Modern bomb disposal equipment has always been vital to efficient counter-terrorist operations in Northern Ireland. Here the latest version of the EOD vehicle Mark VIII is prepared by its operators to investigate a suspected bomb.

10' mortar and had been surrounded by wooden pallets for camouflage.

The IRA, who immediately claimed responsibility for the attack, have had home-made mortars for some years but, until then, had failed to achieve any significant results. Their equipment is unreliable and results are haphazard and are likely to continue to be so. On this occasion they were extremely lucky and the result was a major blow for the Security Forces.

On 27 March a joint RUC/Army patrol was passing St Peter's Block of the Divis Flats in the Lower Falls area of West Belfast when a wire-controlled explosive device was detonated killing Lance-Corporal Anthony Dacre of The King's Own Royal Border Regiment. Two days later, while he was working in his garage in Rathfriland, RUC Reserve Constable John William Bell was murdered by two IRA gunmen who shot him three times, once in the head and twice in the back.

April, May and June 1985 were relatively quiet, the two most notable Security Forces' successes of the period being the discovery of 987kg of home-made explosive in Northern Ireland in April and the frustration of a major IRA plot to plant bombs in twelve seaside resorts in England at the end of June.

Broadly the same pattern of violence by the IRA continued into the late 1980s. December 1986 was characterized by a greater number of IEDs targeted against the Security Forces and commercial targets. Approximately 592kg of explosives were detonated by terrorists and about 927kg recovered from finds or were neutralized. Significantly INLA continued its operations with two IEDs at Killeen. Both were neutralised by the Army. On 11 December, the Garda recovered 700kg of HME from a farmhouse at Tallyvin, County Cavan, six kilometres from the border. And on 13 December, four vehicles were stopped by the RUC at a VCP near Newry. One of the vehicles was found to contain an IED with 600kg of HME which was neutralized. The occupants of all four vehicles were arrested immediately.

By February 1987, the IRA had stepped up their level of activity still further. In the first two weeks of February alone, there was a mortar attack on a Belfast RUC station, two grenade-launcher attacks on RUC patrols, four shooting attacks against the Army, RUC or UDR and several bomb explosions. In March Private O'Conner of the 1st Battalion the Queen's Lancashire Regiment (1 QLR) became the first regular Army fatality since July 1986 when the Land Rover he was driving was attacked in the Divis Flats area. He died instantly when a mortar round lobbed from a third floor corridor exploded above him on the roof of his vehicle. Nor did the situation get any better in April: On the 3rd, Corporal Oldman of the UDR was murdered while sitting in his car outside his place of work at Ederny, County Fermanagh. On the same day Reserve Constable Shaw was killed by IRA terrorists as he left Ballynahinch RUC station. Another two Reserve Constables were shot dead while on duty in Portrush on 11 April. Although all these deaths occurred outside Belfast, the main IRA thrust seemed to be in the city. There were two mortar attacks against RUC stations and eight separate shooting incidents. During one of these attacks two members of the 1st Battalion The Queen's Lancashire Regiment (1 QLR) were seriously wounded while conducting a VCP in the Falls Road. In addition to these attacks, the RUC stations at Springfield Road and North Howard Street were subjected to blast bomb attacks.

On 8 May 1987, the Security Forces scored a notable success against the IRA at Loughgall. Acting on intelligence that the RUC station at Loughgall was to be attacked, the SAS laid an ambush. At 7.20 p.m. a mechanical digger loaded with an explosive device was crashed through the front gate of the police station and detonated. A van following the digger contained gunmen who were caught in the SAS trap. Eight known terrorists were killed and several terrorist weapons were recovered from the scene. This incident was a classic example of the Security Forces acquiring vital intelligence which enabled them to stake out the terrorist target and catch the perpetrators in the act. Although SAS involvement was never admitted, it was an SAS patrol that carried out this operation.

On 19 July the IRA hit back, shooting Lance-Corporal Hewitt of the 1st Battalion The Royal Green Jackets (1 RGJ) dead while on foot patrol in Belleek. A single round hit the soldier in the head and he died a short time later. The same pattern of activity continued until 11 November when the infamous Remembrance Day attack took place at Enniskillen. The IRA detonated an IED inside St Michael's Reading Rooms in Belmore Street as people were gathering outside the building for the Remembrance Day Service at the Enniskillen War Memorial. Eleven people, including six old age pensioners, were killed in the explosion and 61 were injured. The fact that there were no military casualties laid bare the IRA claim to be fighting a war against the British Army. The dead included Marie Wilson, 20, who died under the rubble holding the hand of her injured and trapped father, Gordon Wilson, who subsequently said that he forgave the murderers of his daughter. He has worked fiercely for peace in Northern Ireland ever since. He was appointed a Senator by the Irish Government for his work in the cause of peace and reconciliation.

The year 1988 started much the same. An unusual event occurred on 8 January. Two cars stopped at an RUC checkpoint in Portadown were found to contain no less than 61 Czech 58P assault rifles, 124 rifle mag-

This photograph illustrates just how far the British Army has travelled in terms of weapons, equipment and clothing during the 27 years of the Emergency in Northern Ireland. The Lynx helicopter, the SA80 rifle and the light support weapon, the webbing and other equipment are all 'state of the art'. (*Soldier* magazine)

azines, 11,520 rounds of 7.62mm ammunition, 30 Browning 9mm pistols and 150 Soviet hand- grenades. Three Protestants were arrested.

In March 1988, there were seventeen IED attacks and 20 shooting incidents. Two soldiers, one policeman, one terrorist and five civilians were killed during the month. Kevin McCracken, an IRA member, was shot dead by a soldier who was part of a patrol engaged in cordon duties connected with the funerals of the three IRA terrorists shot dead in Gibraltar by the SAS. McCracken was seen carrying a weapon and taking up a firing position. The soldier gave chase and on hearing McCracken cock his rifle, fired four rounds with his SA 80 rifle. Two rounds hit McCracken who was pronounced dead on arrival in hospital. A Heckler and Koch G3 rifle loaded with a charged magazine was recovered from the scene.

On 19 March, two Royal Signals soldiers, Corporal Wood and Corporal Howes, were travelling in an unmarked military car on a routine military journey when they accidentally blundered into the funeral procession of Kevin Brady. Brady was one of the civilians who had been killed on 16 March in the Mill Town Cemetery during the funerals of Farrell, McCann and Savage, who were terrorists killed by the SAS in Gibraltar on 6 March. The Mill Town Cemetery shooting, caught on camera by the BBC, was in itself an extraordinary incident in which Michael Stone, a Protestant terrorist, threw eight or nine grenades at the 5,000 mourners and then opened fire with a handgun. He was caught by those chasing him, severely beaten and rescued by the RUC who arrested him.

But it was the horrific and brutal murders of Corporals Wood and Howes, which was filmed from a hovering Army helicopter as well as by TV news cameras, that shocked the world. When they realized that they had inadvertently become entangled with an IRA funeral, they attempted to drive clear, but were blocked by other vehicles. A mob of 20–30 mourners attacked the car and dragged the two soldiers from the vehicle. One of them managed to fire one round from his 9mm pistol, although there were no reports of anyone being hit. The two were taken into Casement Park by the mob where they were beaten and stripped to their underclothes. They were then taken away by two gunmen and murdered in a back street. Two members of the IRA were subsequently arrested and convicted of the murder of Corporal Wood and Corporal Howes.

In June 1988, a particularly cowardly IRA attack on off-duty soldiers taking part in a Half Marathon and Fun Run for charity occurred. Six soldiers died when a bomb exploded under their transit van. In August, eight Light Infantry soldiers were killed when a bomb, hidden in a cul-

vert, was remotely detonated under the bus in which they were travelling. In all, between July and September 1988, nineteen soldiers died.
This was a black period for the British Army.

The pattern remained much the same throughout 1989 and 1990,
though 1988 proved to be the worst year in terms of British Army casualties since 1982 and there has never been one to match it since. A corner was turned in 1988. Certainly more innocent civilians were killed in
1991 and 1992, but insofar as the war between the Security Forces and
the IRA was concerned, 1989 was the beginning of the period in which
the IRA came under increasing pressure and that pressure led them
eventually to sue for peace in 1994.

In the 1990s, the Army increasingly took a back seat, as the RUC were
able more and more to operate in many areas without military support.
The Army began to take a more reactive role, remaining in barracks
increasingly unless called upon for support by the RUC. Casualty figures
are instructive: 21 soldiers killed in 1988, twelve in 1989, seven in 1990,
five in 1991, four in 1992 and six in 1993. But the number of terrorists
killed or arrested and weapons found either increased or remained con-
sistent. The tide was turning.

Yet the IRA was by no means broken. In January 1992, for instance,
the IRA targeted contractors who were working on a security force
related contract. Eight contractors were the victims of a command detonated bomb. But at the same time the IRA continued to suffer severe
reverses. On 16 February, four terrorists were shot dead, probably by the
SAS, at Dernagh in the follow-up to a terrorist attack on RUC Coalisland. The level of violence remained relatively high throughout the
remainder of 1992 with parallel attacks on the UK mainland. In April
1993, three Mk 15 mortar bombs, each containing 120kg of home-made
explosive were launched into the Crossmaglen Army base. And throughout the province there were shootings and bomb attacks, though surprisingly few civilian casualties. What was different by 1993 was the
level of attacks on the UK mainland. There had, of course, been attacks
against targets in Britain ever since the early 1970s, but the rate quick-
ened in 1993. One of the more spectacular had been a mortar attack
launched in February 1991 from a van parked in Whitehall and aimed at
10 Downing Street. One of the bombs landed in the garden of No 10 during a Cabinet meeting. It was a serious breach of security and a major
embarrassment for the Security Forces and the Government. The likeli-
hood of killing or injuring a member of the Cabinet was probably fairly
small, but the fact that a mortar attack was even possible in the heart of
London and aimed at the seat of Government stunned the nation. That
there was more serious business in hand, namely the defeat of Saddam

Hussein, had the effect of lessening the impact of this considerable IRA achievement.

On the evening of 2 March 1993, the police arrested two IRA terrorists in Stoke Newington, North London, who were subsequently found to be responsible for a bomb left in a rubbish bin outside Harrods on 28 January. Following the arrests the police found weapons and explosives in a house in Stoke Newington. On 9 March, the police discovered a car in Barnet, North London, containing several hundred pounds of explosives with maps marking various prime targets in London.

Then, on 20 March, a 4-year-old boy was killed and 47 pedestrians injured by two IRA bombs left in rubbish bins in Warrington which exploded within minutes of each other. The atrocity backfired on the IRA and was part of the process which resulted in the IRA being forced to sue for peace.

Nevertheless, the IRA offensive on mainland Britain continued throughout April. On the 7th an explosion occurred in a builder's skip near the Conservative Club in Argyle Square in London. On the 23rd, a device exploded near an oil tank in the Esso terminal at North Shields, causing 600 gallons of crude oil to spill into a drainage ditch. On the 24th, the single most devastating IRA attack (in economic terms) on mainland Britain took place. At approximately 10.30 a.m. a massive bomb containing 1,000–1,500kg of home-made explosive packed in the back of a tipper truck exploded outside the National Westminster Tower and Hong Kong Shanghai Bank in Bishopsgate in the City of London. One person died and 44 people were treated in hospital. In terms of publicity this was a major coup for the IRA: massive damage was caused to the heart of the British economy; three years later the National Westminster Tower is still being repaired and international confidence in London as a Banking and Financial Centre was severely shaken. The same evening two car bombs exploded in Central and North London: armed men hijacked two mini-cabs; one driver was instructed to go to Downing Street, the other to New Scotland Yard, but both drivers abandoned their vehicles and alerted the police. These two bombs caused only minor damage.

The IRA offensive in Britain continued throughout the remainder of 1993 and into 1994, with bomb or incendiary attacks in May and June 1993 and January 1994. But better intelligence enabled the police to frustrate IRA efforts. On 1 June, West Midlands police seized a large quantity of weapons and ammunition in Birmingham. Two men were arrested. In July, London police arrested a man carrying a bomb in a holdall in Hendon. Following this arrest in London a large cache of explosives, bomb-making equipment and ammunition was discovered near Stirling in Scotland. At the same time the Garda in the Republic of Ireland had success after success, finding explosives, mortar tubes and weapons. This was no coincidence; the intelligence effort was being co-ordinated by MI5 from 1992. Increasingly the pressure was building on the IRA.

In Northern Ireland, too, there were fewer security force casualties in 1994, more weapons and explosives finds but at the same time continuing attacks against the Army, RUC and RIR.

But behind the scenes, it had been becoming increasingly clear to the IRA that the tactic of the 'Armalite in one hand and the ballot box in the other' was not working.

British intelligence was beginning to take its toll. A worrying number of IRA operatives, particularly those operating on the mainland, were being detained. The mood in both the Republic and in the North had hardened against the IRA. The end of the cold war had closed several sources of weapons and explosives. Rumours of a cease-fire increased throughout the spring and summer of 1994. And on 31 August, the IRA declared the cease-fire which lasted until January 1996. But it was not as sudden as it seemed. The process had started as far back as 1985 with the Anglo-Irish Agreement which provided for a better relationship between the British and Irish governments. At the same time Gerry Adams, the leader of Sinn Fein, enlisted Father Alex Reid of the Clonard Monastery in Belfast to open a direct line of negotiations with Prime Minister Haughey of Eire. It was then that the possibility of a cease-fire was first glimpsed. The dialogue continued between John Hume of the SDLP and Albert Reynolds, Haughey's successor. In November 1990 Peter Brooke, the Secretary of State for Northern Ireland, stated that Britain 'had no selfish strategic or economic interest in Northern Ireland'. In December 1993, a joint declaration of the British and Irish governments declared the right of the Irish people in both parts of Ireland to decide their own future. Thus it was that the British Government, the Irish Government and the IRA edged towards a cease-fire. The precise sequence of events was as follows:

December 1993
15 Downing Street Declaration signed by British Prime Minister
    Major and Irish Taoiseach Albert Reynolds.
May 1994
20 British government confirms pledge to hold Northern Ireland referendum on any negotiated settlement.
August 1994
31 IRA calls cease-fire, pledging complete cessation of hostilities.

September 1994

16 Major lifts broadcasting ban on Sinn Fein.

24 Adams starts two-week tour of USA. Meets NSC Adviser Anthony Lake.

October 1994

13 Loyalist paramilitaries announce cease-fire.

28 Irish government opens Forum for Peace and Reconciliation in Dublin.

November 1994

23 First British Army troop reduction since cease-fire.

December 1994

1 Major ends 22-year ban on talks with Sinn Fein.

9 Peace talks begin at Stormont.

February 1995

22 Joint framework document welcomed by Sinn Fein, rejected by Unionists.

After that date progress was limited. Despite an agreement between the British and Irish governments in November 1995, on the eve of President Clinton's visit to Britain and Ireland to follow a 'twin track' policy towards all-party talks, the stumbling block of a token decommissioning of terrorist weapons before talks took place remained. A three-man international commission on decommissioning of weapons attempted unsuccessfully to find a route through this impasse.

The period from 1984 to 1994 saw the Army starting to take a lower profile and the RUC beginning to dictate the security agenda in Northern Ireland. And in parallel during this period the slow and agonizing process towards a cease-fire took root and eventually bore fruit. The period also saw a desperate last attempt by the IRA to widen its offensive in the UK mainland, a campaign which caused considerable devastation and loss of life.

After a war lasting 25 years, a 'complete cessation of violence' was nevertheless announced by the IRA at midnight on 31 August 1994.

14
MILITARY CONCLUSIONS AND THE FUTURE

The emergency in Ulster lasted 25 years. There have been eight military phases since the beginning of the current troubles:
1. Civil rights and communal violence, 1967–1969
2. The Army's intervention and temporary peace, 1969–1970
3. PIRA opens its campaign against the Security Forces and the Protestants, 1970–1971
4. The failure of the Whitehall initiatives. The conflict deepens, 1972–1975
5. Sectarian violence and the Peace Movement, 1975–1976
6. PIRA reorganizes for a long war, 1977–1981
7. Full implementation of the 'Way Ahead' policy; Army takes low profile, 1981–1988
8. PIRA attempts to widen the offensive and fails, 1988–1994.

The Northern Ireland emergency has produced a greater variety of threats and challenges across the whole spectrum of unrest and violence in the towns and the countryside than any other internal security situation that the British Army has faced in recent times. The response and tactics of the Army have changed constantly to meet new situations while trying to anticipate the next development. During the early years the Army's primary role was to provide a deterrent to the escalation of violence and to keep the peace between the more extreme elements of both communities. As popular support for PIRA waned and law and order were gradually restored in the main cities and towns and in the majority of the rural areas, it was possible to move to a more active policy with the aim of eliminating the terrorist threat.

With the growing success of the Security Forces, and the heyday of the Peace Movement in the winter of 1976–77, the character of the struggle changed. Despairing of winning popular support among the Catholics, PIRA reorganized on a smaller and more closely-knit cellular structure for a long war. The situation facing the Security Forces in the 1980s was therefore that of a more elusive and still potentially dangerous guerrilla force operating in a more polarized environment. Today the Province is more peaceful than it has been for 25 years. The process of transferring more of the responsibility for maintaining law and order back to the RUC has been continuing steadily.

As the situation in Northern Ireland escalated from rioting to bomb-throwing and so through the whole gamut of sniping, ambushes, car bombs, radio-controlled explosions, kidnapping, hijacking and assassination, the battalions and regiments of the Army have come and gone. Virtually no Army organization or individual has remained untouched by the Northern Ireland experience, the challenge offered being an entirely new one. The parameters of an internal security operation far away from home, of the sort that the Army had been dealing with during the retreat from Empire in various parts of the world, were fairly easy to understand. An internal security situation within the confines of the United Kingdom in which the exact legal position and role of the soldier was not initially precisely established was a different matter altogether. Moreover, it was closer to home. Citizens of the United Kingdom could not be shot.

In a colonial situation it was acceptable to impose curfews, to issue identity cards, to control food supplies and even to move the entire population of a village to a fortified government location to protect it from terrorist intimidation. Well-tried riot-control methods involved platoons adopting a box formation, advancing towards a crowd and laying a white tape on the ground which the crowd were warned not to cross. The crowd were then warned by loud hailer that the assembly was illegal and that they must disperse or fire would be opened. Also, a banner was hoisted which stated, 'Disperse or We Fire'. If the riot persisted, fire was opened at a selected individual. This usually had the desired effect.

In the United States and most Western European countries it is traditional for the police or gendarmerie to use a much greater degree of force to disperse a riot. In the USA the police used tear-gas and shotguns to disperse the Civil Rights riots of the 1960s. The French CRS, the West German police, the Belgian Riot Police, even the Swiss police have consistently used tear-gas, shotguns, water cannon and mounted police to disperse rioters, with little quarter given. But cracking heads with batons or even using tear-gas has never been traditional police practice in the United Kingdom. Even though the RUC were more prepared to use force than their English counterparts, in the main, traditional British police tactics governed the reaction to events. Arguably, if a greater degree of force had been used earlier the problem might not have got out of control. On the other hand, if force had not been resorted to so easily over two decades by the RUC and B Specials, there might have been an easier acceptance of authority by the minority.

Thus outdated riot-control techniques used in far-flung corners of the Empire were tried initially, but found to be inadequate and unsuitable. The main difficulty encountered by troops trying to contain a riot was that of making an arrest. An automatic gap is created between rioters and troops by the range of the missiles used by both contenders, whether it be CS grenade or brick. Alley-ways, side-streets and other avenues of escape are open to rioters. Soldiers are encumbered with heavy equipment. Because of all these in-built disadvantages the methods of riot control inherited from Colonial days were refined and improved. Non-violent methods of persuasion to disperse mobs were attempted first, often with the help of community leaders. Internal security weapons were resorted to if necessary in order to effect the maximum arrests. Rifles were fired only if troops were themselves fired at, and after a riot the area was dominated to prevent any recurrence of disorder. Snatch squads were an early development. Lightly clad, fleet-of-foot soldiers were held in reserve to dart into crowds and arrest rioters.

It was the rules for opening fire which posed the greatest problem. Responsibility for the decision to open fire normally rests with the commander on the spot. In the case of a lone sentry the responsibility can therefore rest with the sentry himself. Soldiers may open fire only in certain carefully laid down circumstances. These are summarized

The latest version of EOD vehicle. This van is designed to carry and deploy the Wheelbarrow EOD vehicle and all its ancillary equipment together with its crew.

on a yellow card, carried by all soldiers in Northern Ireland, giving the Instructions by the Director of Operations for opening fire in Northern Ireland. These orders are clear and comprehensive. The only circumstances in which fire may be opened are if a person is seen carrying what can be positively identified as a firearm and is about to use it for offensive purposes, and refuses to halt and desist from using the weapon when called upon to do so. Fire may also be opened at petrol bombers after due warning if life is in danger. Fire may be opened without warning in self-defence, that is if there is no other way that a soldier can prevent himself being killed or seriously injured. There exist, therefore, very strict rules, and these must be scrupulously adhered to.

The case of Private Ian Thain of 1st Battalion The Light Infantry demonstrates the tightrope which soldiers must walk in Northern Ireland. Thain was involved in a shooting incident in which a civilian died and for which Thain was charged with, and found guilty of, murder. The incident occurred on the streets of Belfast during a riotous situation. And this is an incident that shows how, if a soldier is judged in a court of law to have broken the very strict rules on opening fire, he can be found guilty of murder. Such a risk becomes a frightening responsibility for an 18-year-old soldier, who, under certain circumstances, may have to make up his mind and take a decision on his own. In a situation such as in Northern Ireland, if the Army is to be able to operate effectively in support of the Civil Power, soldiers will require extraordinary powers to stop people and vehicles, to search and to make arrests. When the Army first went to Ulster in 1969, its members had no more legal power than the ordinary citizen. It was soon necessary to introduce the Special Powers Act. This Act, the target of widespread criticism and political protest, was replaced on 8 August 1973 by the Northern Ireland (Emergency Provisions) Act. The 1973 Act has largely been replaced by the Northern Ireland (Emergency Provisions) Act 1978 which became effective in June 1980. Under this Act members of the Armed Forces on duty may:

▷ Stop and question any person about his identity or movements or his knowledge of any recent terrorist incident.

▷ Stop and search any person suspected of unlawful possession of munitions or illegal radio-transmitters.

▷ Arrest without warrant, and detain for up to four hours, anyone suspected of committing any offence. The suspect must be released unless re-arrested by the RMP or RUC within four hours of the original arrest.

▷ Enter premises, under certain conditions, for the purpose of arresting suspect persons.

▷ Enter premises if necessary, in the course of operations, for the preservation of peace or the maintenance of order (such as in hot pursuit).

▷ Enter premises to search for and seize unlawfully held munitions or radio-transmitters. In the case of dwelling-houses (but not other premises) the specific authority of a commissioned officer is required to enter for this purpose.

▷ Enter premises to search for unlawfully held persons whose lives might be in danger. In the case of dwelling-houses (but not other premises) the specific authority of a commissioned officer is required to enter for this purpose.

▷ Control and restrict highways, rights of way and access to buildings.

▷ Stop, and if necessary move, vehicles and vessels to search for munitions and illegal radio equipment.

The art of patrolling, particularly in an urban environment, has developed according to the threat. In the early days patrols tended to go out alone and be up to eight or ten men strong. Section-strength patrols were the traditional method of patrolling for many years. In an urban environment, where fields of view and arcs of fire were limited, and where the enemy was often only one or two gunmen, some members of a large patrol were redundant. It was soon realized that a more efficient way of covering the ground was by multiple and smaller patrols which in time became known as 'bricks'. The four-man 'brick' is now the standard unit of patrol. Any number of 'bricks' can be used to cover an area, the idea being that each provides a measure of mutual support for at least one other, cutting off avenues of escape and, it is to be hoped, preventing ambushes. The art of mobile patrolling in Macrilon Land Rovers and/or Humber 1-ton Armoured Vehicles, commonly known as 'Pigs', was also developed and became a way of covering larger areas quickly.

In the early days, patrols stalked warily around the streets, usually at walking pace. When the shooting started they darted from doorway to doorway, dodging and weaving between each point of cover. This became known as 'hard targeting'. In short, a whole new method of urban patrolling has been developed by the Army over the years. In rural areas, patrolling in some respects has remained traditional. Patrols go out sometimes for days on end to act as observation posts on likely border crossing-points or other similar targets. Platoons are trained in the painstaking and frustrating business of surveillance. A whole new area of expertise has been developed using helicopters. 'Eagle' patrols, using Scout or Lynx helicopters, drop down on country roads to mount instant vehicle check-points or to react to an incident.

'Duet' patrols, employing large RAF Wessex or Puma helicopters and a Command helicopter, usually a Gazelle, are used for more complex operations.

Search techniques have also developed over the years. In 1969 they tended to be haphazard and no special equipment existed. Now, special Royal Engineer Search Teams use dogs and equipment to search both urban and rural areas. But methods have also changed; one, perfected by a young RRF officer called Winthrop in the early 1970s, and which became known as the 'Winthrop Method', provided, when it was first used, several breakthroughs. Teams would look at a house or piece of countryside and attempt to put themselves in the mind of the terrorist. If, looking at a field from a road junction, there was one lone tree along a hedgerow, then it was worth looking underneath it. The method was used by, among others, the QDG with great success in 1976. Equipment has also developed over the years and the Army has learned many lessons.* Special communications, surveillance, riot equipment, body armour, vehicles, weapon sights, bomb-disposal equipment, perimeter protection equipment and much else has been developed particularly by US and British companies.

Command and control of internal security situations has become increasingly more sophisticated. In the July 1969 Belfast riots, when Brigadier Peter Hudson's helicopter was forced to land, command and control of the troops on the ground became strained. Today radio links are secure and simple to operate, and incorporate sufficient redundancy in the system to ensure that a radio net will continue to function despite the failure of some of its constituent parts. ADP systems also provide support in many areas.

The Army had to learn – often painfully – the complications and subtleties of operating in support of the Civil Power with (quite rightly) relatively limited power itself in what has at times amounted to a state of war. During the 25 years of the Emergency, the Security Forces reduced violence, and the potential of the IRA to achieve damage, disruption and destruction, to a degree that in the dark days of the early 1970s often seemed impossible. Within the current constraints of the law, it would have been difficult for the Army and the RUC to have reduced the level of violence much further than was in fact achieved. Unless the – unacceptable – conditions of a police state are imposed, the terrorist can operate with relative ease; there is a limit to what can be achieved by military means alone. The Security Forces' role is, undeniably, to a certain extent reactive. A purely military victory in

---

* The author's *Weapons and Equipment of Counter-Terrorism* (Arms & Armour Press, 1995) highlights British Army counter-terrorist weapons and equipment.

Northern Ireland was never therefore really on the cards. The Security Forces' task was to keep the level of violence as low as possible in order that other influences could work.

The only permanent solution to the Irish problem must be a political one. The alternatives available have been rehearsed many times, but are worth repeating. The methods of government available for Northern Ireland range from total integration into the United Kingdom through various forms of self-government to total absorption into the Irish Republic. Integration of Ulster into the United Kingdom would result in an increased number of MPs for Ulster possibly holding the balance of power between the two major parties. This possible domination of Westminster politics by Ulster politicians would almost certainly not be accepted either by Parliament or the people of the United Kingdom. Perhaps more important it would be quite unacceptable to the Irish Republic.

Devolution is the second alternative. This would involve an elected regional assembly and government operating within the political and legal framework of the United Kingdom. This has always been the chosen option of HM Government but it does, of course, depend on internal consensus and this has eluded successive governments.

Federation would differ from devolution in that, rather than grant Northern Ireland a measure of devolution which can always be taken back at a stroke, Northern Ireland would be a State, with powers and duties vested permanently and inalienably in it, and it would enjoy a statutory relationship with the United Kingdom as the Federal authority, as, for instance, Ontario is to Canada or New South Wales is to Australia. The disadvantage of this option is that it would set a precedent for the rest of the United Kingdom and the Republic would be unlikely to accept it, granting as it does a degree of permanency to the measure of independence.

Another option would be to give Ulster Commonwealth Status; that is to say, the Province would become independent, but the Queen would remain Queen of Ulster. This would solve the problem of the loyalty of many Ulstermen to the Crown, but not to HM Government. Again, however, this would not be acceptable to the Republic granting, as it does, independence to Ulster. The link with the Crown could subsequently be broken. Independence is a further option and indeed it was once fashionable among extremist Protestants. This could be imposed or negotiated independence or take the form of UDI. There is no doubt that, even among the Protestant majority, there is a certain anti-English attitude in Ulster. However, it is unlikely that an independent Ulster could survive economically. More important, independence is not acceptable to the Republic.

Redrawing the border has some attractions. This could be done so as to exclude from Ulster Newry, South Armagh, Strabane and the western parts of Londonderry (the Creggan and the Bogside) so as to leave a smaller but more homogeneous Protestant Ulster. However, these areas account for only 70–80,000 out of 500,000 Catholics. Where would the 100,000 Catholics in West Belfast go? They might not wish to be resettled in the Irish Republic and anyway would the Republic want them?

A patrol deploys from a Lynx helicopter in a rural area of Northern Ireland.

Cantonization has also been suggested as a possible solution. This would involve dividing Ulster into three to five self-governing areas, each with the maximum degree of devolved authority. In this way Catholics could achieve a degree of self-government and of self-respect. But the religious groups are intermingled. It just could not be made to work. More importantly, the total area is too small to be further sub-divided. Unification with the Republic of Ireland is, of course, an option. A new Republic of all Ireland could be formed, or a Federal

Republic of, say, four provinces. There are, however, as is well known, overwhelming Protestant objections to such a plan.

The last two possible options are Condominium and Confederation. Condominiums have been tried in a few instances and in each have been found to be disastrous. In the case of the Republic and the United Kingdom and involving such a sensitive province as Ulster it is unlikely that it would ever be successful. Finally, the Confederation of the Irish Republic and of the United Kingdom would in many ways be the real solution. There could be one monetary policy, full extradition, the same post office and telephone service, one broadcasting service and so on. The Isle of Man and the Channel Islands could be invited to join too. However, history is against such an idealistic solution. The Republic of Ireland has spent hundreds of years fighting to free itself of British domination – it would be unlikely to overturn the gains of 1921.

The British Government has set its sights on devolution and power-sharing as this seems to offer the most hope. There have been some notable recent political developments in Northern Ireland. HMG's initiative on 'rolling devolution' has led to the Northern Ireland Assembly; the SDLP has joined parties from the Republic in the New Ireland Forum; and Sinn Fein has made a dramatic entry into electoral politics. However the same polarized arguments persist.

The Act of 1982 allowed elections to a new 78-seat one-chamber Assembly whose functions, pending devolution of legislative powers to the Assembly and executive power to a local administration, were to be *consultative*. It could make recommendations for the Secretary of State to present in Parliament. The unique feature was the concept of 'rolling devolution'. The idea was that the Assembly could recommend that responsibility for matters in which there is cross-community agreement should be devolved to the Assembly while leaving areas on which there is division in the hands of the Secretary of State. The aim was to encourage and reward what amounts to power-sharing across the sectarian divide. Decisions required the support of 70 per cent of the members of the Assembly. In a further attempt to reduce polarization, elections to the Assembly were by proportional representation.

Elections to the Assembly were held on 20 August 1982 with the results shown in the table. These figures show very clearly that, in Ulster's case, proportional representation would appear to be the best way of securing fair representation for the Catholic minority. There is evidence that there is considerable support for power-sharing in the Province. A *Sunday Times* opinion poll in June 1981 revealed that a majority of Protestants (53 per cent) and Catholics (77 per cent) favoured power-sharing. But while a majority will assent to the general principle,

Result of elections to Northern Ireland Assembly held on 20 August 1982.

Party	Percentage of First Preference Vote	Seats	Remarks
Official Unionist Party (OUP)	29.7	26	Supports Assembly, but anti-devolution.
Democratic Unionist Party (DUP) – Ian Paisley	23.0	21	Supports Assembly, but uses power to block any initiatives leading to devolution.
Social Democratic and Labour Party (SDLP)	18.8	14	Abstains from taking seats – in effect a veto.
Alliance	9.3	10	Supports Assembly.
Sinn Fein	10.1	5	
Workers' Party	2.7	0	
United Ulster Unionist Party (UUUP)	1.7	0	
Others	4.7	2	

the political parties are deeply divided on its practical implementation. A gradual move towards power-sharing could, if both communities were willing, lead to a compromise political solution. If power-sharing devolved government were established, it could provide a way forward.

The basic causes of the fundamental difference between the two communities are perhaps a little clearer now. There is evidence (particularly the Moxon-Browne poll of July–September 1978) to show that Protestant attitudes towards Catholics are essentially religious in nature. They are maintained by misconceptions and fear about the Catholic Church, its organization and its power. Protestantism *per se* is not a serious issue among Catholics, rather Catholic objections centre around Protestant attitudes towards religion. Most Catholics are disillusioned about violence and understand the economic advantages of remaining in the United Kingdom. Theirs is a very pragmatic approach. In a nutshell, Protestants object to Catholics as Catholics but not as people. To some extent Catholics object to Protestants as people and not as Protestants. Perhaps in time the Protestant majority will appreciate that the Catholic minority is not the threat they imagine it to be. If this comes about the Catholic minority will feel less threatened and withdraw its support, tacit or otherwise, from the men of violence. Only then would the circumstances be created for a permanent end to violence.

Until this happens, the Security Forces must remain ready to control a resurgence of terrorism. And while by 1994 the authorities had succeeded in reducing the level of violence from the bad years of 1972–4, they were never able to bring it totally under control. There have been major security force successes and terrorism is not the potent force it was in the 1970s and early 1980s. The Security Forces have become much more professional, have received much more information from a population weary of endless atrocities, and have perfected a much more sophisticated intelligence-gathering machine. On the other hand, the Army has had to learn to come to terms with the tenacity and ingenuity of the terrorists; the UWC strike demonstrated that the Army is not equipped to control a high-technology society at the point of breakdown. The Army has learned that it is the terrorist who nearly always has the initiative. There have been times when the IRA has nearly been defeated but it has bounced back. The IRA can afford not to be too concerned about temporary setbacks. They believe themselves to be engaged in a war that is 800 years old. Unfortunately it is very difficult to defeat an idea.

The Army has learned many practical lessons in Ulster. It will, if necessary, continue to fight terrorism but is unlikely within the context of a liberal democracy to be able to defeat it entirely. In the final analysis all the people of Ulster must want an end to the violence themselves and the politicians must then perpetuate that new-found peace in a framework acceptable to all the people of Ulster of both communities.

Until people of goodwill succeed in constructing peace in Northern Ireland, the Security Forces remain the ultimate bulwark against the breakdown of society. Trying to keep the peace between the two communities is no enviable task, particularly when both these communities are apt to turn against the peacemaker. It is doubtful whether any other Army could have coped without resorting to massive retaliation. The United Kingdom owes an immense debt of gratitude to all those who have served in Northern Ireland, to the Army, to the RIR and to the RUC. One can only hope that the sacrifices they have made will not have been made in vain.

The absence of shootings and bombings from August 1994 to January 1996 transformed life in Northern Ireland. The atmosphere was more relaxed; business confidence surged; foreign investment took off; the police no longer felt the need to check under their cars for deadly booby-traps, and tourism flourished. Security measures were considerably less stringent than they were before August 1994: military vehicles no longer travelled in convoys of no less than three to guard each other against grenade or rocket attack; police officers took off their flak jackets. Far fewer police and troops were seen on the streets.

However the peace did not hold. A massive lorry bomb exploded in London's Docklands, killing two local workers, on 9 February 1996.

There was very little warning, and the damage to several large office blocks was dramatic. In a switch of tactics, the IRA then orchestrated a series of smaller bombings throughout the West End in February and March 1996, which ended with a bomber blowing himself to bits when the bomb he was carrying detonated prematurely in a bus in the Aldwych in London on 18 February 1996. Since then there have been further random bombings in London's West End, including an attempt in late April to damage Hammersmith Bridge with 30lb of Semtex, which failed

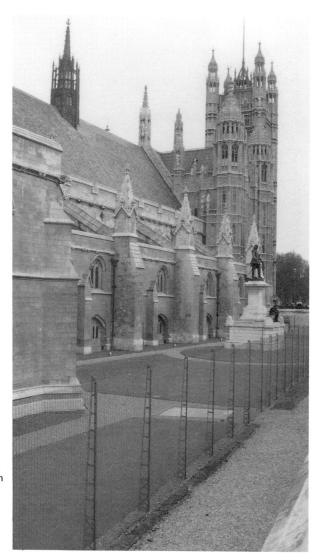

Since the breaking of the IRA 'cease-fire' in January 1996, the protection of potential targets on the UK mainland has become even more important. Here a perimeter protection fence incorporating anti-tamper alarms surrounds the Houses of Parliament in London.

to detonate properly. At the time of writing, however, the IRA has not resumed its campaign in Northern Ireland.

Despite the breakdown of the cease-fire, many Republicans believe they have made significant progress since August 1994. The Sinn Fein leader, Gerry Adams, who until 1994 was banned from both Britain and the USA, completed three triumphant tours of America, where he was treated as an international statesman and raised close on a million dollars. He was seen to shake hands with the Irish Prime Minister, John Bruton, US President Bill Clinton, South African President Nelson Mandela and, perhaps most significantly, Sir Patrick Mayhew, a member of the British Cabinet and Secretary of State for Northern Ireland. He was also allowed into Britain and on to British television after the Government dropped its broadcasting ban on Sinn Fein. In Eire the process of the political legitimization of Sinn Fein went even further. But Sinn Fein was not satisfied with the pace of progress and accused the British Government of putting the whole process at risk by its insistence on the 'decommissioning' of arms before all-party talks. A three-man international commission tried unsuccessfully to manufacture a formula to find a way forward from this impasse. We now know, however, that the IRA was all the while planning to resume its bombing campaign. Clear evidence was uncovered by the Metropolitan Police, in their investigation of the February 1996 Docklands bombing and the Aldwych bus bomb, that planning had commenced for both these atrocities as early as August 1995 – that is, well before the November 1995 visit of President Clinton when the IRA and Sinn Fein were still apparently talking peace. It was during the period when an attempt was being made apparently by all sides to find a peaceful way forward. We now know the IRA and probably Sinn Fein were not engaging in meaningful or sincere negotiations but merely playing for time in order to prepare for a new bombing campaign.

So what is the way forward? The British and Irish Governments are determined to go ahead with the peace process, if necessary without the IRA and Sinn Fein. All-party talks started in June 1996 without Sinn Fein because the IRA refused to reinstate the cease-fire and Sinn Fein made matters worse by refusing to condemn the resumption of bombing. If the IRA insist on remaining outside the political process, then all those who desire peace both north and south of the border must work to isolate the men of violence. If the IRA pin their hopes on driving Britain out of Northern Ireland by force, it would mean that they were shunning all attempts to build political alliances. It would, in other words, represent something close to nihilism.

Certainly the message from the public, including the hardline Republican and Loyalist ghettos, is clear – we have tasted peace and we do not

One of the latest counter-terrorist programmes undertaken by the British Army in Northern Ireland is the building of observation towers close to the border with Eire in order to control cross-border infiltration by IRA terrorists from the Republic.

want a return to conflict. In this respect, the present IRA strategy of not resuming their campaign of violence in Ulster is a clever one. Minimal bombing on the mainland keeps the British Government guessing, while at the same time the Irish are not antagonized. Sooner or later, however, the IRA will have to make up its mind. They will have to join the political process or risk complete marginalization. They will never again command the sympathy or support that they achieved in the 1970s or 80s.

The journey to a lasting and comprehensive peace will probably be long and complex, but it has started and there is no turning back. If in the end a lasting all-inclusive political settlement *is* achieved, no one will be more pleased than Tommy Atkins.

Appendix I
THE NORTHERN IRELAND CAMPAIGN: GENERAL STATISTICS

	1969	1970	1971	1972	1973	1974	1975	1976	1977	1978	1979	1980	1981
Terrorist Incidents													
Bombs	10	170	1515	1853	1520	1113	635	1192	535	633	564	400	529
Incendiaries	-	-	-	-	-	270	56	236	608	115	60	2	49
Shootings	73	213	1756	10564	5018	3206	1803	1908	1081	755	728	642	1142
Casualties													
Regular Army Killed	-	-	43	103	58	28	14	14	15	14	38	8	10
UDR/R Irish *Killed	-	-	5	26	8	7	6	15	14	7	10	9	13
RUC Killed	1	2	11	17	13	15	11	23	14	10	14	9	21
Civilians Killed	10	13	61	223	129	145	196	224	59	43	48	45	52
Terrorists Killed													
Republican	2	10	52	95	37	19	10	18	6	7	3	3	5
Loyalist	-	-	2	3	5	3	10	3	4	-	-	2	-
Finds													
Weapons	14	324	717	1264	1595	1260	825	837	590	400	302	203	409
Explosives (inc neutralized) (tonnes)	.01	1.39	2.61	27.88	32.15	24.14	10.06	17.22	2.72	3.61	2.96	2.73	7.58
Terrorist Charges Loyalist & Republican	-	-	-	531	1418	1362	1197	1276	1308	843	670	550	918

	1982	1983	1984	1985	1986	1987	1988	1989	1990	1991	1992	1993	1994
Terrorist Incidents													
Bombs	332	367	248	215	254	384	458	420	287	367	314	289	24
Incendiaries	36	43	10	36	21	9	8	7	33	237	105	62	45
Shootings	547	424	334	237	392	674	537	566	559	499	426	473	31
Casualties													
Regular Army Killed	21	5	9	2	4	3	21	12	7	5	3	6	-
UDR/R Irish * Killed	7	10	10	4	8	8	12	2	8	8	1	2	-
RUC Killed	12	19	8	23	12	16	6	9	12	6	2	6	-
Civilians Killed	50	37	25	20	33	54	45	37	45	71	59	68	2
Terrorists Killed													
Republican	7	6	11	4	4	13	8	1	4	4	5	1	-
Loyalist	-	1	-	-	-	-	-	1	-	-	-	1	-
Finds													
Weapons	317	201	197	238	215	267	552	327	223	214	199	256	44
Explosives (inc neutralized) (tonnes)	5.61	5.11	6.65	6.844	6.735	9.885	9.461	7.574	8.922	6.867	5.114	10.505	0.381
Terrorist Charges Loyalist & Republican	686	613	528	522	655	468	439	431	380	397	353	366	28

*Ulster Defence Regiment amalgamated with Royal Irish Rangers on 1 July 1992 to form the Royal Irish Regiment.

Appendix II
CHRONOLOGY OF THE MAIN EVENTS
IN NORTHERN IRELAND

c.8000BC	Arrival of first men in Ireland from Scotland.
c.100BC	Arrival of Gaels.
AD432	Arrival of St Patrick.
840	Danes found city of Dublin.
1014	High King Brian Boru killed in battle with the Danes.
1171–72	Norman barons pay homage to Henry II.
	John de Courcy defeats King Dunleavy and assumes title of Earl of Ulster.
1595	Rebellion led by Hugh O'Neill, Earl of Tyrone.
1601	Defeat of O'Neill and Spaniards at Battle of Kinsale.
1609	Plantation of Ulster starts.
1641	Catholic revolt in Ireland against Cromwell.
1649	Cromwell arrives in Ireland. Ruthless suppression of revolt.
1655	Four-fifths of Irish land granted to English owners.
1659	Siege and relief of Derry.
1690	William III of Orange defeats James II at Battle of the Boyne.
1691	Jacobite Army defeated at Aughrim.
1703	Only 14 per cent of land in Ireland remains in hands of Catholic Irish, in Ulster only 5 per cent.
1796	Founding of Orange Order.
1798	Battle of Vinegar Hill and death of Wolfe Tone.
1801	Act of Union.
1829	Catholic Emancipation.
1845–49	The Great Famine.
1848	Battle of Widow MacCormack's Cabbage Patch.
1858	James Stephens founds embryo Irish Republican Brotherhood.
1867	Abortive raid on Chester Castle.

	Fenian Rising in Ireland. Execution of 'Manchester Martyrs'.
1870	Gladstone's First Land Act.
1890	Irish National Land League founded.
1882	Phoenix Park murders.
1886	First Home Rule Bill.
1891	Death of Parnell.
1893	Second Home Rule Bill.
1912	Third Home Rule Bill.
1913	Ulster Volunteer Force founded.
1916	Easter Dublin Rising.
1917	All rebel prisoners released.
1920	Black and Tans join RIC.
1921	Truce between IRA and British Forces. Anglo-Irish Treaty: Constitution of Irish Free State.
1922	Irish Civil War, 77 anti-Treaty IRA executed.
1923	End of Civil War.
1937	Constitution of Eire.
1939	IRA bombing campaign in England.
1949	Republic of Ireland declared.
1956–62	IRA campaign in Ulster.
1967	Northern Ireland Civil Rights Association (NICRA) founded.
1968:	
Summer	Civil Rights marches and demonstrations start and continue to end of year.
22 Nov	Government announces first reforms.
1969:	
Apr	First bombs set off by Protestant extremists.
28 Apr	Prime Minister, Terence O'Neill, resigns and is replaced by James Chichester-Clark.
14 Aug	Rioting in Londonderry and Belfast. Army deployed on peacekeeping duties.

Oct	Government accepts recommendations of Hunt Report including RUC reforms and abolition of 'B' Specials. Protestant rioting in Belfast, first RUC member killed.		Northern Ireland Labour Party, one.
		6–9 Dec	Sunningdale Conference.
		1974:	
Dec	Provisional IRA breaks away from Official IRA.	1 Jan	Power-sharing Executive of Faulkner (Chief Executive) Unionists, SDLP and Alliance formally take office.
1970:			
1 Apr	UDR established.	28 Feb	Westminster General Election: eleven out of twelve Northern Ireland seats won by anti-power-sharing Unionists.
2 Jun	Balkan Street arms find and ensuing Falls riots.		
31 Oct	PIRA kill first British soldier.	14–29 May	UWC Strike against power-sharing and Council of Ireland. Power cuts.
1971:			
Mar	Chichester-Clark resigns; is succeeded by Brian Faulkner.	28 May	Executive collapses. Direct Rule resumed.
9 Aug	Internment without trial introduced.	21 Nov	Birmingham pub bombings: nineteen killed, 182 injured.
30 Oct	Paisley's Democratic Union-ist Party (DUP) formed.	29 Nov	Prevention of Terrorism Act introduced in Great Britain.
		20 Dec–19 Jan	Christmas 'truce'.
1972:			
30 Jan	Bloody Sunday: thirteen killed.	*1975*:	
		9 Feb–7 Apr	Second 'Ceasefire'.
2 Feb	British Embassy in Dublin burned down.	1 May	Constitutional Convention elections: Loyalists win 46 out of 78 seats.
22 Feb	Aldershot bomb explosion; seven killed.		
24 Mar	Direct Rule established. William Whitelaw appointed first Secretary of State for Northern Ireland.	24 July–5 Dec	Internment phased out.
		1976:	
		1 Mar	Special category status abolished.
29 May	Official IRA call ceasefire.	9 Mar	Constitutional Convention dissolved after British Government refused majority report rejecting power-sharing.
20 June	Special category status established for convicted terrorists.		
26 June	PIRA ceasefire; Whitelaw meets PIRA Leaders in London.		
		21 July	British Ambassador to Republic, Christopher Ewart-Biggs, assassinated in Dublin.
9 July	PIRA resume terrorist action claiming British Army had broken ceasefire.		
		10 Aug	McGuire children killed. The birth of the Peace Movement.
21 July	Nine killed and 130 injured by nineteen PIRA bombs in Belfast (Bloody Friday).	1 Sept	Irish Government declares National State of Emergency.
31 July	Operation 'Motorman'.	*1977*:	
24–26 July	Darlington Conference.	11 Mar	Twenty-six UVF men sentenced to a total of 700 years' imprisonment.
1973:			
20 Mar	British White Paper proposes new 80-seat Assembly with power-sharing Executive.	3 May	Short-lived Loyalist strike demanding restoration of majority Government.
28 June	Assembly elections: Faulkner Unionists, 22 seats; other Unionists, 28; SDLP, nineteen; Alliance, eight;	8 June	Roy Mason announces introduction of SAS into Northern Ireland.

27 June	Four killed and eighteen injured in Belfast in feud between OIRA and PIRA.
10 Oct	Betty Williams and Mairead Corrigan awarded Nobel Peace Prize.

1978:

17 Feb	PIRA fire bomb at La Mon House Restaurant: twelve killed, 23 injured.
13 Mar	Republican prisoners at HMP Maze launch 'dirty protest'.
30 Nov	PIRA announces that it is 'preparing for a long war'.

1979:

22 Mar	British Ambassador to The Hague, Sir Richard Sykes, assassinated.
30 Mar	Airey Neave murdered by INLA bomb outside House of Commons.
27 Aug	PIRA bombs kill eighteen soldiers at Warrenpoint and Lord Mountbatten is assassinated near his holiday house in the Republic.
25 Oct	Secretary of State, Humphrey Atkins, initiates talks on restoration of power to locally elected representatives.

1980:

Mar	PIRA admits responsibility for attacks on British Army in West Germany.
18 Apr	Constitutional talks on power-sharing end without reaching any agreement.
21 May	Mrs Thatcher and Charles Haughey reach agreement on close co-operation.
2 June	Atkins begins talks with political parties on devolved government.
27 Oct	Hunger-strikes commence at HMP Maze.

1981:

1 Mar	Bobby Sands begins new hunger-strike campaign.
9 Apr	Bobby Sands elected MP for Fermanagh and South Tyrone.
5 May	Sands dies. Widespread rioting in Londonderry, Belfast and Dublin. Nine more strikers die between 12 May and 20 August.

2 July	Atkins proposes Northern Ireland Advisory Council.
4 Sept	INLA announces no further volunteers will join hunger-strike.
14 Sept	James Prior becomes Secretary of State.
3 Oct	PIRA calls off hunger-strike.
14 Nov	Murder by PIRA of Reverend Robert Bradford, OUP MP for South Belfast.
Oct–Nov	PIRA bombing campaign in London.
23 Nov	Paisley-led day of action in support of tougher security measures. Paisley announces formation of 'Third Force'.

1982:

20 July	Bomb explosion in Regent's Park kills six bandsmen. Second bomb kills men and horses of the Household Cavalry in Hyde Park.
6 Dec	Ballykelly bomb kills seventeen.

1983:

May	Direct Rule extended for a further twelve months.
12–17 July	Serious riots in Londonderry.
25 Sept	Thirty-eight Republican prisoners escape from Maze.
20 Nov	Three innocent worshippers killed in INLA attack on Mountain Lodge Pentecostal Gospel Hall.
17 Dec	Harrods bombing in London.

1984:

6 Mar	William McConnel, Assistant Governor of HMP Maze, is shot dead.
14 Mar	Attempt by UFF on life of Gerry Adams, MP.
Apr–May	Attacks on RUC and UDR intensify.
Oct	Bombing of Grand Hotel at Brighton during Conservative Party conference.
24 Dec	Dominic McGlinchey captured in the Republic and extradited to Northern Ireland.

1985:

1 Feb	Third of three Graham brothers shot dead by IRA. All were members of the UDR.

Nov	Anglo-Irish Agreement concluded.

1986:

16 Jan	Dutch police arrest William Kelly and Maze Prison escapees Brendan MacFarlane and Gerard Kelly, all members of the IRA, and seize a quantity of arms and bomb-making equipment including fifteen rifles.
Dec	Intensive bombing campaign against military targets in Northern Ireland. Security Forces in Northern Ireland and Eire find large quantities of explosives.

1987:

8 Feb	UFF claim responsibility for a number of incendiary IEDs that had exploded in Dublin and Donegal.
Mar	Private O'Conner of 1 QLR killed in Belfast, first Army fatality since July 1986.
15–30 Apr	Three members of Security Forces and three civilians murdered. 25 April Lord Chief Justice Gibson and his wife murdered.
8 May	SAS ambush and kill eight known PIRA terrorists at Loughgall.
19 July	Lance-Corporal Hewitt of 1 RGJ shot dead by IRA sniper in Belleek.
11 Nov	Eleven civilians killed and 61 injured by IRA bomb at Remembrance Day Service at Enniskillen.

1988:

8 Jan	61 assault rifles, 30 pistols and 150 hand-grenades seized by Security Forces; three Protestants arrested.
Mar	Two soldiers, one policeman, one terrorist and five civilians killed during the month.
6 Mar	SAS ambush and kill three IRA terrorists (Farrell, McCann and Savage) planning a bombing in Gibraltar.

16 Mar	Michael Stone, Protestant terrorist, opens fire and throws grenades at Mill Town Cemetery during funeral of Farell, McCann and Savage, killing three civilians.
19 Mar	Corporals Howes and Wood dragged from their car and murdered.
15 June	Six soldiers taking part in a charity run murdered by a bomb detonated under their van.
20 Aug	Eight Light Infantry soldiers killed by a CWIED while travelling in a bus near Omagh.

1989:

20 Oct	Constable Marshall of the RUC shot dead in his police car when overtaken by a lorry with a 12.7mm heavy machine-gun mounted in the back.
Nov–Dec	Six soldiers and one civilian murdered and twenty-four civilians injured in 'punishment' shootings.

1990:

July	Three RUC officers and five civilians murdered during the month.
7 & 19 July	Co-ordinated attempts to disrupt Belfast with scares of hoax vehicle bombs.
Nov	Peter Brooke, Secretary of State for Northern Ireland, states 'Britain has no selfish strategic or economic interest in Northern Ireland'.

1991:

Feb	Mortar attack on 10 Downing Street.

1992:

16 Feb	Four terrorists shot dead by SAS at Dernagh.
Sept	Large finds of weaponry, munitions and explosives by Security Forces at Strabane and Castlewellan.
Nov	Bombing campaign on UK mainland starts.

1993:

28 Jan	Bomb explodes in rubbish bin outside Harrods, London.
2 Mar	Police arrest two IRA terrorists in North London.
9 Mar	Police uncover terrorist bomb factory in North London.
20 Mar	IRA bomb explodes in Warrington, killing 4-year-old boy and injuring forty-seven pedestrians.
7 & 23 Apr	Bombs explode in London and North Shields.
24 Apr	Bishopsgate bomb explodes, causing massive damage in City of London.
1 June	Police seize large quantity of weapons and ammunition in Birmingham. Two arrested.
14 July	IRA terrorist in possession of a bomb arrested in Hendon, North London.
17 July	Bomb factory uncovered by police near Stirling in Scotland.
Dec	Joint Declaration of British and Irish governments that the Irish people in both parts of Ireland had the right to decide their own future.

1994:

31 Aug	IRA calls cease-fire.
13 Oct	Loyalist paramilitaries announce cease-fire.
23 Dec	First British troop reduction.

1995:

Feb	Joint framework document welcomed by Sinn Fein, rejected by IRA.
June	Further British troop reductions.
Nov	President Bill Clinton visits Britain, Northern Ireland and Eire.
Dec	Punishment beatings intensified by IRA.

1996:

9 Feb	1,000lb bomb in London's Docklands marks end of cease-fire.
15 Feb	Bomb Squad officers make safe bomb in London's West End.
18 Feb	Semtex bomb explodes in London's Aldwych, killing the bomber, Edward O'Brien.
8 March	Bomb explodes in London's West End.
17 April	Small bomb explodes in Kensington, London.
24 April	32lb Semtex bomb under Hammersmith Bridge in London fails to explode.
10 June	All Party Talks commence in Belfast.
15 June	IRA explode 1,000lb bomb in Manchester, injuring over 200.

Appendix III
EXTREMIST ORGANIZATIONS IN
NORTHERN IRELAND

Catholic Ex-Servicemen's Association (CESA) and League of Ex-Servicemen (LES)
CESA was formed to protect the Catholic enclaves from Protestant attacks. The organization was started by the Provisional IRA and initially restricted its membership to ex-servicemen, though this was widened to include 'honorary members'. LES was started in late 1973 with the aim of removing the more extreme members of CESA to form a genuine ex-Servicewomen's organization. It is by no means clear how successful LES has been in this venture. Recent reports indicate that as a result of leadership problems neither organization is particularly active, but they retain the potential to produce vigilante street patrols in Catholic areas when under threat of Protestant attack. Their main strength is in Belfast, where they have an estimated membership of 2,000, some of whom have access to arms.

Cumann Na Bann
The Cumann Na Bann is the women's section of the IRA. Their members are integrated into the IRA and some hold officer posts. Although women have taken part in shooting incidents, their main use has been as arms and bomb carriers, couriers and incendiary device and bomb planters.

Doomsday Organizations
There are a number of organizations in existence with the stated aim of providing a means of defence for the Protestant community in the event of an outbreak of civil war (probably as a result of complete British withdrawal from Northern Ireland).
ORANGE VOLUNTEERS (OVs). Founded in 1969 by militant members of the Orange Order, the OVs are well equipped (by Protestant standards) with the usual range of weapons, a basic collection of mortars and a good selection of modern radio equipment on which members carry out regular training. Morale is good and members regard themselves as a cut above other Protestant groups.
DOWN ORANGE WELFARE (DOW). First came to notice in 1973 as a 'secret army' of 5,000 men, commanded by a retired British Army Officer, Lieutenant-Colonel Peter Brush. DOW is allegedly ready for action in the event of civil war or a breakdown in law and order. The force is not believed to have taken part in any violence, but Brush is respected by a number of active paramilitary leaders.
(ULSTER) VOLUNTEER SERVICE CORPS ((U)VSC). Formerly the Vanguard Service Corps (Craig's Private Army), the (U)VSC effectively performs a bridging function between the Loyalist paramilitary organizations and Loyalist political groups.
ULSTER SERVICE CORPS (USC). The military wing of the Ulster Special Constabulary Association which sprang briefly to fame in May 1976 when it decided to mount vigilante patrols in rural areas with the aim of curtailing Republican attacks on Protestants. Patrols have been mainly concentrated in County Armagh, County Tyrone and County Fermanagh.
LOYALIST DEFENCE VOLUNTEERS (LDV). An umbrella group, now defunct, which encompassed the Orange Volunteers (OVs), Down Orange Welfare (DOW), Ulster Special Constabulary (USCA) and Ulster Service Corps (USC). These groups are now separate entities although the USC in the County Tyrone/Fermanagh area utilizes the LDV chain of command.

Fianna N Eirrean (FNE)

The FNE is the youth movement of the IRA. It is organized on a paramilitary basis and works closely with the IRA and provides the main recruiting base. Their members are used to provoke street disturbances, as look-outs, bomb planters and weapon carriers.

Irish National Liberation Army (INLA)

INLA's aims are quite straightforward: through armed warfare it intends to compel the British to withdraw militarily from Northern Ireland, which would then unite with the South. The new Republic would then withdraw from the European Economic Community and would practise 'socialist' principles. INLA members, who have probably never numbered more than 50, are Marxist–Leninists, although they were fiercely critical of the pro-Soviet stance of the Officials.

The organization is based in Dublin, where at first it picked up recruits expelled by the Provisionals. The quality proved poor, however, so that the leadership quickly turned to more careful screening of candidates, which led to a tighter organization. The majority of their weapons and explosives came from Communist sources via the Middle East.

Quite the most outrageous murder undertaken by the INLA, was that of Airey Neave, the Conservative Party spokesman on Northern Ireland, in his car on the forecourt of the House of Commons in March 1979.

INLA continues to operate in 1985 although with nothing approaching the incidence attributable to PIRA. Their targets have included Protestant paramilitaries as well as members of the security forces. In their misguided determination there is little to distinguish INLA militants from PIRA; both groups had members who died on hunger-strike in 1981.

Irish Republican Army (OIRA)

The IRA is split between the so-called Officials (OIRA) and the Provisionals (PIRA), a distinction born in 1969.

In the mid 1960s, under the influence of Cathal Goulding, a Marxist wing of the IRA was resurrected. Goulding's followers involved themselves in exploiting social issues and were not prepared for the armed struggle which emerged from the communal violence of the mid and late 1960s in Northern Ireland.

While not ruling out military actions, the Marxist wing indulged in relatively little terrorism, and in May 1972 declared a unilateral ceasefire. Since then the bulk of their activity has taken place through their political front, known as the Official Sinn Fein, which was registered in the Republic as a party with a national organization. In Northern Ireland, however, the Officials worked through the Republican clubs. Both in the North and the South the Officials fielded candidates in all elections during the 1970s, winning the support in the north on an average of less than 2½ per cent of the vote.

They argued that class politics should supersede sectarian issues, and that the violence practised by the Provisionals merely entrenched reactionary attitudes. The most prominent Official leader in the late 1970s was Thomas MacGiolla, who in 1977 became leader of the new Sinn Fein – The Workers' Party (SFWP) – in the Republic. By 1979 the links with Sinn Fein were dropped completely so that the party contested the 1982 Ulster Assembly elections as The Workers' Party (WP).

In the North, the Officials, through the Republican clubs, supported the establishment of devolved government within the United Kingdom, but in the long run they looked forward to a united socialist Ireland 'where all the people of Ireland own and control the wealth and run their own affairs'.

Irish Republican Socialist Party (IRSP)

Violence ensued between the Official IRA and the dissidents who formed the break-away IRSP in December 1974. Six people died and several dozen received injuries following the break led by Seamus Costello. These men were Marxist–Leninists, former Officials, who had come to believe that the Irish Revolution could only be accomplished with militant action. For them the 'national struggle' was inseparable from the 'class struggle', and they did not condemn the terrorist campaign waged by the Provisional

IRA. The IRSP journal, *The Starry Plough*, carries news of Provisional activities and the party acts as a political front for the Irish National Liberation Army (INLA). Ideologically the new party was closer to Trotskyism than to Moscow's Communist line, and it sought to establish contact abroad with like-minded groups. Prominent in these efforts was Bernadette Devlin (married name, McAliskey), who quarrelled with Costello for reverting to 'the sterile nationalism of traditonal Republicanism'. In late 1976 she left the party to found the Irish Socialist Party in February 1977. Costello was assassinated in Dublin in October 1977.

Loyal Citizens of Ulster (LCU)
The LCU emerged in Northern Ireland in 1968 under the leadership of Ronald Bunting, a former British Army Officer. He taught mathematics at Belfast College of Technology and was a member of the Ulster Protestant Volunteers in East Belfast. LCU membership was largely drawn from the Volunteers and had no formal structure of its own. Bunting was an eccentric figure, organizing, among other bodies, the Knights of Freedom. He was a close associate of Ian Paisley. Together they organized counter-demonstrations against the Civil Rights marchers in 1968. He was sentenced in 1969 to three months in jail, together with Paisley, for organizing an unlawful assembly in Armagh.

Loyalist Association of Workers (LAW)
Billy Hull of Belfast, then 60 years old, was behind the setting up of LAW in 1971. The organization drew support from the industrial workers employed at Harland & Wolff's shipyards, Short's military engineering plant, Mackie's foundry and Gallagher's tobacco factory. That year LAW was able to rally as many as 25,000 workers to an open-air loyalist meeting.

Most LAW supporters gave their political sympathy in 1972 to William Craig's Vanguard party, a new umbrella movement for traditional loyalist groups. By 1974 nothing remained of Billy Hull's organization, which suffered from poor leadership and was discredited following cases of embezzlement.

Yet the power of Protestant industrial workers was only too clearly displayed in the 1974 general strike, which was called by the Ulster Workers' Council (UWC) and on which several LAW members sat.

Northern Ireland Civil Rights Organization (NICRA)
NICRA is the Irish manifestation of the civil rights movement. It has been penetrated by the Communist Party and the Official IRA, the latter using it on occasions as a front organization. It is poorly organized, financially weak and no longer effective in street politics.

People's Democracy (PD)
In Ireland, as in other countries of Europe, 1968 was the year of student revolution, and it was among students of Queen's University, Belfast, that the People's Democracy was born in October. In January 1969 PD staged a Civil Rights march against the inequities practised by the Protestant establishment of Northern Ireland on the Roman Catholic minority. Members infiltrated the Northern Ireland Civil Rights Association (NICRA), which had initiated the 1968–69 marches, and exploited grievances so as to foment disorder and violence in the guise of supporting a non-violent movement. By this time it had fallen rapidly under the influence of the Trotskyist Young Socialist Alliance, which broadened PD's original Irish Perspective to embrace world revolution. Thenceforth it existed as a revolutionary splinter group, sympathetic to the Provisional Sinn Fein and to the Irish Republican Socialist Party, with whom PD toured Europe on behalf of the Irish Republican cause in 1975.

Protestant Action Force (PAF)
In the mid 1970s, when it was active as a sectarian murder gang, the PAF drew its members from the Ulster Volunteer Force. It chose its first victim from Belfast, but later carried out sectarian murders in Armagh and East Tyrone. With the flare-up of violence

in mid 1982 the group surfaced again, murdering a Sinn Fein election worker, Joseph Corrigan in October.

Provisional Irish Republican Army (PIRA)

The IRA split in December 1969 into Provisional and Official wings, the latter being Marxist–Leninist and sympathetic to the Soviet Union. Conscious that the Officials were putting ideology before nationalism, the Provisionals decided to go their own way. They were led by John Stephenson (Sean MacStiofáin), Rory O'Brady (Ruairi O' Bradaigh), Leo Martin, Billy McKee, Seamus Twomey and Francis Card (Prionnsias MacAiart), who together formed the Provisional Army Council.

PIRA's goal in the 1970s was to unite the North with the South into a 32-county island of Ireland, which would be republican and socialist. Adopting a non-aligned posture, the 'New Ireland' would neither form part of the European Economic Community, nor would it belong to NATO. PIRA advocated the nationalization of key industries and severe limitations on foreign investments, largely, it appeared for nationalistic reasons. The political programme was put across by PIRA's political front – the Provisional Sinn Fein (Ourselves Alone), which published a newspaper, *An Phlobacht*.

PIRA is a revolutionary organization, in that its members believe that 'a revolutionary movement does not depend on a popular mandate as a basis for action. Its mandate comes from the justice and correctness of its cause . . .'

The tactics employed by PIRA have included petrol and nail bombs in the early days, car bombs – from a few pounds of explosives to more than 1,000 pounds – left outside public buildings, incendiary devices in shops and department stores, letter bombs, assassination, kneecapping, and tarring and feathering. Snipers have picked off individual soldiers, mortars have been employed on specific targets like barracks and airports, while delayed-action explosive devices and booby traps have stretched the ingenuity of the Security Forces. In assassinating Earl Mountbatten of Burma in 1979 and narrowly failing to murder the Prime Minister in Brighton in 1984, PIRA reached out and struck at the highest in the land.

Most of the Provisionals' modern arms come from the USA and include the Armalite, the M1 carbine, the Garand rifle and latterly (1978) the M-60 machine-gun. Little was done in the early 1970s to stop this traffic, but security was tighter from 1975 onwards. Apart from the USA, three consignments have been intercepted: from Czechoslovakia in 1971, from Libya in 1973 and from the Palestine Liberation Organization (PLO) in 1977.

Outside Northern Ireland, PIRA has been active in England. The first bombs exploded in London and Birmingham in 1973. Others followed in 1974, when a coach carrying soldiers and their families was blown up, killing twelve people. Targets that year included Heathrow Airport, the National Defence College, Westminster Hall, the Tower of London, and three public houses known to be frequented by servicemen off duty. The worst act was a revenge bombing in Birmingham in November, when 21 people were killed and 180 injured in two blasts.

With bomb attacks on a local pub in Caterham, Surrey, and explosions at the Hilton Hotel in Park Lane and in three London restaurants, 1975 was no quieter. As he opened his front door, the writer, Ross McWhirter, was shot dead, and a car bomb killed a renowned cancer specialist in Kensington. When four Provisionals surrendered to police after the six-day Balcomb Street siege, the London terror ended. There have been further bombing campaigns since then including the Regent's Park, Hyde Park and Harrods outrages.

Today PIRA is variously estimated to have about 400 active adherents. This number is considerably less than, possibly half, the number of activists operating in the early 1970s. PIRA, though smaller, is still an effective terrorist organization.

Red Hand Commandos

After being forced out of the Ulster Defence Association, John McKeague set up this paramilitary clandestine group in Belfast in mid 1972. It consisted of the uglier elements of Society. McKeague was shot dead in January 1982, reputedly by militants from the Irish National Liberation Army.

Saor Eire

Saor Eire is an extremist organization of about 50 members, mainly criminals. Their activities in the main have been bank robberies and wage snatches motivated as much for personal gain as for political idealism. The group has operated in the North, but has not posed a serious threat. Although there have been claims that this organization has been involved in bombing outrages in Britain there has been no definite evidence to support this.

Shankill Defence Association (SDA)

Established in 1969, the SDA was largely the creation of its chairman, John McKeague (shot dead 1982), and his deputy, Fred Proctor. Originally a community association, the new SDA in Wilton Street, Belfast, became a Protestant armed vigilante group in one of the city's toughest areas. It soon boasted a thousand members, who patrolled the upper Shankill. Members wore arm bands and crash-helmets and carried cudgels, using them to intimidate isolated Catholic families, so as to force them to move from a predominately Protestant area to a Catholic one, and to encourage Protestants to leave predominately Catholic communities.

The worst rioting where SDA men were involved took place in front of Unity Flats, a Catholic complex, near Shankill road, on 2 August 1969. Police battled with a crowd several thousand strong, under McKeague's direction. Shops were looted, cars burned, windows broken, and a police water cannon was attacked with petrol bombs and gelignite. The fighting lasted until the early hours, when fires were eventually quenched. Some 70 policemen and 200 civilians were injured. The incident put the SDA beyond the political pale; thenceforth the Reverend Ian Paisley, who came to symbolize loyalist politics, dissociated himself from the movement.

Undoubtedly, many SDA members were also members of the Ulster Volunteer Force (UVF). Wearing anoraks and hoods and in defiance of the Army, vigilantes threw up barricades in the summer of 1969.

In response to increasingly ugly SDA terror tactics, the Provisional IRA was born that year in the Clonard District of Belfast. Under SDA auspices gun clubs were formed in the Shankill, Oldpark, Crumlin and Glencairn areas of Belfast. But the armed potential of the SDA was never realized: the movement was overtaken by the Provisionals' armed offensive against the British Army. In this encounter the militant loyalists took a ringside seat only.

As an organization, the SDA broke up in factional quarrelling; McKeague himself was prosecuted unsuccessfully in 1971 for inciting racial hatred in a Loyalist Song Book. Most of its members joined either the UDA or UVF.

Sinn Fein (Ourselves Alone)

Sinn Fein was the original Irish nationalist party, founded in 1905, when all Ireland was still British. The party won overwhelming support in the elections of 1918 (73 out of 105 seats), but the elected MPs, instead of attending at Westminster, convened a revolutionary parliament in Ireland, the Dail Eireann. Their stand was supported by armed militants who, from mid 1919 until the truce in July 1921, attacked the British administration, earning for themselves the title of Irish Republican Army (IRA).

Some members of Sinn Fein accepted the partition of Ireland in 1921, others did not, so that a civil war was fought between June 1922 and May 1923. Those who lost became today's Sinn Fein, a nationalist party dedicated to reuniting Ireland. Their armed branch was the IRA, but whereas today the IRA is illegal in both Northern Ireland and the Republic, Sinn Fein is not. Their aims are identical, but their methods differ, although in fact members of the one are often members of the other.

When in 1969 the IRA split into a Provisional and an Official wing, Sinn Fein split too. The Provisional Sinn Fein organized itself with regional committees and local branches covering all 32 counties of Ireland. It took no part in any of the elections held in the North, urging a general boycott. In the Republic too it abstained from general elections, largely because of the party's minimal following. The principal personalities include Rory O'Brady, Provisional Sinn Fein President, Seamus Twomey and Martin McGuiness.

Since 1980 Sinn Fein has enjoyed some political success. Gerry Adams, MP, is the most obvious example of this.

The Official Sinn Fein is led by Thomas MacGiolla in the Republic and Seamus Lynch in the North, where the party operates through the Republican clubs, which became an integral part of a new Official party, known as Sinn Fein the Workers' Party (1977). By this time the Officials had renounced all links with paramilitary or terrorist organizations, and in 1979, so as to avoid further confusion with Provisional Sinn Fein, they dropped 'Sinn Fein' from the title. Thereafter it was known simply as the Workers' Party, leaving the provisionals' political front to contest the Northern Ireland Assembly Elections as Sinn Fein.

Troops Out Movement (TOM)

TOM was formed in September 1973 to lobby the Trades Union movement into supporting the withdrawal of British Troops from Northern Ireland. Trotskyists soon penetrated the group, a development which led ultimately to a split in mid 1977 and the creation of United Troops Out Movement (UTOM). TOM ceased to exist; UTOM, although Trotskyist, drew close to the Provisional Sinn Fein. Most of its supporters were drawn from the International Marxist Group (IMG) and the Socialist Workers' Party (SWP).

Ulster Defence Association (UDA)

The UDA was formed in 1971 to group the various Protestant defence associations in Belfast, particularly the Shankhill, Woodvale, Ormeau, Carrick, Donnegall Pass, Hammer, Newtownabbey, Abbots Cross, Woodburn, Lisburn Road, Seymour Hill, Suffolk, Castlereagh, Beersbridge, Upper Woodstock and Dundonald areas. The initiative was taken by Charles Harding-Smith. Members were to call themselves Ulster Volunteers, and to publish a UDA Bulletin.

From the start the UDA was faction-ridden, with the principal contestants being John McKeague, with his base at Shankhill, and Harding-Smith, strongly supported in Woodvale. In 1972, with the formation of William Craig's Vanguard Party, the UDA virtually became its paramilitary wing.

Harding-Smith, spent most of 1972 in prison, accused of negotiating an illegal purchase of arms. He was acquitted, however, and in January 1973 was reinstated as joint-chairman of an organization that had grown to 60,000 strong. Within months he was back in custody, and a glazier, Jim Anderson, then 42 years old, took over the UDA. He reorganized the UDA along military lines; on that council sat the commander of the UDA.

It was the UDA which manned the Protestant barricades of 1972, wearing their combat jackets and hoods. They aped the IRA purposefully, even to copying the Provisionals' funeral ceremony. Like the UVF, members were drawn from the Protestant urban working classes.

Afterwards the UDA took to making up explosives in Belfast and bombing south of the border. These explosions continued intermittently throughout the mid 70s; the bombs were often placed in hotels and known meeting-places of the IRA. Sometimes these actions were claimed by the Ulster Freedom Fighters, an off-shoot of the UDA.

In 1974, the UDA opposed the political reform based upon power-sharing, and took part that year in the general strike, which the Ulster Workers' Council co-ordinated. Consequently, the British Government resumed direct rule of the Province, and abandoned its attempts to set up a new Assembly to replace the old Stormont Parliament. The UDA maintained its place throughout the decade as the most important Protestant paramilitary group in Ulster. It also has strong links with Scotland, whence it derives support. It has not shrunk from murder for which several members have been tried, found guilty and sentenced. Most acts of violence by its members are claimed in the name of the UFF or the Young Militants – both 'flags of convenience' for the UDA Active Service Units.

Ulster Freedom Fighters (UFF)
The UFF emerged in the summer of 1973 from the Ulster Defence Association in Northern Ireland. It was a militant paramilitary Protestant organization, loosely composed of violent firebrands anxious to take the law into their own hands, more for kicks than through fear of the Provisional IRA. Members carried out assassinations across the political divide, and may have numbered several dozen hard-core members. Sporadic activity continued throughout the decade and into the 1980s. UFF activities were a constant reminder of the terrorism which might surface with a vengeance were the British Army to withdraw from Ulster. In March 1984 the UFF attempted to murder Gerry Adams, MP.

Ulster Protestant Volunteers (UPV)
Set up in early 1966 by Noel Doherty, the UPV was quickly submerged in the Ulster Constitution Defence Committee (UCDC), which formed the political nucleus of Ian Paisley's Democratic Unionist Party. Doherty was Paisley's political organizer in the early days, responsible for producing his propaganda at the Puritan Printing Company in Ravenhill Road, opposite Paisley's Free Presbyterian Church, which he had joined in 1956. He became a Protestant Unionist Candidate at the age of 23, and was a member of the B Specials. The UPV adopted as their own, the motto of the proscribed Ulster Volunteer Force (UVF), 'For God and Ulster'.

The UCDC was defined as the 'governing body' of the UPV, for which only 'born Protestants' were eligible. Following the descent into bloody violence by the UVF, the link was broken by Paisley himself in June 1966. He and the vice-chairman of the UCDC, James McConnell, summarily expelled Doherty from the movement he had helped found.

But with divisions all over the province, the UPV continued to exist, and was closely involved in the demonstrations against the 1968 Civil Rights marches. Among the organizers were Douglas Hutchinson, Frank Mallon, John McKeague and Major Ronald Bunting. The UPV remained a legal organization after the UVF had been proscribed in 1966, and was used as a front by UVF sympathisers.

Ulster Volunteer Force (UVF)
Throughout the decade of the 1970s, the UVF was a force of militant Protestant loyalists, whose origins went back to 1912 when, from manpower supplied by Orange lodges, Edward Carson founded the UVF which in 1929 became the Ulster Special Constabulary. In 1966 Augustus Spence set up the present organization, which within weeks was proscribed under the Special Powers Act by the Northern Irish Government at Stormont.

Spence defined the UVF as a 'military body dedicated to upholding the constitution of Ulster by force of arms if necessary'. At its height in Belfast in the late 1960s and early 1970s, it probably claimed the allegiance of 500 members, who financed their activities largely through protection rackets.

'Gusty' Spence came from the notorious lower Shankill area of Belfast, of tough Protestant working-class antecedents. He had served in the British Army as a military policeman in Cyprus, and in 1966 was 33 years old. Together with Ian Paisley and Noel Doherty, he reconstituted the UVF in March 1966 at the time of the foundation of Paisley's fortnightly *Protestant Telegraph*, printed by Doherty's new Puritan Printing Company. He was a member of the Apprentice Boys and of the Royal Black Preceptory, both arch-Orange organizations.

The first recorded UVF action took place on 16 April 1966, when bullets were fired at the door of Unionist MP, John McQuade, in the Shankill area. Further UVF petrol bomb attacks took place in March, April and May.

On 21 May 1966, the UVF declared war against the IRA. 'Known IRA men will be executed mercilessly and without hesitation. Less extreme measures will be taken against anyone sheltering or helping them, but if they persist in giving them aid more extreme measures will be adopted. Property will not be exempted in any action taken.' The first UVF murder occurred on 26 May, when John Scullion was shot on his way home from a pub. A second murder attempt followed on 4 June.

On 25 June, Spence was involved with two other men in the cold-blooded murder of a Catholic barman in Belfast. Within hours he was arrested and later convicted and sentenced to life imprisonment. Paisley denied all contact with the UVF, and steered well clear of political violence. But the Ulster Constitution Defence Committee (UCDC), of which Paisley was chairman, remained tainted by the early association.

With Spence in Crumlin Road jail, the UVF fell apart in 1967. But in 1969 a series of blasts, which damaged an electricity pylon and the control valves and supply pipes of Belfast's water supply, saw the re-emergence of the UVF as a sabotage unit.

Thenceforth the potential membership of the UVF was more important than its actions. The spirit which had led to its formation was channelled in 1971 into the Ulster Defence Association, although the UVF still operated as an independent organization in 1972, helping to establish a Protestant 'No-Go' area in Londonderry that June.

When 'Gusty' Spence was briefly released on parole that year, he was kidnapped by his well-wishers and hidden from the police for some months. The UVF enjoyed a revival, with members adopting a uniform of black berets and leather jackets. A number were arrested and stood trial, but refused to recognize the court. To a man the UVF remained a working-class organization, and without intellectual or middle-class political leadership. With Spence in jail, Kenneth Gibson became the leading personality.

The most savage killings took place in the autumn of 1974, after the murder of a judge and a magistrate in Belfast by teenage Provisional gunmen. Within a month, sixteen Catholics had been shot dead in the city. Subsequently, UVF gunmen also settled personal scores with the rival Protestant Ulster Freedom Fighters.

There was little Protestant violence after 1976, when the UVF suspended 'military activity' in May. Eight men belonging to the UVF were sentenced to life imprisonment for murder in March 1977, and 23 others were convicted of attempted murder, armed robberies, bombing and illegal possession of arms. Further convictions followed in 1978, when one UVF member was sentenced to life imprisonment sixteen times over, and in 1979, when the 'Shankill butchers' (eleven men) were given a total of 42 life sentences for nineteen killings.

Ulster Workers' Council (UWC)

The UWC emerged in Belfast in 1973 on the same lines as the Loyalist Association of Workers, which it replaced. By 1974 the UWC covered the whole province, so that each of its seven sections held regular meetings and elected three deputies to the 21-man council. Most prominent was Glen Barr, then 31, a former shop-steward and a Vanguard Assembly member for Londonderry.

The UWC concentrated upon recruiting key workers in key industries, a policy which gave it the power in 1974 to shut down all activity in Ulster, and thus compel London to abandon its political reform programme. The elected leaders of the Trades Union movement condemned the strike which the UWC called in May, but, undeterred, workers brought the province to a standstill.

The UWC ran the strike with a 15-man co-ordinating committee. Barricades of vehicles stopped public transport. Commerce ceased, with banks and offices closed. The strike committee authorized chemists to stay open; food could be sold in the mornings. Volunteers manned advice centres, and pensioners received free candles, tea and butter. Streets were swept and rubbish regularly collected; order reigned throughout. Outside Belfast, farmers co-operated by bringing in supplies of milk, butter, eggs and fuel.

The unanimity displayed brought about the resignation of Brian Faulkner's power-sharing Executive, and the collapse of Westminster's attempt to reform Ulster's political system. London assumed responsibility for government in the province, and immediately the UWC called off the strike.

Appendix IV
TWELVE HOURS IN THE LIFE OF A GUNNER REGIMENT

081800–090600 hrs Aug 74

On the 8th August 1974, 4th Light Regiment RA (reinforced by T (Shah Sujah's Troop) and a troop from 9 (Plassey) Battery, both from 12th Light Air Defence Regiment RA) was nearly halfway through its second tour in Northern Ireland. The hub of its area this time was the hard Republican New Lodge district of Belfast. Two soldiers, Sgt Bernard Fearns and Gnr Kim MacCunn, had been killed in separate shooting incidents in the New Lodge earlier in the tour; 4 am on the 9th of August was the third anniversary of the start of internment.

The twelve hours started peacefully enough with a local band playing round the area while children built bonfires for the night's celebrations. Supporters, mostly women and children, many carrying placards with the names of internees or convicted criminals, gathered together, followed the band for a little while and then, led by six children carrying dustbin lids, marched to North Queen Street Police Station, where the regiment's headquarters was co-located. Speeches concerned with opposition to internment, the RUC and the Army were made. At 8.45 pm the marchers dispersed and the bonfires were lit.

At 9.35 pm in the so called Republican 'Little America' area north of the New Lodge, a youth threw a petrol bomb into a car and the Fire Brigade was called to the scene. Two Landrovers which were nearby drove there at once to provide cover. As the soldiers began to cordon the area, a gunman concealed in a garden hedge shot at them, and one bullet, ricochetting off the road, struck LBdr John Dolphin in the leg. Using tracker dogs an immediate search for the gunman was made but proved fruitless.

Street lights are never lit in the New Lodge, and, as dusk fell, only the flames of the bonfires lit up the dingy streets.

Scattered throughout the area were a network of army observation posts. Some were permanent, solidly built structures sited on top of the high rise flats or in shops (including a disused funeral parlour); others were in temporary positions concealed in waste ground or in occupied or derelict houses.

The next shootings were at 10.20 pm in the heart of the Lodge but the site and the target were never found. Childen were on the streets, round the bonfires, and at half past eleven a stranger was seen organising a group of about 30 boys into groups of seven, each of which was sent off in a different direction.

The first gunman was seen just before midnight. He was wearing a mask, carrying a rifle and, escorted by two youths, ran through the centre of the Lodge. He was seen by three of the OPs but he was moving too fast for an effective shot to be fired at him.

The light from the bonfires was by now increased by flames from two shops and the Post Office, set on fire by petrol bombs. An effigy was also burnt at one of the bonfires, which was reported by a certain BC[1] to be that of the Commanding Officer!

The 9th of August opened with the discovery of the body of a man in a street to the north of New Lodge. He had five bullets in the head.

At about half past midnight in a dark street two soldiers hidden upstairs in a derelict house glimpsed their second gunman of the evening. Their observation was through a crack in a sheet of corrugated tin which offered only a very narrow arc of fire. The sentry had to engage the terrorist by firing sharply downwards through the tin, a difficult shot which missed. The gunmen, for there were three of them, had evidently been setting an ambush for a foot patrol. They all opened up on the house from their three separate

[1] Battery Commander

directions. The sound of the first shots brought a foot patrol to the corner, a hundred yards away, in time to see the last of the flashes from the fusillade. The patrol fired from the south end of the street at the flashes while another hidden OP did the same from the north. For 30 minutes the patrol searched the back alleys with the aid of a searchlight mounted on a helicopter, but found nothing; as usual the gunmen had shot and run.

Along the north edge of the New Lodge runs Duncairn Gardens, more popularly known as 'the Buffer' as it forms the interface with the Loyalist Tiger Bay area. Shooting had started here at half past midnight when a gunman fired a sub machine gun at a foot patrol. Fire was returned but the patrol did not have enough evidence to report any hits.

After these incidents it took the gunmen two hours to work out their next move. Having detected a patrol lying up north of the Buffer on Hallidays Road, near the biggest bonfire, they momentarily increased the light level by adding petrol bombs to the fire. Their single round was returned by the soldiers which, as the gunman was seen to fall, produced our first reported hit of the night. Another hour passed, another shot was fired at an OP, fire was returned, and four o'clock was almost with us.

Just before 4 am a rifleman fired up Edlingham Street at an OP placed near the spot where Sergeant Fearns had been murdered two weeks before. The Sergeant on duty fired back. Soon afterwards, one street further west, a foot patrol on the Buffer fired at a gunman running into the New Lodge and again, 15 minutes later, as he ran back. The second time he was seen to stagger and clutch his leg – 'one hit reported', bringing the night's total to three. The gunman having failed, his friends came out on the street, broke up paving stones and started bottling and stoning the patrols. Firm action by the soldiers was all that was necessary to sent this gang packing.

The banging of dustbin lids on the pavement and the blowing of whistles were the signals used in 1971 to report the arrival of the Army to arrest the terrorist suspects; in 1974 the symbolism was repeated and was kept up continuously. The din was enlivened by the sound of 17 separate shootings in the next hour. Half of these involved the Funeral Parlour OP, manned by a Sergeant and five soldiers. The Sergeant reports: 'At approximately 0400 hrs the sound of dustbin lids being banged, seemed to be the signal for the fun to start. Remembering the shooting we had earlier in the evening, and the tensions which now seemed to be building up in the Lodge, I decided to stand-to the OP. The first shots directed at us came from Stratheden Street, three rounds probably a pistol. We did not return fire. Five minutes later three rounds were fired at us from Phoenix Alley, and we opened fire. The next contact came from the alley in Donore Place and again three rounds were fired at us. This I think was an M1 carbine, and again we fired back. At about the same time a gunman with a high velocity weapon opened fire with four or five rounds from Singleton Street and again fire was returned. There was then a slight lull in the battle as far as we were concerned, although shooting was still going on elsewhere. Battle recommenced with the slow rattle of a Thompson. We had a good laugh at this because the gunman jumped out from Hartwell Street and fired a quick burst obviously directed as us. Sadly for him he had overlooked the large van parked between us and him and all he succeeded in doing was to fill the van full of holes. (Next day we counted 17 holes in the front of this vehicle, and a shattered windscreen). This man, unfortunately for him, was a tryer because again he came back, this time up Shandon Street and fired another burst at the Parlour. This was the only time during the night that we were able to fire at a seen target, rather than flashes, and he was seen to fall. Things then got hot for a few minutes when we were fired at by three gunmen simultaneously, but all three targets were engaged. I had sent one man to our little kitchen for the last ten minutes to make tea and sandwiches so light refreshments were served at the firing line. For the next half an hour we just had the cowboy firing the odd shots from a pistol, until at around 0500 hrs with a final volley of shots from the alleyway behind Lynch's bar the gunman called it a day. After the shooting had died away, the crowds began to come back onto the streets and at approximately 0545 hrs we were subjected to a hail of bottles, bricks and verbal abuse from a crowd of 50–60, mostly young lads.'

While all this was going on, back at the Police Station a rather different crowd from that of the evening before had assembled. This time a concerted attack was made, under cover of a hail of bottles and stones, to break through the compound walls. Considerable damage was done and a subaltern required four stitches when he was struck on the forehead by a brick. Six baton rounds had to be fired before the attack was repelled.

Further south, the sangar in Unity Flats was also under attack. Here the weapons used were petrol bombs, but the choice was poor and the 16 which were thrown had no effect. A blast bomb was placed against the external wall of the sangar and the resultant explosion, which was heard all round the regiment's area, caused a sizeable crater. Two women living nearby were taken to hospital, but the sangar's imperturbable inmates were entirely unaffected. Just before dawn, some Catholic youths broke through the locked gate in the wire fence separating Unity from the Lower Shankill and began throwing stones at the Protestant Flats. They were soon driven off by our patrols, leaving behind them only four broken windows as evidence of their abortive foray.

The first scene in the final act took place at 'the stumps' which is an alleyway towards the east end of the Buffer. There had been two shootings here earlier in the tour, in one of which a Protestant boy had been killed. Just after 4.30 am, gunmen in the attics of houses on the New Lodge side of the Buffer opened fire on a foot patrol. The patrol twice tried to cross Duncairn Gardens and each time was driven back by terrorist fire. A private gun battle developed in which about 20 shots from the gunmen were answered by fire from the soldiers before the former withdrew.

By 5 am the gunmen were losing heart, and, in a last attempt to have something to show for the night's work, fired a dozen rounds from three street corners at an OP on the top of the high rise flats. Their range was nearly 200 metres and the rounds were nowhere near the target. A single round returned was enough to send them running and bring the proceedings to an end just after 5 o'clock.

The follow-up action to incidents is always time consuming, tedious and often unproductive. On this occasion it produced an M1 Carbine loaded with 15 rounds apparently disposed of hurriedly in a back garden.

During the night we had confirmation that at least one of the gunmen was hit – he was seen being half-dragged, half-carried by three women and his chest and abdomen were covered in blood.

LBdr Smith is recovering well in hospital where his pride and joy is a get-well card signed by the whole Aston Villa football team. By the time you read this he will be back on duty, and his account of the 'Night of the Long Knives' will be growing taller by the minute.

Appendix V
OPERATION 'VEHEMENT', SOUTH ARMAGH
by Major A. R. D. Pringle, 1 RGJ

Operation Vehement was a protracted operation, conducted by Support Company 1 RGJ in the Camlough area of South Armagh in June 1981.

This account of Operation Vehement starts with the fortuitous discovery of a command wire and finishes, some fifteen months later, in the Crown Court in Crumlin Road, Belfast, with the conviction and sentencing of five bombers.

I returned from R and R[1] on the evening of Tuesday 9th June 1981, to be met by my Company Sergeant-Major, CSM Condon, with the news that we had just received information via the RUC, that there was thought to be a suspect command wire on the Quarter Road about a mile North of Camlough. Before a plan could be made we had to have confirmation. Late that night, past midnight, I took the Sergeant-Major, Rfn Love, my signaller, and two search-trained buglers, Cpl Evans and Rfn Sanderson, to recce the area; Evans and Sanderson were armed with equipment to help us detect buried wires in the dark. We knew where the wire was thought to be, and we knew the area. We had already worked out where the likely firing point would be, and it was to this point that we headed. We arrived in the area at about 0230 in the morning. The searchers set to work whilst Love and I approached the road to where we thought the bomb might be. First light was just appearing. There was not much time if our presence was not to be noticed. It all happened at once. Love and I got to about 15 metres from the road when I noticed a white plastic sack propped up against the road embankment in the field we were in on the other side of a small stream. The bag was held in place by a stick and there were signs of digging in the embankment. We thought this must either be a marker, or the bomb itself. We retraced out steps back up the hill to the corner of the field where we had left the searchers and the Sergeant-Major. They had found the wire and the firing point. The wire ran along a hedgerow down the field towards the road. The firing point was a hole in the hedge, covered on top and hidden by a dead bush which had been pulled in front of it. The wire, cut into the turf, ran directly to the firing point. From the firing point the white plastic bag on the road embankment was clearly visible.

There was no doubt in my mind that we had confirmed the presence of a command wire bomb. By now it was light and we had to quickly get clear of the area if our discovery was not to be compromised. We returned to Bessbrook well pleased with the night's work.

The Quarter Road had been placed out of bounds to ourselves and the RUC so there was no danger of anyone becoming the victim of another culvert bomb. The problem was; how to catch the bomber. After breakfast I devised Op Vehement. The plan was to insert two mutually supporting OPs covering the firing point and then to attempt to lure the bomber to his bomb, by providing a tempting target. This we were going to achieve by deploying RUC patrols in Camlough during the day. These RUC vehicles often returned to Bessbrook via the Quarter Road from Camlough. Their presence in Camlough, we hoped, would provide the trigger required to attract the bomber to his bomb. Having attracted the bomber the plan was to allow him to get really comfortable in his firing point, all the while taking photographs. There was to be no question of the bomber claiming he was out bird-watching! Meanwhile the reaction force would mount in a Scout and a Wessex. The Scout, stripped down, was to carry a four-man patrol together with a war dog and handler. The war dog was a 110 lb Alsatian with huge teeth! The Scout would land immediately in rear of the firing point. If the bomber fled towards

---

[1] Rest and Recuperation.

the road, depending on circumstances, he would either be shot, or the OPs would cut him off, in the unlikely event of the war dog not having brought him to ground! The Wessex, carrying a further three four-man patrols, was to land one field to the East of the firing point, thus completing the encirclement. In theory, the first the bomber would have known was when the helicopters suddenly arrived around his position. The helicopters would then return and fly out an outer cordon on all road escape routes. That was the theory anyway, but like all the best-laid plans what actually happened was somewhat different!

Shortly before midnight on Wednesday 10th June I led the same patrol, but without the Sergeant-Major, back to the firing point. A member of the Surveillance Section accompanied us. We were to take him to the firing point, whereupon he would insert unattended ground sensors (UGS) at the position and on its approaches. This was accomplished successfully and tested. We returned to Bessbrook. Meanwhile, the Company Sergeant-Major led two four-man patrols on a circuitous route round Bessbrook to approach the selected OP positions from the West. They also carried one of the "other ends" of the UGS[1] inserted. By 0400 the two OPs were in position. The forward OP, led by the Sergeant-Major and consisting of Cpl Butcher (photographer), Rfn Loftus (machine gunner) and Rfn Rowland (sniper), buried themselves in a clump of gorse only 25 metres from the Quarter Road and directly opposite the firing point. The second OP, led by L/Cpl Sanders, found a position to their rear.

Throughout the day of Thursday 11th June RUC patrols were active in the Camlough area. The UGS never stopped alarming and had to be discounted! I was beginning to wonder whether the plan would work. Maybe the bomber was away for the day. Maybe it might work tomorrow. The reaction force was all briefed and ready to go. We were not sitting in the helicopters because we couldn't tie down the only helicopters we had; and because we anticipated getting warning from the OP that the bomber had arrived. They were going to give us a coded running commentary, and then when all was ready the reaction would be sprung. "Bingo" was the codeword for the helicopter reaction force, and this I anticipated sending the Sergeant-Major once he had confirmed the presence of our target.

At 2020 hrs, still daylight, just as I was sitting down to dinner, the telephone rang in the Mess. Men with machine guns, M79s, radios and rifles were sprinting for the helipad. Thanks to the air cell, run by Ken Gray, the rotors were already turning by the time we arrived. Bear, the war dog, was literally hanging out of the Scout. Miraculously, by the time the helicopters were ready to take off we were all aboard. Away we went, flying low and fast. The pilots were to approach from two directions and arrive simultaneously. I could hear them chatting to each other over the headphones. Ten seconds, nine, eight . . . we landed. The patrols sprinted for their cut-off positions. We saw the Scout land one field away just behind the firing point. I imagined Bear leaping the fence and rushing for the unfortunate's throat. I called the Sergeant-Major on the radio and told him to direct us on to the suspects. Two men were apprehended on the Quarter Road. There was no one at the firing point. There was no one in the adjacent field. I wondered what on earth had happened. Several suspects were arrested and taken back to Bessbrook. Meanwhile I met up with the Sergeant-Major who explained what had occurred.

The move into position had gone according to plan. They had not been detected and were in position by 0430 hrs. They were about 25 metres from the road, looking directly up towards the firing point which was about 125 metres away. At 1815 hrs that evening a farmer entered the field they were in to tend some cattle; at one stage he approached a cow that was actually eating the gorse in which their OP was concealed. They remained undetected. At 2015 hrs they heard voices coming from behind them. Two men passed close to their position, heading for the firing point. Shortly afterwards a third man appeared from behind them. The leading two turned and shouted to him to hurry up. He ran past their position. The men walked up to the firing point where they were met by another two men who approached from the opposite direction. What the Sergeant-Major thought he was seeing was the initial ground clearance and hedge beating that would

---

[1] Unattended Ground Sensors.

precede the arrival of the bomber. Cpl Butcher started to take photographs. He was equipped with a camera with a high-powered telescopic lens. At one stage a helicopter flew overhead and all five men dashed for cover into the bushes. All this was recorded on film. At 2040 hrs, having beaten all the surrounding hedgerows, three of the men walked down the hill towards the road where the bomb was thought to be. The other two men had disappeared through the hedge. The three men disappeared out of sight into dead ground in front of the OP. One of the men then appeared standing on the bank of the road about 15 metres in front of the OP. He was obviously acting as look-out. He was so close that Cpl Butcher could not take any photographs for fear of him hearing the camera mechanism. Whenever a car came down the road he would shout at the other two men and then hide behind the bank of the road. Rfn Loftus, who was observing through a Swiftscope, suddenly exclaimed that two men were pulling up the command wire. At this stage the lookout was still only 15 metres away and the OP could neither take photographs nor use their radio. As the men pulling up the wire backed up towards the firing point, the look-out left the road to rejoin them. Cpl Butcher again started to take photographs and the Sergeant-Major called "Bingo" over the radio. The three men collected up the wire, stowed it away in a plastic bag and departed through the hedge in the opposite direction from the OP. Shortly after this the helicopter reaction force arrived on the ground.

What had actually happened could not have been further from that which we had expected. We had expected a bomber to come to his bomb. What we witnessed was a party of five men taking in the command wire. None was armed.

Having met up with the Sergeant-Major's party, the area was thoroughly checked. The OP parties, soaked to the skin, returned to Bessbrook. Cpl Butcher developed his photographs. WO2 Lucas, my Company Intelligence SNCO, attended to the detailed "continuity of evidence" requirements. I prayed the pictures would come out! In clearing the area I confirmed that the whole command wire appeared to be removed, and noticed that the bank where the plastic bag had been beside the road appeared to have collapsed. Whether the bomb was there or not was not clear. A cordon remained in position that night for the EOD clearance that would be required the following morning. Meanwhile, Cpl Butcher developed his film. The photographs taken at 125 metre range showed all five men quite clearly. Some we knew. Some we didn't. Those we didn't know the RUC did! Success. The RUC decided that before they were arrested, as much forensic evidence as possible should be recovered from the scene.

The next day, Friday 12th June, we carried out a full EOD clearance of the Quarter Road area. The bomb had gone! Clear imprints of the milk churns could be seen in the soil by the collapsed bank. A considerable amount of soil had been thrown in the stream. The cut in the turf where the command wire had been ran clearly from the position of the bomb, up the hedgerow to the firing point. Once the area had been cleared by ATO, swarms of RUC Scenes of Crime Officers, photographers and mappers arrived. Casts of footprints were taken, cigarette butts recovered and fibres collected. This took all day. Finally the area was cleared of every conceivable shred of potential evidence. That evening the simultaneous arrests of the five suspects were planned. Each man was to be arrested by a dedicated RUC team. They would then all be taken to Castlereagh by separate routes, arriving at separate times. None would know that all the others had also been arrested. A special interrogation team was assembled at Castlereagh. The house of each suspect was then to be searched by our search teams. All clothing remotely resembling that worn by the suspects, and recorded in the photographs, was to be collected together, bagged and taken away for forensic analysis.

At 0400 hrs on Saturday 13th June all five suspects were arrested at home. Their houses were searched according to plan. Police vehicles departed fully laden with plastic bags of clothing, boots, wire and miscellaneous potential evidence. One of the men arrested had been identified from an RUC photograph taken at a H block rally. This photograph had been incorrectly annotated as Lewis. At Castlereagh when Lewis was shown this photograph, he instantly identified the suspect, not as himself, but Jennings! At 0400 hrs on Sunday 14th June Jennings was arrested and the same procedure followed. Now we had all five men. It was now up to Castlereagh.

All day 14th and 15th June we searched the area for the command wire and explosives. They had to be somewhere close by. At 22.30 on the night of 15th June we received information from Castlereagh that the explosives might be hidden in a dung heap at Crilly's farm about 500 metres from the scene. Two OPs were inserted that night to ensure that if this was so, then no one was going to remove it! Early the next morning we started a search and EOD clearance of the farm surroundings. The OPs returned to Bessbrook for breakfast. The area was cordoned off and the Sapper Search Teams started work. The first deep probe into the dung heap indicated the presence of metal. Carefully the search team started to dig. The top of the first milk churn appeared. We had found it. Mr Mitchell, our ATO, had a field day. Churn after churn was removed from the dung heap and neutralised by ATO. As the clearance continued we received information from Castlereagh about exactly how many churns we could expect to find. We were told there would be seven milk churns and a beer keg. This was exactly right. Approximately 700 lbs of explosives were recovered from the dung heap, with sufficient cordtex to link all the churns together. The bomb was a similar size to the one that had earlier destroyed our patrol on the Chancellors Road, Newry, throwing pieces of Saracen 500 metres across the countryside. The clearance lasted all day. All forensic evidence was recovered.

All day on 17th and 18th June we continued our search for the command wire. At 1700 hrs on 18th June we received further information from Castlereagh. The command wire was hidden behind a barn about 800 metres from the original scene. We searched the area and found the command wire, detonating cord and detonator, initiation pack and bell push plus a test kit, all in a haversack. In a pipe there was a pair of black leather gloves. Later that night I received a call from Castlereagh saying that one of the suspects was to be brought to Bessbrook to point out a weapon hide. At 2300 hrs, hidden in a civilian van, we escorted a police vehicle to a spot about three miles from Camlough, on the hill above Camlough Reservoir. The suspect indicated where to stop. The marker was a prominent dead tree. He took ten paces up the road, and revealed in a ditch heavily overgrown with bracken, a classic pipe hide. Sadly it was empty, but had contained weapons a month before. I surmised that these may have been the weapons we recovered after the McCreesh funeral.

All day on 19th June, acting on information coming from Castlereagh, we searched the fields around the suspects' houses, and also the graveyard of Carrickcroppen Chapel where the hunger strike funeral had taken place. Nothing was found in the fields. Several hides were discovered in the graveyard and one live round was found in the hedgerow.

On the afternoon of 19th June 1981 we heard that all five men had been charged. The next phase of Operation Vehement was not to come for some fifteen months.

Having left South Armagh at the end of July 1981, the Battalion was to return to Ireland for a two-year resident tour in November the same year. We were to be based at Aldergrove. It is now September 1982. Meanwhile, since June 1981, the five Camlough bombers have been residing on remand at Her Majesty's pleasure. On Monday 20th September 1982 they were brought to trial at the Crown Court, Belfast, opposite Crumlin Road Prison. The court house has just been renovated and repainted – orange! Military witnesses called for the case were Rfn Love, Cpl Evans, Rfn Sanderson, WO2 Condon, Cpl Butcher, Rfn Loftus, WO2 Lucas, WO1 Mitchell and myself. The trial lasted for ten days. As Support Company was based at Girdwood Park for a month it was easy for me to get to court each day. Girdwood Park adjoins the prison to the North. The court house is opposite the prison to the South. To watch the "due process of law" unravelling was an education. The five bombers were in the dock; short-haired, well-dressed and all wearing (obviously borrowed) ties. We knew they were guilty. Now the prosecution had to prove it!

The five accused were variously charged on six counts; one, conspiracy to murder; two, conspiracy to cause an explosion; three, possession of explosive substances with intent on 10th June; four, possession of explosive substances in suspicious circumstances on 10th June; five, possession of explosive substances with intent on 11th June; six, possession of explosive substances in suspicious circumstances on 11th June. Counts 3 and 4 related to the milk churns. Counts 5 and 6 related to the detonation pack.

The five accused appeared in the dock, having been brought direct from the Crumlin Road jail via the underground tunnel that links jail and court house. The court rose for the judge's entry. Judge Rowland was an ex-Punjabi, and had apparently been the last surviving officer in the Regiment at the Battle of Arakan. He looked the part, sitting under the Royal Coat of Arms resplendent in his purple and red robes, and wig. Through the four large windows above us could be seen the grey skies of Belfast and the ubiquitous helicopter hovering overhead. The inside of the court was painted a depressing grey and olive drab. The acoustics were abominable, the accents worse. The court exhibits were piled on a table, all produced in labelled plastic bags; that corner of the court resembled an auction room! A battery of microphones protruded from every desk and dock, so that the proceedings could be recorded. Prison Warders were lounging everywhere, caps on the back of their heads as usual. That is until the judge appeared! Armed policemen sat at every door, and in the public gallery. One could not help but think that the defendants looked exactly like the repressed "republicans" they claimed to be. About twenty supporters trooped in to the public gallery. Many we knew from Camlough, including inevitably the local "godfathers" who we knew well. The trial lasted ten working days spread over three weeks. I kept a day by day account of the proceedings, of which the following is an abbreviated version.

DAY 1
Counsel for the prosecution opened the case by outlining the evidence against the defendants; Lynch (20), Jennings (19), Graham (20), Declan Murphy (20) and Connor Murphy (19). This was followed by a lengthy introduction of maps, air photographs, and photographs taken at the scene. Cpl Butcher was the first to be called to take the stand. He was led by the prosecution counsel through the events of the OP and then in detail through the photographs he had taken at the time. The photographs were presented by counsel as an illustrated record of the events that had occurred in full view of the OP. The people depicted in the photographs were the people observed by the OP, and were the five men in the dock before the court. Lengthy cross-examination of Cpl Butcher concerning identification "at a range of 150 metres", a detailed cross-examination on photographic technique and evidence handling, and a mass of suggestions by each of the defence counsel in turn that "you could not possibly have identified these men" failed to break Cpl Butcher's resolve. "Those were the men I saw in the field that day, those were the men I photographed and there they are in court," Cpl Butcher maintained.

I then took the stand and outlined the events of the night of the 9th/10th June when we went out to confirm that there was a command wire bomb in situ. Defence counsel declined to cross-examine and the court was adjourned until the following day.

DAY 2
Before the court opened it was apparent that the South Armagh Supporters' Club was much reduced in numbers. That this was due to the fact that many of them had been stopped on leaving the court the evening before, and had been invited to Girdwood base to witness a thorough four-hour search of their cars, is naturally mere supposition.

The case opened with each defence counsel in turn quoting legal references concerning identity procedure, and seeking that either the judge should now dismiss the case; or at the least strike Cpl Butcher's evidence in toto from the record. One of the references quoted was an identification issue in a handbag snatching case in 1955 when a witness had been asked to identify a suspect from a photograph! Prosecuting counsel however maintained that this particular case was not similar to the references quoted. It was, he claimed, analogous to a bank robbery where the bank manager being robbed had himself taken pictures of the robbers who he had seen at the time. It was in effect a visual record of events taken and compiled by himself.

The judge ruled that there was no precedent for dismissing the case, and that the identity issue was an issue he would have to decide upon in the light of the total sum of all evidence to be produced.

Having overcome this legal hurdle, the case continued. Cpl Evans was called to give further evidence concerning the discovery of the command wire on the night of 9th/10th June. Counsel declined to cross-examine him.

CSM Condon was called next. He was to be a vital continuity witness, having accompanied the initial recce on 9th/10th June, and then having commanded the close OP from which the photographs were taken; and subsequently been present throughout the clearance of the area and the discovery of the bomb in the dung heap. Condon opened his statement with a description of the initial recce and the finding of the firing point and the command wire. He then described the events in the OP, pointing out the accused in the dock as the men he had seen that night. Defence counsel were instantly on their feet objecting in strong terms, one after the other. The judge ruled this as admissible, but when the prosecution began to lead CSM Condon through what in his opinion "his observations had meant to him" another barrage of objections from defence counsel were sustained. CSM Condon was not allowed to say that the events before him, the command wire, the firing point, the marker and presumed bomb, were exactly similar to the events on the Chancellors Road less than a month previously, in which a Saracen and a complete patrol had been totally destroyed. CSM Condon was then subjected to lengthy cross-examination lasting, in all, about an hour. At one stage when erroneously accused by defence counsel of omitting to mention in his statement "the seemingly vital swiftscope", Condon quickly retorted that he hadn't mentioned "the machine gun or the sniper rifle either". Defence counsel asked him whether he had "any more humorous remarks to make", whereupon the judge had to step in and separate the verbal combatants. Detailed cross-examination on the "impossibility of identification" followed. This was firmly rebutted by Condon who kept returning to "the man I saw is (pointing) that man in the dock there". Questions of identity from the photographs such as "are his eyes open or closed", "is that a shadow or a day's growth of beard" failed to shake Condon. "The man I saw, is that man there!" We adjourned for lunch.

After lunch Condon again took the stand. We produced a swiftscope and the 60 times magnification seemed to convince the judge that whether or not you could tell if the accused's eyes were open or closed in the photograph was irrelevant. With a swiftscope at 150 metres you can count his eyelashes! Condon and the cross-examiners parted agreeing to disagree. Condon maintained throughout that he was positive that the men in the dock were the men observed that day fifteen months earlier. Defence counsel could only "suggest" that they were not.

Rfn Loftus was the next to be called. He described exactly the observations made from the OP, Defence counsel declined to cross-examine him.

Rfn Love was "tendered" by the prosecution counsel as he could produce no more evidence than Cpl Evans, CSM Condon and I had already given concerning the initial recce on the night of 9th/10th June. The defence counsel, however, chose to call Rfn Love for cross-examination. The line of questioning was designed to intimate that there was no bomb on the Quarter Road that night – just a wire and a plastic bag. Rfn Love confirmed his part in the recce, what he did and what he saw.

Next to the stand was WO2 Lucas, who at the time had been my Company Intelligence Cell SNCO. He gave evidence concerning continuity of evidence pertaining to the film taken by, and later developed and printed by Cpl Butcher. Lucas had not been in court the previous day when Butcher had explained that not only had he taken the photographs, he had also processed and printed the film. Lucas finished by stating that the film was handed to "the dark room technician for printing". Immediately the defence counsel pounced. "Who, Mr Lucas, was the dark room technician." Lucas, completely unperturbed, and totally deadpan, answered "Cpl Butcher". Even the judge laughed!

WO1 Mitchell, our ATO at Bessbrook at the time, then gave his evidence. He described the clearance of the Quarter Road subsequent to the OP operation, and the discovery and clearance of the 700 lbs of explosive in the dung heap, followed by the subsequent clearance of the detonation pack and command wire found at the farm. Cross-examination then commenced. Defence counsel appeared to be intimating that there was a strong possibility that the explosives in the dung heap had been placed there by the Security Forces. ATO was further cross-examined on his opinion "based on considerable experience" that such a bomb would completely destroy any vehicle under which it was detonated, almost certainly kill all the occupants, and make a considerable crater in the road. "Was it true," defence counsel asked. "that people had been known to survive such an explosion?" "Was it not true that the force of the explosion depended on the specific ground conditions at the time?" Had Mr Mitchell ever heard of explosives simply being used to crater roads? This line of cross-examination continued. Defence counsel appeared to be trying to suggest that the explosives need not necessarily have caused loss of life, and indeed may not have been placed with the intention of causing loss of life at all, but simply to make a hole in the road, Mr Mitchell disagreed.

Mr Mitchell was the last military witness to appear. Before adjourning at the end of the second day the first two of a long line of police witnesses were called. A constable was called to give continuity of evidence concerning the handling of the film taken by Cpl Butcher and to rebut the defence counsel's suggestion that two of the negatives had been scratched deliberately to prevent correct identifications being made; the suggestion being that the only photographs that could disprove the presence of the accused had been defaced! Before adjourning for the day the first of the RUC Scenes of Crime Officers gave evidence concerning the removal of numerous items of clothing from the accused's houses at the time of their arrest.

DAYS 3 TO 9
The next seven days involved an endless succession of witnesses from the RUC; scientists from the forensic laboratories, Castlereagh interrogators and others. Their evidence was accepted verbatim. None of it was challenged by the defence counsel. To do so would risk putting the accused in to the dock, and then the evidence of one could be used against another. By avoiding this step the prosecution could rely only on the evidence of any of the accused against himself. One could not implicate the other; or more accurately his implications could not be taken as evidence against another. The Crown's case ended on the eighth day. The defence submissions were then made. The defence cases relied on the degree of evidence required to prove conspiracy; and those requirements needed to prove intent. Each of the defence counsel made lengthy statements, claiming that the evidence produced was neither sufficient to prove conspiracy, nor intent, despite the admissions all the accused had eventually made at Castlereagh. Much was made of the fact that the five had been discovered in the course of removing a bomb, "a laudable act"! Amongst the revelations that came out in court was that the bombers had removed the bomb from the road to the dung heap about an hour before we "ugged"* the firing point. At one time we must all have been just two fields apart in the dark!

DAY 10 – FINDINGS AND SENTENCE
Judge Rowland opened the day's proceedings by announcing that he acquitted Lynch, Jennings and Graham of charges 1 and 2, conspiracy, on the grounds that the elements of conspiracy could not be proven beyond reasonable doubt. As to all other charges, however, he found all defendants guilty. He then proceeded to run through each of the charges, outlining both prosecution and defence counsels' case and highlighting critical evidence, in particular the photographs Cpl Butcher took. The process was lengthy and unexciting, everyone's attention being centred on the sentences to come. However, before summary and sentence respective defence counsels had to be allowed the opportunity to submit their pleas in mitigation.

All pleas emphasised the youth of those convicted and were common in alluding to the promise and potential of those involved that would be unfulfilled whilst they were imprisoned. Equally, all pleas stressed the standing of the families and individuals in their communities. Graham, it was said, had ambitions to attend university and would undoubtedly be heir to his father's business. Lynch, apparently, had shown promise as an apprentice plumber and had not only co-operated fully with the police, but also assisted in the uncovering of the explosives. Lynch in no way intended to cause or be party to the injury of anyone. Jennings' counsel produced written references from a source that remained anonymous, but very evidently impressed Judge Rowland. Counsel for Jennings also added that his involvement was only peripheral and in recognizing his previous conviction four years before, on a firearms charge, detailed that the arm in

*From UGS (Unattended Ground Sensors).

question was "only" an air pistol and that Jennings, again, was victim of his youth. The Murphys' counsel did not expand on Declan Murphys' previous conviction of possession of a firearm and membership of the Fianna, other than to say that the consequent award of a £25 fine and two years' suspended sentence only reflected the "minor nature" of the crimes. Needless to say, Declan Murphy, like Jennings, had at the time fallen victim to youth. Connor Murphy's involvement was, according to his counsel, only peripheral.

As an aside, all pleas were notable for their extreme brevity.

The judge in summarising, described the case as a "tragedy" in that not one of the defendants was over the age of 21 and that the majority were obviously in possession of a promising future. Despite the contrary evidence contained in the photographs and the clothes of the now convicted terrorists produced during the trial, he stressed that he had not often seen defendants appear so well dressed and presented in court. He forcibly questioned why potentially useful and youthful citizens should have been involved in such an act of terrorism, but emphatically recognised that more sinister forces and personalities were behind the operation. He recognised that all were incriminated during the course of the bomb's removal rather than its laying, but stressed that he could not ignore that its removal was only to allow it to be used elsewhere against the army or police. He described the act as one of dangerous folly, ruinous to both the lives of those convicted and those of their families. (No reference here to the danger to the Security Forces!) In concluding, he recognised that some individuals were more involved than others and that Connor Murphy of all was least so, but that Declan Murphy was at the heart of the operation. The sentences, therefore, recognised these facts.

Declan Murphy was sentenced to concurrent charges of 14 years and 7 years for possession of explosives with intent and in suspicious circumstances on 10th June (the milk churns), and 10 years and 7 years for possession of explosive with intent and in suspicious circumstances on 11th June (the detonation pack). He also received 5 years for membership.

Connor Murphy was sentenced to concurrent charges of 5 years and 3 years for possession of explosive substances with intent and in suspicious circumstances. He also received 5 years for membership.

Lynch, Jennings and Graham were each sentenced to concurrent charges of 12 years and 5 years for possession of explosives with intent and in suspicious circumstances on 10th June, and 8 years and 5 years for possession of explosive substances with intent and in suspicious circumstances on 11th June. In addition Lynch and Jennings received 5 years for membership.

The now convicted terrorists have been held on remand awaiting trial for fifteen months. Remission in Ulster, even for terrorist crimes, is currently 50 per cent. Taking into account the period served on remand, Declan Murphy could be released in July 1988, Lynch, Jennings and Graham in July 1987, and Connor Murphy in January 1984! Put it another way; by the time we return to South Armagh again all five will probably be out of prison. Whether they will have seen the error of their ways, or whether they will be older, more experienced, more hardened terrorists remains to be seen. I have my suspicions as to what the answer will be.

Appendix VI
TOURS OF DUTY IN NORTHERN IRELAND

1 Grenadier Guards
29.12.69–20.4.70 Londonderry
19.8.71–7.10.71 Belfast (Ligoniel)
27.11.72–27.3.73 Londonderry
26.3.74–26.7.74 Londonderry
27.10.76–27.1.77 Armagh
16.11.78–7.3.79 Bessbrook
6.10.83–20.2.84 Bessbrook
26.9.86–31.1.87 Operation 'Cara Cara'
28.9.93–28.3.94 Armagh Resident

2 Grenadier Guards
23.8.69–23.1.70 Londonderry
1.3.73–25.3.73 Belfast (Emergency)
9.7.73–14.11.73 Belfast (Ardoyne)
10.11.77–13.3.78 Londonderry
7.3.80–15.7.80 Fermanagh
16.2.86–14.3.88 Ballykelly

1 Coldstream Guards
15.12.70–22.4.71 Londonderry and rural area
17.10.71–18.2.72 Londonderry
29.7.72–30.9.72 Londonderry
1.11.75–1.3.76 (Ballymurphy/Spring-field/Whiterock)
29.10.78–27.2.79 Belfast (Springfield/Falls)
8.9.82–22.1.83 Bessbrook
11.9.88–29.1.89 Belfast Roulement Bn
7.92–28.12.92 East Tyrone

2 Coldstream Guards
27.7.70–19.11.70 Belfast
11.12.72–31.3.73 Belfast (Springfield)
15.9.76–15.3.78 Londonderry (Resident Bn)
28.3.82–12.8.82 West Belfast
5.7.86–29.9.86 Operation 'Cara Cara'

1 Scots Guards
25.8.71–29.12.71 Belfast (Clonard/Bally-murphy)
1.5.73–5.9.73 Armagh
3.4.75–5.8.75 Belfast (Falls/Divis/Sandy Row/Unity/Shankill)

6.8.77–15.8.77 Belfast (Royal Visit)
28.8.78–30.12.78 Armagh
15.3.80–10.11.81 Aldergrove (Resident Bn)
10.9.86–21.1.87 Armagh Roulement Bn
7.6.89–18.10.89 Lisnaskea Incremental Roulement Bn
4.92–2.11.92 Belfast Roulement Bn
28.6.94–12.94 Detail Not Available

2 Scots Guards
1.7.70–18.7.70 Belfast and rural area
28.7.72–30.11.72 Londonderry
27.11.73–29.3.74 Belfast (Ballymurphy/Springfield)
17.11.76–16.3.77 Londonderry
28.5.80–12.10.80 Belfast (Springfield/Falls)
14.10.87–23.2.88 Armagh Roulement Bn
11.3.90–24.9.90 Province Reinforcement Bn

1 Irish Guards
11.92–4.93 Fermanagh

1 Welsh Guards
25.3.71–28.7.71 Belfast (Carnmoney)
17.6.72–25.10.72 Belfast (City)
14.11.73–8.3.74 Bessbrook (two Coys in Belfast)
25.10.79–27.2.80 Bessbrook
4.3.86–4.7.86 Belfast Roulement Bn
4.92–4.94 Ballykelly Resident Bn

1 Royal Scots
9.3.70–29.7.70 Belfast
25.5.71–28.7.71 Drumahoe
17.10.71–29.12.71 Belfast (Ligoniel)
17.6.72–7.8.72 Londonderry
16.12.75–16.4.76 Bessbrook
16.2.80–29.5.80 Belfast (Springfield/Falls)
1.3.81–24.3.83 Ballykinler (Resident Bn)
18.12.87–29.4.88 Belfast Roulement Bn
9.92–5.93 Armagh Roulement Bn

1 Royal Highland Fusiliers
7.2.70–21.5.70 Londonderry

16.2.71–17.6.71 Belfast
27.2.74–28.6.74 Belfast
  (Andersonstown/Suffolk/Twinbrook)
2.7.75–1.11.75 Belfast
  (Ballymurphy/Springfield/Whiterock)
16.12.76–19.4.77 Bessbrook
2.8.80–9.12.80 Armagh
5.3.83–3.85 Belfast (Holywood Resident
  Bn)
28.8.88–28.9.88 Lisnaskea Incremental
  Roulement Bn
12.91–2.92 Operation 'Luff'

1 King's Own Scottish Borderers
4.5.70–10.9.70 Belfast
9.7.71–13.7.71 Belfast (12 July Marches)
28.2.71–26.4.72 Belfast (Springfield)
17.11.72–2.3.73 Belfast (Andersonstown)
16.5.75–15.11.76 Belfast (Holywood/
  Ballymacarrett Resident Bn)
26.6.79–23.10.79 Belfast
  (Springfield/Falls)
16.3.85–6.8.85 Bessbrook
2.2.86–12.4.86 Operation 'Cara Cara'
18.10.89–3.3.90 Fermanagh Roulement
  Bn
5.4.92–4.94 Province Reinforcement Bn
  – Weeton

1 Black Watch
28.6.70–16.7.70 Belfast
8.8.70–19.8.70 Londonderry
9.2.71–25.6.71 Rural tour in border area
7.10.71–22.11.71 Belfast (East Belfast)
26.6.74–4.10.74 Belfast
  (Andersonstown/Suffolk/Twinbrook)
24.6.75–27.10.74 Belfast (Andersons-
  town/Suffolk/Twinbrook)
25.7.76–26.1.78 Ballykinler (Resident Bn)
22.12.82–10.5.83 West Belfast
17.12.85–27.4.86 Armagh Roulement Bn
28.7.89–8.91 Ballykinler Resident Bn

1 Queen's Own Highlanders
21.11.71–22.3.72 Belfast
28.7.72–6.10.72 Dungannon
4.12.73–4.4.74 Belfast (Falls/Divis/Sandy
  Row)
27.4.78–28.8.78 Armagh
5.7.79–25.10.79 Bessbrook
20.11.83–15.11.85 Aldergrove (Resident
  Bn)
1.3.90–17.11.90 Belfast Roulement Bn

1 Gordon Highlanders
2.5.72–6.9.72 Armagh

2.3.73–1.7.73 Belfast (Andersonstown)
15.11.76–20.5.78 Belfast (Holywood
  Resident Bn)
6.8.79–6.12.79 Armagh
13.2.85–26.6.85 West Belfast
17.7.90–18.12.90 Belfast Roulement Bn

1 Argyll and Sutherland Highlanders
26.7.72–29.11.72 Bessbrook
15.3.73–27.3.73 Belfast (HMS *Maidstone*)
12.11.73–25.2.74 Belfast (Shankill,
  Ardoyne Spearhead
  Deployment of part of battalion only)
2.12.75–4.4.76 Belfast (Falls/Divis/Sandy
  Row)
28.10.77–1.3.78 Belfast (Springfield/Falls)
6.3.80–10.3.82 Ballykelly (Resident Bn)
12.4.86–28.7.86 Operation 'Cara Cara'
18.12.90–11.5.91 Belfast Roulement Bn
3.92–6.92 Operation 'Luff'

1 Queen's Regiment
17.8.69–13.12.69 Londonderry
16.10.72–16.2.73 Belfast (New
  Lodge/Unity)
15.10.73–15.2.74 Belfast (New
  Lodge/Unity)
23.5.74–4.6.74 Belfast (UWC Strike)
4.2.75–29.5.75 Belfast (New
  Lodge/Ardoyne)
10.7.76–17.11.76 Londonderry
20.6.78–12.10.78 Belfast (Monagh)
25.11.82–3.85 Omagh (Resident Bn)
3.6.87–14.10.87 Armagh Roulement Bn
19.10.89–1.3.90 Belfast Roulement Bn

2 Queen's Regiment
3.3.69–25.8.70 Belfast (Holywood Resident Bn)
5.8.71–17.9.71 Belfast (East Belfast)
29.7.72–29.11.72 Londonderry
26.11.73–29.3.74 Londonderry
7.1.76–14.1.76 South Armagh (Spearhead
  Whitecross Murders)
22.2.77–21.6.77 Belfast (Monagh,
  Andersonstown)
2.4.80–2.8.80 Armagh
25.1.83–25.11.84 Londonderry
28.4.88–8.9.88 Belfast
1.92–2.92 Operation 'Gypsy'

3 Queen's Regiment
20.4.70–22.12.71 Ballykinler (Resident
  Bn)
30.3.72–6.4.72 Belfast
6.8.72–31.8.72 Londonderry

27.10.75–27.2.76 Belfast (Andersons-
town/Suffolk/Twinbrook)
7.3.79–5.7.79 Bessbrook
3.2.84–15.6.84 Belfast (North Queen
Street)
2.2.87–30.5.87 Operation 'Cara Cara'
26.1.88–16.3.90 Aldergrove Resident Bn

1 Royal Regiment of Fusiliers
16.6.70–22.10.70 Belfast (Shankill/Lower
Falls)
5.2.71–25.2.71 Belfast (Holywood)
19.6.71–21.6.71 Belfast (Long Kesh)
11.8.71–19.8.71 Belfast (Ballymurphy)
1.9.73–10.3.75 Londonderry (Resident Bn)
2.3.76–19.6.76 Belfast(Springfield
Road/Whiterock/Ballymurphy)
2.5.77–12.6.77 (Spearhead/Province-wide
UUAC Strike)
12.10.80–26.2.81 Belfast (Springfield
Road/Falls)
10.1.84–4.2.86 Londonderry (Resident Bn)
30.11.88–12.4.89 Armagh Roulement Bn
6.91–7.91 Operation 'Aladdin'
9.91–10.91 Operation 'Bronski'

2 Royal Regiment of Fusiliers
19.10.71–16.2.72 Belfast (New
Lodge/Unity)
11.7.72–10.11.72 Belfast (Suffolk)
1.3.73–27.3.73 Belfast (Carnmoney Border
Bn)
26.6.73–30.10.73 Belfast (Andersonstown)
23.10.74–26.2.75 Belfast (Andersons-
town/Suffolk/Twinbrook)
24.6.76–26.10.76 Armagh
10.7.78–10.11.78 West of River Foyle
15.11.79–6.4.81 Belfast (Holywood
Resident Bn)
7.91–2.94 Ballykinler Resident Bn

3 Royal Regiment of Fusiliers
27.1.72–22.5.72 Dungannon
13.7.72–2.2.9.72 Londonderry
3.1.73–4.5.73 Armagh
2.1.74–3.5.74 Armagh
2.1.74–3.5.74 Armagh
15.8.75–15.12.75 Bessbrook
9.3.76–6.4.76 Co Armagh Spearhead
(Whitecross Murders)
20.10.77–22.2.78 Belfast (Monagh)
7.11.79–6.3.80 Londonderry
6.4.81–5.3.83 Belfast (Holywood Resident
Bn)
6.8.85–17.12.85 Armagh Roulement Bn

1 Royal Anglian Regiment
23.7.70–10.3.72 Londonderry (Resident
Bn)
2.9.74–17.12.74 Portadown
13.5.79–16.9.79 Belfast (Ardoyne/City
Centre)
25.8.81–4.1.82 Fermanagh
25.11.84–15.6.87 Londonderry (Resident
Bn)
25.8.89–10.1.90 Armagh Roulement Bn
12.93–6.94 Londonderry (Resident Bn)

2 Royal Anglian Regiment
20.10.70–11.2.71 Belfast
2.8.72–6.12.72 Belfast (Hastings Street)
27.7.73–29.11.73 Londonderry
4.8.75–3.12.75 Belfast (Hastings Street)
16.3.77–28.6.77 Belfast (Springfield/Falls)
25.1.81–25.1.83 Londonderry (Resident
Bn)
1.1.86–2.3.86 Operation 'Cara Cara'
28.4.86–10.9.86 Armagh Roulement Bn
29.1.89–9.6.89 Belfast Roulement Bn
12.92–6.93 East Tyrone Bn

3 Royal Anglian Regiment
11.4.72–4.8.72 Belfast (Hastings Street)
27.3.73–27.7.73 Londonderry
19.11.74–21.3.75 Londonderry
20.5.78–15.11.79 Belfast (Holywood
Resident Bn)
10.11.86–25.3.87 Belfast Roulement Bn
4.91–9.92 Londonderry Resident Bn

1 King's Own Royal Border Regiment
10.3.71–31.3.71 Rural tour border area
11.1.72–5.7.73 Ballykinler (Resident Bn)
3.12.74–5.4.75 Belfast (Falls/Divis/Sandy
Row/Unity/Shankill)
17.6.76–20.10.76 Belfast (Springfield
Road)
13.9.78–14.1.79 Belfast (Ardoyne/New
Lodge/City Centre/ Markets)
27.2.80–17.6.80 Bessbrook
10.3.85–2.87 Belfast (Holywood Resident
Bn)
24.4.87–12.5.87 Armagh
25.4.89–6.9.89 Operation 'Fondant'
9.92–8.94 Londonderry Resident Bn

1 King's Regiment
1.9.80–5.1.70 Belfast
25.4.72–25.8.72 Belfast (Springfield)
1.3.75–15.9.76 Londonderry (Resident Bn)
27.2.79–26.6.79 Belfast (Springfield
Road/Falls)

15.6.84–4.10.84 West Belfast
25.5.87–26.9.87 Operation 'Cara Cara'
9.2.90–3.92 Ballykelly Resident Bn

1 Prince of Wales's Own Regiment of
Yorkshire
28.4.69–21.8.69 Londonderry
20.5.72–30.11.73 Belfast (Holywood
Resident Bn)
9.7.75–11.11.75 Londonderry
16.3.77–14.7.77 Londonderry
25.4.85–19.5.87 Ballykinler (Resident Bn)
11.91–4.92 Belfast Resident Bn

1 Green Howards
30.6.70–3.9.70 Belfast
29.7.71–30.11.71 Belfast (Ardoyne)
23.10.72–24.2.73 Belfast (Suffolk/MPH)
1.5.74–4.9.74 Portadown
15.4.75–15.8.75 Bessbrook
6.4.76–5.5.76 Spearhead (Whitecross
Murders)
20.9.78–15.3.80 Aldergrove (Resident
Bn)
3.6.85–5.11.85 Belfast
20.1.87–27.3.89 Londonderry
6.91–7.91 Operation 'Clifford'
6.91–8.92 Londonderry
8.92–19.1.93 Drummond and Girdwood
Roulement Bn

1 Queen's Lancashire Regiment
19.5.70–18.9.70 Londonderry
29.11.71–29.3.72 Belfast (Ardoyne)
4.12.72–4.4.73 Belfast (Hastings Street)
1.1.75–25.7.76 Ballykinler (Resident Bn)
5.8.77–9.12.77 Bessbrook
30.10.80–13.3.81 Bessbrook
25.3.87–30.7.87 Belfast Roulement Bn
22.9.90–4.92 Province Reinforcement Bn
– Weeton

1 Duke of Wellington's Regiment
15.6.71–29.10.71 Belfast (New
Lodge/Unity)
27.4.72–28.7.72 Bessbrook
10.3.73–30.9.74 Londonderry
14.1.76–9.3.76 Armagh Area Spearhead
(Whitecross Murders)
9.7.77–9.11.77 Londonderry (West of
Foyle)
23.10.79–16.2.80 Belfast
(Springfield/Falls)
13.12.81–25.4.82 Bessbrook
12.2.87–24.2.89 Belfast (Holywood Resident Bn)

1 Devon and Dorset Regiment
26.7.70–26.8.70 Belfast
18.1.72–2.5.72 Armagh
30.10.73–1.3.74 Belfast
(Andersonstown/Suffolk/Twinbrook)
20.1.77–19.5.77 Belfast (Ardoyne/New
Lodge)
14.1.79–13.5.79 Belfast (Ardoyne/City
Centre)
27.7.81–13.12.81 Bessbrook
24.3.83–25.4.85 Ballykinler (Resident Bn)
11.4.89–28.8.89 Ballykinler (Resident Bn)
1.5.93–8.11.93 Belfast Resident Bn

1 Cheshire Regiment
31.3.70–1.8.70 Londonderry
24.2.73–24.6.73 Belfast (Suffolk)
27.3.74–26.7.74 Belfast
(Ballymurphy/Springfield/Whiterock)
15.3.76–19.7.76 Londonderry
13.3.78–13.7.78 West of River Foyle
10.3.82–5.1.84 Londonderry
24.5.90–19.10.90 Armagh Roulement Bn
3.91–4.91 Emergency Tour

1 Royal Welch Fusiliers
6.3.72–8.9.73 Londonderry
17.10.74–27.10.74 Belfast
28.2.75–30.6.75 Belfast
(Ballymurphy/Springfield/Whiterock)
20.10.76–22.2.77 Belfast (Fort Monagh)
1.5.77–19.5.77 Belfast (UUAC Strike)
10.11.78–8.3.79 West of River Foyle
26.2.81–8.7.81 Belfast (Springfield
Road/Falls)
15.6.86–28.9.86 Operation 'Cara Cara'
12.5.87–20.7.89 Ballykinler Resident Bn
5.93–11.93 Fermanagh Resident Bn

1 Royal Regiment of Wales
28.7.69–11.9.69
20.10.70–18.2.71 Belfast (Hastings Street)
27.3.72–28.7.72 Belfast (Ardoyne)
20.11.73–15.5.75 Belfast (Holywood
Resident Bn)
29.12.78–26.4.79 Armagh
6.5.81–9.6.81 Belfast (Spearhead Funeral
of Mr B. Sands)
21.9.83–3.2.84 Belfast (North Queen
Street)
6.9.86–31.1.87 Operation 'Cara Cara'
9.94 Ballykelly Resident Bn

1 Gloucestershire Regiment
2.12.69–12.4.70 Londonderry
7.12.71–13.4.72 Belfast (Hastings Street)

2.4.73–3.8.73 Belfast (Hastings Street)
5.8.74–13.12.74 Belfast (Falls/Divis/Sandy
Row)
20.9.77–6.3.79 Londonderry (Resident Bn)
10.3.88–11.2.90 Ballykelly Resident Bn
12.91–12.91 Operation 'Trip 2'
3.94–9.94 Aldergrove Resident Bn

1 Worcestershire and Sherwood Foresters
Regiment
15.3.72–9.6.72 Londonderry
20.9.74–27.3.76 Londonderry (Resident
Bn)
19.4.77–14.8.77 Bessbrook
12.8.82–22.12.82 West Belfast
21.1.89–2.91 Omagh Resident Bn

1 Royal Hampshire Regiment
19.8.69–28.11.69 Belfast
27.11.72–27.3.73 Bessbrook
3.9.73–4.1.74 Armagh
27.3.76–4.10.77 Londonderry (Resident
Bn)
8.3.79–14.7.79 Londonderry
4.1.82–19.5.82 Fermanagh
21.1.87–3.6.97 Armagh Roulement Bn
12.3.89–4.91 Ballykelly Resident Bn
20.11.93–29.5.94 Fermanagh Resident Bn

1 Staffordshire Regiment
4.9.72–5.1.73 Armagh
23.7.74–22.11.74 Londonderry
4.4.76–3.8.76 Belfast (Falls/Divis/Sandy
Row)
7.9.79–25.1.81 Londonderry (Resident Bn)
5.2.84–2.7.84 Bessbrook
4.92–11.92 Fermanagh Roulement Bn

1 Duke of Edinburgh's Royal Regiment
22.4.71–28.5.71 Londonderry
1.7.73–10.1.75 Ballykinler (Resident Bn)
8.7.79–7.11.79 Londonderry
5.6.83–6.10.83 Bessbrook
7.11.85–7.2.88 Aldergrove Resident Bn
10.12.90–5.5.91 Fermanagh Roulement
Bn
29.3.93–9.93 Aldergrove Resident Bn

1 Light Infantry
26.2.68–24.4.70 Belfast (Resident Bn)
23.3.71–31.7.71 Belfast (Ardoyne)
26.7.72–24.11.72 Belfast (Ardoyne)
16.7.73–16.11.73 Bessbrook (two Coys to
Belfast)
20.5.74–3.6.74 Belfast (UWC Strike)
6.9.75–7.10.75 South Armagh Spearhead

(Sectarian Murders)
28.6.78–29.10.78 Belfast
(Springfield/Falls)
6.5.83–21.9.83 Belfast (Belfast North
Queen Street)
25.11.86–20.1.89 Omagh Resident Bn
29.5.94–11.94 Fermanagh Roulement Bn

2 Light Infantry
13.9.69–17.1.70 Belfast
24.6.71–28.10.71 Armagh
5.2.72–10.2.72 Rural tour in border area
19.6.72–20.10.72 Londonderry
29.3.73–27.7.73 Belfast
(Springfield/Clonard)
18.3.75–9.7.75 Londonderry
2.8.76–2.12.76 Belfast (Falls/Divis/Sandy
Row/Shankill)
25.1.78–27.7.79 Ballykinler (Resident Bn)
25.4.82–8.9.82 Bessbrook
30.7.87–18.12.87 Belfast Roulement Bn
10.1.90–25.5.90 Armagh Roulement Bn
11.90–12.90 Operation 'Derivable'
9.91–10.91 Operation 'Bronski'
2.92–7.92 Armagh Roulement Bn
7.93–12.93

3 Light Infantry
15.8.69–15.11.69 Belfast
6.2.71–25.3.71 Belfast
22.11.72–11.3.73 Aldergrove
3.4.74–7.8.74 Belfast (Falls/Divis/Sandy
Row)
13.11.75–18.3.76 Londonderry
28.6.77–28.1.77 Belfast (Springfield/
Falls)
10.10.82–16.2.83 Fermanagh
25.1.85–11.11.86 Omagh (Resident Bn)
10.5.91–13.11.91 Belfast Roulement Bn

1 Royal Green Jackets
20.8.69–18.12.69 Belfast
4.5.71–10.9.71 Belfast (Hastings Street)
30.7.72–19.11.79 Belfast (Andersonstown)
3.8.73–5.12.73 Belfast (Falls/Divis/Sandy
Row/Village)
15.12.74–17.4.75 Bessbrook
19.5.77–20.9.77 Belfast (Ardoyne/New
Lodge)
13.3.81–27.7.81 Bessbrook
10.11.81–15.11.83 Aldergrove (Resident
Bn)
13.3.81–7.7.86 Operation 'Cara Cara'
15.7.87–19.11.87 Operation 'Fondant'
7.91–1.92 DRB
8.92–2.93 Armagh Resident Bn

2 Royal Green Jackets
1.6.71–10.3.73 Ballykelly (Resident Bn)
4.4.74–1.5.74 Armagh
1.11.74–2.3.75 Belfast
  (Ballymurphy/Springfield/Whiterock)
9.12.77–8.4.78 Bessbrook
26.4.79–15.8.79 Armagh
15.11.81–18.3.82 West Belfast
5.11.85–5.3.86 West Belfast
4.2.89–7.6.89 Lisnaskea Incremental
  Roulement Bn
2.91–8.92 Omagh Resident Bn

3 Royal Green Jackets
29.6.70–16.7.70 Rural tour
23.8.72–13.12.72 Belfast (Springfield)
27.7.73–29.11.73 Belfast
  (Springfield/Clonard/Beechmount)
24.7. 74–3.11.74 Belfast
  (Ballymurphy/Springfield)
2.5.77–22.5.77 Belfast (UUAC Strike)
15.3.78–6.9.70 Londonderry (Resident Bn)
4.10.84–13.2.85 West Belfast
12.9.91–16.3.92 Armagh Roulement Bn

1 Parachute Regiment
12.10.69–19.2.70 Belfast
21.9.70–25.5.72 Belfast (Holywood
  Resident Bn)
29.7.72–29.11.72 Belfast (Ardoyne)
8.4.78–16.7.78 Bessbrook
18.11.81–27.1.82 Armagh/Border Spearhead
18.5.82–2.10.82 Fermanagh
18.7.88–30.11.88 Armagh Roulement Bn
2.91–6.93 Belfast (Holywood Resident Bn)
8.5.94–11.94 Belfast Resident Bn

2 Parachute Regiment
28.2.70–24.6.70 Belfast
21.4.71–26.8.71 Belfast (Springfield)
15.2.72–15.6.72 Belfast
  (Carnmoney/Unity)
29.7.72–28.9.72 Belfast (Springfield)
27.3.73–18.7.73 Bessbrook
31.5.75–27.9.75 Belfast (New
  Lodge/Ardoyne Area)
2.12.76–16.3.77 Belfast
  (Ballymurphy/Springfield/Whiterock)
27.7.79–6.3.81 Ballykinler (Resident Bn)
13.11.84–26.3.85 Bessbrook
2.3.90–26.3.83 Fermanagh Roulement Bn
7.92–10.92 Girdwood Roulement Bn

3 Parachute Regiment
19.1.71–3.6.71 Rural area

11.3.73–14.7.73 (Belfast (Ardoyne)
23.2.74–22.6.74 Belfast
  (Shankill/Ardoyne)
15.4.76–18.8.76 Bessbrook
21.2.78–20.6.78 Belfast (Monagh)
9.13.80–20.4.81 Armagh
21.2.89–2.91 Belfast (Holywood Resident
  Bn)
3.92–6.92 Operation 'Gypsy'

40 Commando
14.6.72–18.10.72 Belfast (Unity/New
  Lodge)
15.6.73–17.10.73 Belfast (Unity/New
  Lodge)
24.2.75–25.6.75 Belfast
  (Andersonstown/Suffolk/Twinbrook)
18.8.76–16.12.76 Bessbrook
7.3.79–5.3.80 Ballykelly (Resident Bn)
22.1.83–8.6.83 Bessbrook
23.2.88–18.7.88 Armagh Roulement Bn
6.1.93–7.5.93 Belfast (Resident Bn)

41 Commando
29.9.69–13.11.69 Belfast
27.8.70–13.11.70 Belfast
1.3.78–28.6.78 Belfast (Springfield/Falls)
17.8.80–30.10.80 Bessbrook
Disbanded 5.8.81

42 Commando
28.10.71–1801.72 Armagh
28.7.72–1.9.72 Belfast (East Belfast)
16.2.73–15.6.73 Belfast (New
  Lodge/Unity)
13.2.74–14.6.74 Belfast (New
  Lodge/Unity)
5.10.74–13.10.74 Portadown/Newry/
  Bessbrook (N. Ireland General Election)
7.10.75–5.11.75 Armagh Spearhead
  (Sectarian Murders)
28.2.76–24.6.76 Belfast (Fort
  Monagh/Andersonstown)
15.7.78–16.11.78 Bessbrook
3.7.84–13.11.84 Bessbrook
28.5.87–19.7.87 Spearhead
7.6.89–23.10.89 Belfast Roulement Bn
11.91–9.5.92 Fermanagh Roulement Bn
10.94–4.95 Aldergrove Resident Bn

45 Commando
29.5.70–3.9.70 Belfast
10.8.71–1.9.71 Belfast and rural area
17.10.71–16.2.72 Belfast (Carnmoney)
10.7.72–28.7.72 Belfast
1.7.74–5.11.74 Bessbrook

21.6.77–20.10.77 Belfast (Monagh)
4.8.78–30.8.78 Spearhead Bn
8.7.81–15.11.81 Belfast (Springfield
  Road/Falls)
2.7.86–12.11.86 Belfast Roulement Bn
18.10.90–12.3.91 Armagh Roulement Bn

1 Royal Irish
21.9.88–5.2.89 Lisnaskea Incremental
  Roulement Bn

2 Royal Irish
10.6.90–12.12.90 Fermanagh Roulement
  Bn

NB. A small number of independent
  companies have also completed tours
  in Ulster.

Life Guards
24.7.72–1.12.72 East Belfast (Infantry
  Role)
1.5.74–11.9.74 Armagh

Blues and Royals
29.12.76–27.4.77 Londonderry
2.2.79–5.6.79 Belfast (Monagh)

Queen's Dragoon Guards (Infantry Role)
25.2.74–2.6.74 Londonderry
6.1.76–3.5.76 Armagh
15.11.80–25.11.82 Omagh (Resident
  Regiment)

Scots Dragoon Guards
1.5.74–28.8.74 Long Kesh (Infantry Role)
3.5.76–28.8.76 Dungannon
28.9.80–27.11.80 Belfast (Ardoyne/City
  Centre)

4/7 Dragoon Guards
28.12.77–1.2.78 Fire Fighting

5 Inniskilling Dragoon Guards
10.4.81–25.8.81 Fermanagh

Queen's Own Hussars
24.6.73–27.10.73 Belfast (Suffolk/
  Dunmurry/Lisburn)
24.5.77–27.9.77 Armagh
5.6.79–2.10.79 Belfast (Monagh)

9/12 Lancers
6.1.75–4.5.75 Armagh
22.5.76–25.11.77 Omagh (Resident
  Regiment)

Royal Hussars (Infantry Role)
26.8.74–17.12.74 Long Kesh
27.8.76–29.12.76 Dungannon
2.6.78–2.10.78 Belfast (City Centre/
  Markets)

13/18 Hussars
11.1.72–10.5.72 Long Kesh
4.9.75–3.1.76 Armagh/Aughnacloy
25.11.77–25.5.79 Omagh (Resident
  Regiment)

14/20 Hussars
12.10.78–2.2.79 Belfast (Monagh)

15/19 Hussars (Infantry Role)
3.8.71–9.12.71 Long Kesh
18.11.74–21.5.76 Omagh (Resident
  Regiment)

16/5 Lancers
3.11.71–17.5.73 Omagh (Resident
  Regiment)
28.7.76–28.11.76 HMP Maze
27.3.80–14.7.80 Lurgan/Maze

17/21 Lancers
May 70–5.11.71 Omagh (Resident
  Regiment)
3.11.75–3.3.76 Belfast (City Centre/
  Markets)

1 Royal Tank Regiment
17.5.73–22.11.74 Omagh (Resident
  Regiment)
28.4.77–29.8.77 Londonderry

2 Royal Tank Regiment
5.5.75–5.9.75 Armagh
29.8.77–28.12.77 Londonderry

25.5.79–15.11.80 Omagh (Resident
  Regiment)

3 Royal Tank Regiment
10.1.73–4.5.73 Long Kesh (Infantry Role)
9.9.74–4.1.75 Armagh

4 Royal Tank Regiment
6.4.76–28.7.76 Long Kesh
12.2.78–2.6.78 Belfast (City Centre/
  Markets)

Note: Many RAC sub-units (ie. detached
squadrons) completed tours independent
of their parent units, particularly in the
early 1970s.

1 Royal Horse Artillery
12.11.69–14.3.70 Belfast (City Centre)
12.9.72–12.1.73 Long Kesh
6.3.74–5.7.74 Belfast (City Centre)
2.3.76–9.6.76 Belfast (Grand Central/City
Centre)

3 Royal Horse Artillery
7.9.70–21.1.71 Rural tour
1.7.71–15.7.71 Rural tour
21.7.71–17.8.71 Ballykelly
28.12.71–27.4.72 East Belfast (Andersons-
town/Lower Falls)
1.9.72–16.11.72 Londonderry
24.1.76–25.5.76 Belfast (North Queen
Street Belfast) Now Disbanded

7 Royal Horse Artillery
16.2.72–19.6.72 Belfast (Ligoniel)
8.11.72–11.3.73 Belfast (City Centre)
6.3.74–3.7.74 Bessbrook
31.3.78–29.7.78 Lurgan

2 Field Regiment
16.3.72–21.7.72 Belfast (Lisburn/
Dunmurry/Andersonstown)
3.9.73–4.1.74 Long Kesh
5.7.75–6.11.75 Londonderry
29.3.77–28.7.77 Lurgan/HMP Maze

4 Light Regiment now 4 Field Regiment
1.8.71–9.11.71
9.5.72–14.9.72 Long Kesh
12.6.74–23.10.74 Belfast (Unity/New
Lodge)
25.5.76–24.9.76 Belfast (Ardoyne/New
Lodge)

5 Light Regiment now 5 Heavy Regiment
4.4.70–27.8.70 Londonderry
20.3.71–26.4.71 Londonderry
16.8.71–14.9.71 Ballykelly
6.3.75–4.7.75 Londonderry
27.9.77–24.1.78 Armagh (Redesignated 5
Heavy Regiment with effect from 1977)
15.5.80–28.9.80 Belfast (Ardoyne/City
Centre)

12 Light Air Defence Regiment now 12 Air
Defence Regiment
25.11.71–17.3.72 Belfast (Lisburn/
Dunmurry/Andersonstown)
25.1.77–24.5.77 Armagh (Redesignated 12
Air Defence Regiment with effect from
1977)
27.11.79–27.3.80 Lurgan/HMP Maze/
Portadown

16 Light Air Defence Regiment now 16
Air Defence Regiment
28.6.70–28.10.70 Belfast
15.11.72–16.3.72 Londonderry
13.3.74–15.7.74 Londonderry
29.6.76–24.9.76 Londonderry (Redesignated 16 Air Defence Regiment with
effect from 1977)
6.12.79–2.4.80 Armagh

19 Field Regiment
19.7.72–16.11.72 Belfast (Musgrave Park)
7.11.73–6.3.74 Belfast (City Centre/
Markets)
14.7.80–24.11.80 Fermanagh/Maze

20 Medium Regiment
7.6.72–11.10.72 Londonderry
23.6.73–27.10.73 Londonderry
20.6.74–20.9.74 Belfast (Shankill/
Ardoyne) Since Disbanded

22 Light Air Defence Regiment now 22 Air
Defence Regiment
24.11.71–16.3.72 Drumahoe
15.3.73–7.7.73 Londonderry
5.11.74–5.3.75 Londonderry (Redesignated
22 Air Defence Regiment with effect
from 1977)
29.11.78–28.3.79 Long Kesh/Lurgan

25 Light Regiment now 25 Field Regiment
25.7.71–27.11.71 Belfast (Lisburn/
Andersonstown)
18.10.72–24.2.73 Londonderry
2.7.75–4.11.75 Belfast (City Centre/
Markets)
11.2.77–9.6.77 Belfast (City Centre/
Markets)
16.9.79–14.1.80 Belfast (Ardoyne/City
Centre)

26 Field Regiment
6.8.75–4.12.75 Long Kesh
29.11.77–31.3.78 Lurgan/Maze

27 Medium Regiment now 27 Field
Regiment
7.9.71–13.1.72 Enniskillen
9.4.75–7.8.75 Long Kesh
28.7.77–29.11.77 Lurgan/Maze (Redesignated 27 Field Regiment with effect from
1977)
14.1.80–16.5.80 Belfast (Ardoyne/City
Centre)

32 Light Regiment now 32 Guided

Weapons Regiment
5.1.71–6.5.71 Belfast
2.5.73–5.9.73 Long Kesh
9.10.74–4.2.75 Belfast (Ardoyne/New
Lodge)
24.9.76–20.1.77 Belfast (Ardoyne/New
Lodge) (Redesignated 32 Guided Weapons
Regiment with effect from 1977)

36 Heavy Air Defence Regiment
28.3.73–31.7.73 East Belfast
26.11.76–29.3.77 HMP Maze (Disbanded
with effect from 31.1.78)

39 Medium Regiment then 39 Field
Regiment now 39 Heavy Regiment
25.10.73–27.2.74 Londonderry
4.12.75–6.4.76 HMP Maze
12.1.78–11.5.78 Belfast (Ardoyne/New
Lodge) (Redesignated 39 Field Regiment
with effect from 1977)
24.11.80–11.4.81 Fermanagh/Maze
(Redesignated 39 Heavy Regiment with
effect from 1.4.82)

40 Field Regiment
22.2.73–25.6.73 Belfast (Ballymurphy)
3.3.75–4.7.75 Belfast (City Centre/
Markets)
20.9.77–12.1.78 Belfast (Ardoyne/New
Lodge)

42 Heavy Regiment
4.4.70–4.5.70 Belfast
26.9.70–14.12.70 Rural tour
6.7.71–16.7.71 Belfast
8.8.71–31.8.71 Ballykinler
8.7.73–9.11.73 Belfast (City Centre)
4.11.75–8.3.76 Londonderry (Since
Disbanded)

45 Medium Regiment now 45 Field
Regiment
26.7.71–25.11.71 Drumahoe
3.7.74–6.11.74 Belfast (City Centre/
Ballymacarratt)
9.6.76–10.10.76 Belfast (City Centre/
Ballymacarratt) (Redesignated 45 Field
Regiment with effect from 1977)
26.7.79–27.11.79 Lurgan/HMP Maze/
Portadown

47 Light Regiment now 47 Field Regiment
16.7.73–16.11.73 Londonderry (Victoria
Barracks/Drumahoe/Bogside/City
Centre/Brandywell)
27.9.75–24.1.76 Belfast (Ardoyne/New
Lodge) (Redesignated 47 Field Regiment

with effect from 1.4.77)
11.10.77–13.2.78 Belfast (City Centre/
Markets)

49 Field Regiment
8.3.73–15.7.73 Belfast (City Centre)
5.11.74–5.3.75 Belfast (City Centre/Unity)
11.10.76–11.2.77 Belfast (City Centre/
Markets)
11.5.78–13.9.78 Belfast (Ardoyne/New
Lodge)

94 Locating Regiment
14.11.73–15.3.74 Londonderry

21 Engineer Regiment (Infantry Role)
30.4.71–5.8.71 Long Kesh
15.12.74–11.4.75 Long Kesh
25.9.76–29.12.76 Londonderry

23 Engineer Regiment (Infantry Role)
20.3.72–24.7.72 East Belfast

25 Engineer Regiment
1.8.73–30.11.73 East Belfast

26 Engineer Regiment (Infantry Role)
8.7.74–8.11.74 Londonderry

32 Engineer Regiment (Infantry Role)
2.1.74–3.5.74 Long Kesh
9.3.76–30.6.76 Londonderry

35 Engineer Regiment (Infantry Role)
29.12.72–30.3.73 East Belfast

36 Engineer Regiment (Engineer Role)
21.10.74–7.12.74 Maze (Rebuild)

2 Armoured Division Engineer Regiment
(Infantry Role)
9.6.77–11.10.77 Belfast (City Centre/
Markets)
2.10.79–2.2.80 Monagh

3 Armoured Division Engineer Regiment
29.7.78–29.11.78 Lurgan/HMP Maze

4 Armoured Division Engineer Regiment
24.1.78–27.4.78 Armagh

1 Armoured Division Engineer Regiment
28.3.79–26.7.79 Lurgan/HMP Maze/
Portadown

HQ 22 Engineer Regiment
1.8.72–16.9.72

HQ 36 Engineer Regiment
21.10.74–7.12.74 Long Kesh (Maze Rebuild)

23 Amphibious Squadron
25.10.78–22.2.79 Ballykelly

64 Amphibious Squadron
24.2.77–23.6.77 Shackleton Barracks
27.3.80–14.7.80 Lurgan/HMP Maze

73 Amphibious Squadron/73 Independent
Field Squadron
8.7.74–8.11.74 Londonderry
9.3.76–30.6.76 Londonderry
25.10.77–22.2.78 Shackleton Barracks
23.10.79–23.2.80 Ballykelly

2 Armoured Engineer Squadron
25.9.76–31.12.76 Londonderry

26 Armoured Engineer Squadron
21.1.74–3.5.74 Long Kesh
30.7.72–31.7.72 Operation 'Motorman'

31 Armoured Engineer Squadron
12.12.74–11.4.75 Long Kesh

Detached 40 Army Support Regiment
8.3.76–8.7.76 HMP Magilligan

6 Field Support Squadron
30.7.72–16.9.72

43 Field Support Squadron
23.6.77–25.10.77 Shackleton Barracks

60 Field Support Squadron RE
7.9.70–12.1.71 Long Kesh
1.11.72–28.2.73 Long Kesh

Troop 60 Field Support Squadron RE
9.3.76–11.4.76 Castledillon

Detachment 61 Field Support Squadron
RE
19.5.74–1.6.74
21.10.74–12.12.74 Long Kesh (Maze
Rebuild)

1 Field Squadron
8.11.72–6.3.73 Ballykelly
19.12.74–11.4.75 Long Kesh
23.6.78–25.10.78 Ballykelly

Troop 1 Field Squadron
18.8.72–18.9.72
21.7.81–6.12.81 Castledillon

3 Field Squadron
17.8.69–16.1.70 Antrim
11.5.71–14.9.71 Antrim
20.11.72–22.3.73 Antrim
10.6.74–14.10.74 Castledillon
9.6.76–11.10.76 Castledillon
2.5.77–17.5.77 UUAC Strike
11.10.78–8.2.79 Castledillon
8.3.81–22.7.81 Castledillon

4 Field Squadron
4.7.73–7.11.73 Shackleton Barracks
Troop 4 Field Squadron
6.12.81–20.4.82 Castledillon

5 Field Squadron
6.3.73–6.7.73 Ballykelly and Long Kesh

7 Field Squadron
10.7.72–9.11.72 Ballykelly
8.3.76–30.6.76 Londonderry
6.11.80–20.3.81 Ballykelly

8 Field Squadron
7.1.70–13.5.70 Antrim
15.10.71–29.11.71 Lurgan
11.1.72–29.3.72 Antrim
17.7.72–16.9.72 Long Kesh
21.11.73–22.3.74 Antrim
11.10.75–10.2.76 Castledillon
14.6.77–11.10.77 Castledillon
8.6.79–9.10.79 Castledillon
6.12.81–20.4.82 Castledillon

Troop 10 Field Squadron
21.10.70–12.1.71 Antrim
29.7.72–1.11.72 Long Kesh

11 Field Squadron
19.10.71–8.2.72 Castledillon
12.6.73–17.10.73 Castledillon
27.5.74–3.6.74 Castledillon
5.11.75–13.12.75 HMP Maze
31.3.78–30.11.78 Ballykinler
9.10.79–9.2.80 Castledillon
Troop 11 Field Squadron
23.6.70–18.7.70

12 Field Squadron
26.2.75–26.6.75 Ballykelly
22.2.79–21.6.79 Ballykelly

16 Field Squadron
26.6.74–1.11.74 Ballykelly
Troop 16 Field Squadron
30.5.83–16.10.83 Omagh

20 Field Squadron
18.2.71–18.6.71 Castledillon
13.10.72–13.2.73 Castledillon
21.10.74–12.12.74 Long Kesh (Maze
  Rebuild)
2.5.77–17.5.77 UUAC Strike
9.2.78–9.6.78 Castledillon
Troop 20 Field Squadron
3.9.82–18.1.83 Armagh

25 Field Squadron
29.12.72–30.3.73 East Belfast
24.6.76–22.10.76 Ballykelly
21.6.79–23.10.79 Ballykelly

29 Field Squadron
5.3.74–28.6.74 Shackleton Barracks
23.2.76–22.6.76 Shackleton Barracks
23.6.80–6.11.80 Shackleton Barracks

30 Field Squadron
8.11.71–9.3.72 Ballykelly
8.3.76–1.7.76 Londonderry

32 Field Squadron
5.6.72–14.10.72 Castledillon
6.10.74–5.2.75 Belfast (Ardoyne)
8.2.79–7.6.79 Castledillon
20.4.82–3.9.82 Castledillon

34 Field Squadron
12.1.71–11.5.71
27.3.72–29.7.72 Antrim
24.7.73–23.11.73 Antrim
12.6.75–11.10.75 Castledillon
9.2.80–10.6.80 Castledillon
|
Troop 34 Field Squadron
15.9.69–14.1.70
19.8.71–22.10.71 Long Kesh
11.4.72–29.7.72 Belfast
17.10.74–26.10.74 Antrim

37 Field Squadron
5.11.73–7.3.74 Shackleton Barracks
23.10.75–23.2.76 Shackleton Barracks
23.2.80–24.6.80 Ballykelly
Troop 37 Field Squadron
18.1.83–30.5.83 Armagh/Omagh

39 Field Squadron
8.3.72–11.7.72 Ballykelly

28.6.75–24.10.75 Ballykelly

42 Field Squadron
30.10.74–28.2.75 Ballykelly
22.10.76–24.2.77 Ballykelly
23.2.78–23.6.78 Ballykelly
20.3.81–21.7.81 Ballykelly

48 Field Squadron
29.6.71–29.11.71 Long Kesh
13.2.73–14.6.73 Castledillon
11.10.77–9.2.78 Castledillon
21.7.81–6.12.81 Castledillon
Troop 48 Field Squadron
20.3.74–24.7.74
10.1.75–8.3.75
15.6.76–15.7.76

50 Field Squadron (Construction)
8.2.72–6.6.72 Newtownbreda
3.8.72–16.9.72 Carnmoney
19.5.74–1.6.74
21.10.74–12.12.74 Long Kesh (Maze
  Rebuild)

51 Field Squadron (Construction)
13.2.75–12.6.75 Castledillon
9.6.78–11.10.78 Castledillon
Troop 51 Field Squadron (Construction)
29.6.71–29.11.71 Castledillon

52 Field Squadron (Construction)
6.2.74–12.6.74 Castledillon
2.5.77–17.5.77 UUAC Strike

53 Field Squadron (Construction)
30.11.71–14.3.72 Long Kesh
10.2.77–14.6.77 Castledillon

59 Independent Commando Squadron
24.7.72–21.11.72 Antrim
20.3.74–24.7.74 Antrim
12.2.76–11.6.76 Castledillon
10.6.80–23.10.80 Castledillon

Condor Troop 59 Independent
  Commando Squadron RE
17.10.71–8.1.72 Under Comd 9 Indep Para
  Sqn
28.6.72–19.7.72 With 45 Cdo RM
2.7.74–6.11.74 With 45 Cdo RM
12.5.76–12.6.76 With 45 Cdo RM
21.6.77–20.10.77 With 45 Cdo RM

33 Independent Field Squadron RE
25.8.70–17.12.70 Belfast
17.6.71–19.10.71 Long Kesh

29.7.72–1.11.72 Ballykelly
15.10.73–15.2.74 Castledillon
23.7.74– Antrim (Resident Unit)

9 Independent Para Squadron/9 Para
 Squadron
12.5.70–8.9.70
14.9.71–11.1.72 Antrim
22.3.73–24.7.73 Antrim Bridging Camp
12.10.74–14.2.75 Castledillon
10.10.76–10.2.77 Castledillon
23.10.80–8.3.81 Castledillon
Troop 9 Para Squadron
25.1.76–9.3.76

Troop 28 Amphibious Engineer
 Regiment
16.10.83–28.2.84 Omagh
12.7.84–22.11.84

Troop 21 Engineer Regiment
1.3.84–12.7.84 Omagh

Troop 25 Engineer Regiment
22.11.84–5.4.85 Omagh

**Recent Royal Armoured Corps and Royal
 Artillery Tours**

3 RHA
9.10.92–9.4.93 Drummond Roulement Bn

2 Regt RA
19.2.93–21.6.93 Girdwood Roulement Bn

22 Regt RA
9.4.93–7.10.93 Drummond Roulement Bn

9/12L
21.6.93–21.1.94 Girdwood Roulement Bn

26 Regt RA
07.10.93–11.4.94 Drummond Roulement
 Bn

4 Regt RA
21.1.94–20.6.94 Girdwood Roulement Bn

32 Regt RA
11.4.94–12.10.94 Drummond Roulement
 Bn

KRH
20.7.94–1.95 Girdwood Roulement Bn

5 Regt RA
12.10.94–4.95 Drummond Roulement Bn

Prison Guard Force Tours

4 Bty RA: 7.11.74–7.12.74
6 Sqn RCT: 28.10.76–28.3.77
6 Bty 27 Regt RA: 11.77–3.78
76 Bty 14 Regt RA: 3.78–7.78
57 Bty 32 Regt RA: 7.78–11.78
2 Sqn 2 Engr Regt: 11.78–3.79
42 Bty 22 Regt RA: 3.79–7.79
5 Sqn 16 Sig Regt: 28.3.79–26.7.79
45 Sqn 21 Engr Regt: 7.79–11.79
52 Bty 45 Regt RA: 11.79–3.80
T Bty 12 Regt RA: 3.80–7.80
13 Bty RA: 15.7.80–24.11.80
13 Bty 19 Regt RA: 24.11.80–10.4.81
29 Bty 4 Regt RA: 10.4.81–25.6.81
A Sqn 1 RTR: 25.6.81–8.9.81
G Bty 7 RHA: 8.9.81–21.11.81
D Sqn LG: 5.2.82–22.4.82
B Sqn 3 RTR: 22.4.82–7.7.82
C Sqn 9/12 L: 7.7.82–21.9.82
A Sqn 15/19 H: 21.9.82–4.12.82
A Sqn 17/21 L: 4.12.82–17.2.83
Ajax 2 RTR: 17.2.83–3.5.83
E Bty 1 RHA: 3.5.83–17.8.83
L Bty 2 Regt RA: 17.8.83–1.10.83
31 Bty 47 Regt RA: 1.10.83–15.12.83
C Sqn QRIH: 15.12.83–27.2.84
156 Bty 94 Regt RA: 2.84–5.84
A Sqn 15/19 H: 5.84–7.84
34 Bty 14 Regt RA: 11.84–12.84
34 Bty 39 Regt RA: 12.11.84–19.12.84
A Sqn 4/7DG: 19.12.84–14.2.85
13 Bty 19 Regt RA: 14.2.85–4.85
C Bty 3 RHA: 4.85–7.85
P Bty 5 Regt RA: 7.85–9.85
B Sqn 13/18 H: 6.9.85–21.11.85
49 Bty 27 Regt RA: 21.11.85–1.86
C Sqn RH: 1.86–4.86
88 Bty 4 Regt RA: 4.86–6.86
Sqn 4 RTR: 19.6.86–28.8.86
9 Bty 12 Regt RA: 28.8.86–6.11.86
B Sqn 1 RTR: 6.11.86–12.1.87
A Sqn QOH: 12.1.87–26.3.87
O Bty 2 Regt RA: 26.3.87–2.6.87
D Sqn 4/7DG: 2.6.87–8.87
74 Bty 32 Regt RA: 8.87–10.87
137 Bty 40 Regt RA: 10.87–26.12.87
Sqn 16/5L: 26.12.87–12.3.88
127 Bty 49 Regt RA: 12.3.87–18.5.88
64 Sqn 28 Engr Regt: 5.88–7.88
518 Coy RPC: 28.7.88–7.10.88
3 Bty 47 Regt RA: 7.10.88–15.12.88
187 Coy RPC: 15.12.88–22.2.89
Huntsman 2 RTR: 22.2.89–4.5.89
A Sqn QDG: 4.5.89–14.7.89
C Sqn 1RTR: 14.7.89–28.9.89

518 Coy RPC: 28.9.89–30.11.89
K Bty 5 Regt RA: 30.11.89–10.2.90
159 Bty 36 Regt RA: 10.2.90–20.4.90
143 Bty 49 Regt RA: 20.4.90–20.7.90
B Sqn 12/20H: 20.7.90–19.10.90
43 Sqn 2 Engr Regt: 19.10.90–21.1.91
D Sqn QOH: 21.1.91–21.4.91
C Sqn 4/7DG: 21.4.91–7.91
A Sqn 1RTR: 8.91–11.91
Sqn 5 INNNIS DG: 19.1.92–21.4.92
Sqn 9/12L: 21.4.92–22.7.92

36 Bty RA: 22.7.92–20.10.92
17 Bty 26 Regt RA: 20.10.92–21.1.93
D Sqn QOH: 21.1.93–19.4.93
12 Bty 12 Regt RA: 19.4.93–20.7.93
32 Bty 16 Regt RA: 20.7.93–21.10.93
B Sqn QDG: 21.10.93–19.1.94
21 Bty 47 Regt RA: 19.1.94–19.4.94
43 Bty 47 Regt RA: 10.4.94–23.7.94
D Sqn 1RTR: 23.7.94–21.10.94
201 Sig Sqn: 21.10.94
1 (UK) Div Sig Regt

SELECT BIBLIOGRAPHY

Literally hundreds of books have been written about Northern Ireland though, as I make clear in my Foreword, none has adequately described the role of the British Army in Northern Ireland. The following list is grouped under different aspects of the subject to aid those who wish to specialise. It is intentionally selective in order to focus on books which I have found to be informative and helpful.

Historical background
BECKETT, J. C. *A Short History of Ireland.* London, 1952
BUCKLAND, PATRICK. *A History of Northern Ireland.* Dublin: Gill & Macmillan, 1981
BUCKLAND, PATRICK. *Ulster Unionism and the Origins of Northern Ireland, 1886–1922.* Dublin: Gill & Macmillan, 1973
HICKEY, D. J. and DOHERTY, J. E. *A Dictionary of Irish History Since 1800.* Dublin: Gill & Macmillan, 1980
KEE, ROBERT. *Ireland, A History.* London: Weidenfeld, 1980
MOODY, T. W. (ed.). *Irish Historiography, 1936–70.* Irish Committee of Historical Studies, 1971
WALLACE, MARTIN. *Northern Ireland: 50 Years of Self Government.* David & Charles, 1971

Military aspects
BARZILAY, DAVID. *The British Army in Ulster* (4 vols.). Belfast: Century Services, vol. I 1973, vol. II 1975, vol. III 1978, vol. IV 1981
CLARKE, A. F. N. *Contact.* London: Secker & Warburg, 1983
DEWAR, MICHAEL. *Brush Fire Wars: Campaigns of the British Army Since 1945.* London: Robert Hale, 1984
DEWAR, MICHAEL. *Internal Security Weapons and Equipment of the World.* London: Ian Allen, 1979

ELLIOT, R. J. 'Countering Urban Terrorism', in *British Army Review* (April 1980), pp. 16–24
EVELEGH, ROBIN. *Peacekeeping in a Democratic Society*, The Lessons of Northern Ireland. Hurst & Co., 1978
HAMILL, DESMOND. *Pig In The Middle*, The Army in Northern Ireland 1969–1984. London: Methuen, 1985
Pegasus (Journal of the Parachute Regiment), 1969–85
The Globe and Laurel (Journal of the Royal Marines), 1969–85
The Gunner (Journal of the Royal Regiment of Artillery), 1969–85
The Royal Green Jacket Chronicle, 1969–85

Political and social aspects
ARTHUR, P. *The Government and Politics of Northern Ireland.* London: Longman, 1980
BECKETT, J. C. *The Ulster Debate*, Report of a Study Group of the Institute for the Study of Conflict. London: Bodley Head, 1972
BIRRELL, W. D. and MURIE, A. S. *Policy and Government in Northern Ireland*, Lessons of Devolution. Dublin: Gill & Macmillan, 1980
BOULTON, D. *An Anatomy of Loyalist Rebellion.* Dublin: Gill & Macmillan, 1973
BURTON, F. *The Politics of Legitimacy*, Struggles in a Belfast Community. London: Routledge & Kegan Paul, 1978
CALLAGHAN, JAMES. *A House Divided*, The Dilemma of Northern Ireland. London: Collins, 1973
DARBY, JOHN. *Conflict in Northern Ireland*, The Development of a Polarised Community. Dublin: Gill & Macmillan, 1976
FAULKNER, BRIAN. *Memoirs of a Statesman.* London: Weidenfeld, 1978
FISK, R. *The Point of No Return*, The

Strike which broke the British in Ulster. London: Deutsch, 1975

GRAY, TONY. *Psalms and Slaughter, A Study in Bigotry*. London: Heinemann, 1972

GRAY, TONY. *The Orange Order*. London: Bodley Head, 1972

HOLLAND, JACK. *Too Long A Sacrifice*, Life and Death in Northern Ireland since 1969. New York: Dodd, Mead & Co., 1981

MAGEE, JOHN. *Northern Ireland, Crisis and Conflict*. London: Routledge & Kegan Paul, 1974

O'BALLANCE, EDGAR. *Terror in Ireland*. Praesidio Press, 1981

O'DOWD, LIAM, ROLSTON, B. and TOMLINSON, B. *Northern Ireland Between Civil Rights and Civil War*. London: CSE Books, 1980

O'NEILL, T. *Ulster at the Crossroads*. London: Faber, 1969

Revolutionary Communist Group. 'Ireland: Imperialism in Crisis, 1968–1978' in *Revolutionary Communist*, No. 8, 1978, pp. 5–33

Sunday Times Insight Team. *Ulster*. London: Deutsch, 1972

UTLEY, T. E. *Lessons of Ulster*. London: Dent, 1975

WALLACE, MARTIN. *Drums and Guns*, Revolution in Ulster. London: Geoffrey Chapman, 1970

The Republican viewpoint

BROWNE, V. 'H–Block crisis: Courage, Lies and Confusion'. Magill, August 1981

BRADY, B., FAUL, D. and MURRAY, R. *British Army Terror Tactics, West Belfast, September–October 1976*. Dungannon, 1977

COOGAN, T. P. *On The Blanket: The H–Block Story*. Dublin: Ward River Press, 1980

DASH, S. 'Justice Denied: A challenge to Lord Widgery's Report on Bloody Sunday'. London: NCCL, 1972

FALIGOT, R. (transl.). *Britain's Military Strategy in Ireland*, The Kitson Experiment (from Guerre Spéciale en Europe). 1980

MOXON-BROWNE, E. 'Terrorism in Northern Ireland, The Case of the Provisional IRA', in LODGE, J. (ed.). *Terrorism: A Challenge to the State*. London: Martin Robertson, 1981

High Intensity Subversion: A speculative look at the ideas of Brigadier Frank Kitson's *Low Intensity Operations*. Ronin, Anarchist Press, 1981

Government Reports

Disturbances in Northern Ireland, Cameron Commission, Cmd 532, Belfast: HMSO, 1969

Report of the Inquiry into allegations against the Security Forces of Physical Brutality in Northern Ireland arising out of events on 9 August 1971, Cmd 4823, London: HMSO, 1971

Report of the Commission to consider Legal Procedures to deal with Terrorist activities in Northern Ireland, Cmd 5185, London: HMSO, 1972

Report of the Committee of Privy Councillors appointed to consider Authorised Procedures for the Interrogation of Persons suspected of Terrorism, Cmd 4901, London: HMSO, 1972

Report of the Tribunal Appointed to inquire into the Events on Sunday 30 January 1972 which led to loss of life in connection with the Procession in Londonderry on that day, HC 220, London: HMSO, 1972

In addition to this very selective list I have consulted many pamphlets, regimental journals, broadsheets, leaflets and HMSO political and economic fact sheets and reports. These are too numerous to list.

INDEX